Listening Subjects

LISTENING SUBJECTS

Music,

Psychoanalysis,

Culture

DAVID SCHWARZ

Duke University Press

Durham & London

1997

© 1997 Duke University Press

All rights reserved

Printed in the United States of America

on acid-free paper ∞

Typeset by Tseng Information Systems, Inc.

Typeset in ITC Carter and Cone Galliard

Library of Congress Cataloging-in-

Publication Data appear on the last

printed page of this book.

for Jakob and Marlies

CONTENTS

ACKNOWLEDGMENTS

I would like to thank my wife, Marie-Luise Gättens, for inventing the phrase *listening subjectivity,* for her clear and critical readings of the manuscript from its inception to the final manuscript, and for her support and encouragement. Special thanks as well to dear and brilliant friends without whom this book would never have been conceived and written: Eric Santner, Anahid Kassabian, Dennis Foster, and Nina Schwartz. Thanks as well to Jenny Kallick, Lew Spratlan, and David Reck of the Music Department at Amherst College for their support and invaluable criticism of several drafts of the manuscript. Thanks also to Patrick McCreless for his thoughtful comments on the manuscript. Thanks as well to Raphael Atlas.

Special thanks to Barbara Riecke, Rolf Suhl, Vito Avantario, and Matthias Weber for help, support, and invaluable criticism of the manuscript during various stages of the writing. Very special thanks as well to Jenny Gättens for generous emotional support during several summers of writing and research in Hamburg, Germany.

Thanks to Lisa A. Raskin, Dean of the Faculty, Amherst College, for generous financial assistance in the preparation of the final manuscript. Thanks to Robert Frank of the University of North Texas for his diligent work in preparing the music examples. Thanks to Mark Abbott and Lew Spratlan for generous help with music examples. Thanks to Richard Morrison and Ken Wissoker of Duke University Press for their long-standing support of this project. I am grateful to the cds Gallery in New York for permission to use the Morales painting on the cover.

Thanks as well to my young son, Jakob, whose early development confirmed many of the psychoanalytic claims on which the book is based. Special thanks as well to my mother, Jean Chalmers, and father, Joseph Schwarz, who, from a very early age, taught me about painting, music, and beauty.

INTRODUCTION

I have been fascinated for some time by the goose bumps I sometimes get while listening to music. What exactly is happening when they occur? How important is familiarity with the music or lack of familiarity to the experience? Are goose bumps universal? Is the experience contingent on a cultural context? Is there something in our childhood or infancy that makes the experience possible? Why are goose bumps so powerfully at the *skin*—the boundary separating our bodies from the rest of the world? How can classical and popular music, even music I would call sentimental trash, give me goose bumps?

The chapters of *Listening Subjects* probe questions like the ones above. "Music as Sonorous Envelope and Acoustic Mirror" asks, Why does music often sound so good when heard "all-around"? "Scatting, the Acoustic Mirror, and the Real in the Beatles' 'I Want You (She's So Heavy)'" began with the question, (How) can the white noise at the end of the song mean anything? "Why Notes Always Reach Their Destination (at Least Once) in Schubert's *Winterreise*" asks, (How) can music represent a crisis within conventionality? "Music and the Gaze: Schubert's 'Ihr Bild' and 'Der Doppelgänger'" interrogates the representation of doubles. "Peter Gabriel's 'Intruder,' a Cover, and the Gaze" examines structures within which a male listener can relate to the song's representation of a violent sexual fantasy. "Oi: Music, Politics, and Violence" asks, What is the musical, textual, and ideological structure of the German postrock Oi Musik? And "Lamentation, Abjection, and the Music of Diamanda Galás" explores how music can produce terror and awe, displeasure and pleasure at the same time.

These are some of the personal questions that got *Listening Subjects* started. Addressing these questions involved engaging scholarship in "new" musicology, psychoanalysis, music theory, and history. I would like this book to participate in a growing body of criticism that brings these fields together as equal partners. For well over a decade, the work of Slavoj Žižek has influenced film studies, literary studies, and cultural studies, drawing together Lacanian psychoanalysis, Marxism, history, and popular culture. *Listening Subjects* introduces his techniques into music studies for the first time. Why psychoanalysis? In part, I am drawn to psychoanalysis temperamentally; much of it just seems right, particularly with daily confirmation from the experiences of raising a small child.

But I also feel that it is only through the psychoanalytic techniques outlined in this book that one can get into a nuanced discourse of music as a visceral experience to explain what happens to listeners of music. Throughout *Listening Subjects,* I discuss music and the body as a fantasy of being enclosed in a second skin of all-around sound (chapter 1), as music and representations of sexual desire (chapter 2), as music and fantasies of breached skin (chapter 5), as music and violent sexual fantasy (chapter 6), and, finally, as music and abjection (chapter 7).

Psychoanalytic criticism can also ground a wide variety of textual claims in social space. Throughout *Listening Subjects,* I implicitly or explicitly discuss music as cultural artifact. For example, two of the chapters of this book address music by Franz Schubert from a psychoanalytic point of view. For me and many music scholars, much nineteenth-century classical music is about alterity: the formal and harmonic "experiments" of Beethoven, the song cycles of Franz Schubert, the song-like piano music of Chopin and Schumann, the exquisite temporal complexities of Richard Wagner, and music as rewriting in the music of Franz Liszt. Historically, the nineteenth century opens the space of modernism, and its music explores the epistemological doubt of the era. Also, music is so important in collective contexts in the West —at funerals, sporting events, popular and classical concerts, the opera, political rallies, etc. For me, psychoanalysis offers a precise technique to name and explore in nuanced discourse how history sounds in music.

"New" musicologists have powerfully influenced this book. Lawrence Kramer's *Music as Cultural Practice* offers a convincing example of how to apply traditional comparative techniques to subordinate music and poetry to a single unifying principle. I follow Kramer's work, grounding musical-cultural claims both within musical texts and in their historical contexts.[1] In the chapter on German Oi Musik, I discuss the structure of the Oi subject in music, texts, and historical contexts of right-wing appropriation of left-wing music in German history, on the one hand, and in the contemporary subjective positions made possible by postrock, on the other. The Oi chapter is also based on a belief that one can theorize Oi subjectivity only by getting into it, by acknowledging its seductive power, and by entertaining the possibility that unpleasant structures of desire might be a part of listening to music.

Susan McClary's *Feminine Endings* cuts against the grain of traditional musicology to suggest ways in which community, the body, and a plurality of textual voices (re)produce gender in music and musical responses. *Listening Subjects* owes much to McClary's work. In the chapter on the music of Diamanda Galás, I listen to music twice: once historically and once (more) psychoanalytically. Both approaches focus on music and the representation of a woman's voice. The first approach describes the Greek lament, its history, structure, and gender specificity. The second approach rereads the first as representation of abjection from the point of view of Julia Kristeva's *Powers of Horror*.[2] I am also indebted to Carolyn Abbate's *Unsung Voices* for the idea that musical voices cross and enunciate thresholds.

Music theory has carved out a small, relatively exclusive space in contemporary academic circles. In recent years, some music theorists have become interested in grounding music theory in semiotics, such as V. Kofi Agawu in his *Playing with Signs*.[3] I would like *Listening Subjects* to accelerate this process, showing that music theory and cultural studies reciprocally produce meaning for one another.

For me, *listening* is the process of unpacking the musical-theoretical, musical-historical, cultural, psychoanalytic, and personal dimensions of music. Throughout the book (particularly in the first two introductory chapters), I discuss two registers of listening—as a fantasy *thing* and as a fantasy *space*.

Listening as a fantasy thing is produced when attributes of a structure represented in music are described and related to one another. Listening as a fantasy space is produced when musical-theoretical, musical-historical, cultural, psychoanalytic, or personal thresholds are crossed and enunciated. Both listening thing and listening space are always *retrospective* fantasies since we have direct access to neither events that structured our developing subjectivity nor historical contexts as immanent experiences of reality. These experiences and contexts have left traces, however, in how we listen to music.

For me, listening things and listening spaces are unevenly and indistinctly marked at their boundaries since music theory, music history, culture, psychoanalysis, and personal experiences (both actively and passively "remembered" and represented) occupy different logical classes. For example, if I described and analyzed the pitch structure of "The Star Spangled Banner" as a composing-out of the overtone series in a particular key, then I would produce a fantasy of a listening thing—not necessarily stable, but treated, for a moment, from a certain perspective *as if* the relation between the overtone series and the pitch structure of the song were objectively "there" on the page, in the music, in our ears. Interrogating the ideological structure of the "natural status" of the overtone series would turn the fantasy thing into a fantasy space—a threshold between pitch structure, form, and musical language, on the one hand, and a historical context that makes pitch structure, form, and musical language possible, on the other. These two critical gestures clearly occupy different registers: a fantasy *thing* can be formalistic, "whole," hierarchical, subordinate, transhistorical, "purely" textual; a fantasy *space* can be heterogeneous, fragmented, coordinated, culture specific, and personally specific.

There can be no single point of entry into the space of listening, no diachronic trajectory that will take us across it. The chapters of this book are thus not like the terraced structure of traditional hermeneutic rhetoric. Each chapter unpacks its own interrogation of listening things and spaces, beginning with chapters that emphasize the psychoanalytic and ending with chapters that emphasize the cultural conditions that make music as listening possible.

After the initial chapters of the book, however, I stop referring explicitly to fantasy things and fantasy spaces. This happens, in part, because, the closer one interrogates musical, theoretical, historical, psychoanalytic, and personal registers, the more imbricated in one another fantasies of "things" and "spaces" become.[4]

Since the book proposes that listening can be both fantasy things and fantasy spaces in which representations of structures in different logical classes (re)sound, it can have no single, unified *reader*. Some chapters will address and ponder the experience and concerns of people who have read current cultural criticism, have worked with Romanticism, modernism, and postmodernism, and know some of the basics of music. Other chapters will address and ponder the experience and concerns of professional music scholars. I hope that the book starts to explore what is happening to our bodies, our sense of identity, both individually and collectively, when we listen to music.

I

Music as Sonorous

Envelope and

Acoustic Mirror

I have been curious about another simple phenomenon and my response to it for some time—how music sounds in the Musikhalle in
Hamburg, Germany. The hall was built in the early twentieth century;
it has plaster walls, gold ornaments, translucent glass ceilings, and
wooden seats with velvet cushions. If you sit anywhere in the hall on
the side, music comes at you, remains "in front." But, if you sit in the
middle, from the first few seats of the orchestra all the way back to the
gallery, even in seats behind pillars, music is "all around" and seems
to embrace your entire body. I experienced this again during a recent
performance of Bruckner's Ninth Symphony with Giuseppi Sinopoli
conducting the Hamburger Philharmonisches Staatsorchester.

The all-around pleasure of listening to music is one of many
"oceanic" fantasies (some pleasurable, displeasurable, or ambivalent)
such as sleeping, swimming, having sex, being absorbed by a movie,
by a religious experience, by a landscape, etc. Although these fantasies are quite different from one another in obvious ways, they share a
common feature: the boundary separating the body from the external
world seems dissolved or crossed in some way. What makes such fantasies possible? How and why can oceanic fantasies be pleasurable, displeasurable, or ambivalent?[1] How does sound function in these structures? This chapter will attempt to answer some of these questions.

Recent film theory based on psychoanalytic research has related a
wide variety of "oceanic" representations to "the sonorous envelope."[2]
The French writer Guy Rosolato says, for example: "The maternal

voice helps to constitute for the infant the pleasurable milieu which surrounds, sustains, and cherishes him. . . . One could argue that it is the first model of auditory pleasure and that music finds its roots and its nostalgia in [this] original atmosphere which might be called a sonorous womb, a murmuring house."[3] On an elementary level, then, the experience of being embraced by the all-around sound of music in Hamburg's Musikhalle was made possible by my experience of the sonorous envelope in the early stages of my developing subjectivity. But, even though the experience in the Musikhalle was visceral, it was a *fantasy*—a representation of an experience to which neither I nor anyone else can have direct access. Thus, representations of the sonorous envelope are always retrospective; they are produced by a wide variety of theoretical, historical, psychoanalytic, and personal contexts. Given its retrospective structure, the sonorous envelope can be described as a *thing,* an immanent experience whose features represent how we imagine the sonorous envelope might have sounded. The sonorous envelope can also produce *threshold crossing*—a crucial component of listening as *space.* In the experience described above, I crossed the threshold between my clearly marked-off adult body and a fantasy of a familiar but archaic body less distinctly marked off from the external world than its adult counterpart. Goose bumps at my skin marked the crossing of this sonorous threshold.

On the one hand, the sonorous envelope is a fantasy of a thing, a representation of having been at one with the touch, smell, and voice of the mother to which we do not have direct access; on the other hand, it is a space in which thresholds are crossed and enunciated. Music represents the sonorous envelope as a fantasy *thing* when there are one-to-one correspondences between musical details and an archaic, oceanic fantasy. Music represents the sonorous envelope as a fantasy *space* when attributes of the thing are related to other conventional registers in which the subject finds him/herself. The conventionality in my experience was my adult self-awareness and all the baggage associated with my social identity, knowledge of the music, status as a foreigner in Germany, etc.

This is an elementary introduction to the sonorous envelope as a fantasy of a thing and threshold-crossing space. Perhaps, as Rosolato suggests, the sonorous envelope supports *all* musical experience. But, beyond the universal claim, new minimal music in particular represents the sonorous envelope both as fantasy thing and as fantasy space. Much new minimal music relies on two structures that can easily sound "oceanic." The music often has familiar and simple *rhythmic* structures with small and large groupings of eighth or sixteenth notes pervading entire scores. And the music's *pitch content* often consists of drawn-out versions of traditional harmonies from the canon—particularly the semitonal voice leading of the German tradition of the mid-nineteenth century.[4] It is precisely this familiar but archaic quality that makes "new" minimal music work so well as a representation of the sonorous envelope. The minimal rhythmic patterns are nothing more than an elevation to primacy of a common secondary feature of canonic music, particularly Lieder and sonatas—accompanying figuration.[5] Consider the opening measures of John Adams's opera *Nixon in China*, shown in ex. 1 in piano-vocal arrangement.

The passage creates a fantasy of the sonorous envelope as thing through very repetitive and metrically regular fragments, on the one hand, and irregular entrances of sustained pitches, on the other. A predictable pattern of ascending A natural-minor scales fills each *measure* with eighth notes that fill in the *octave* with "white notes." The piece sounds as if in A minor until the bass enters with an F♮ in m. 6, making the piece sound as if in F Lydian. With the C♯ in m. 31, Adams hints at a cycle of major thirds as an organizing principle. Each of these bass notes, A♭-F♮-C♯, thus shifts the perception of the harmonic organization of the music. These bass notes thus slowly open the music's sonorous *space*. Conventional materials emerge gradually during the first several hundred measures of the piece, as shown in ex. 2.

So far, I have described the musical representation of the sonorous envelope in two mutually dependent ways: music that is structured as a representation of the sonorous fantasy thing and music that articulates a crossing of thresholds, the sonorous fantasy space.[6] Spaces also open when the stability of the text shifts at the emergence of half-formed quotes—not so much of specific pieces, but more an appropriation of a preexisting style. Since the turn of the nineteenth century, quoting in Western canonical works has become more and more self-conscious; Adams relies on this tradition in his music. Indirect quoting is thus another familiar technique that supports this "new" mini-

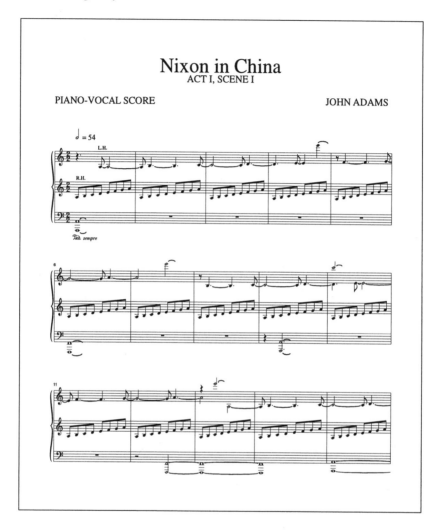

Example 1. John Adams, *Nixon in China*, mm. 1–35. *Nixon in China* Copyright 1987 by Hendon Music, Inc., a Boosey & Hawkes Company. Reprinted by permission.

mal music. There are many examples of self-referential quoting among movements of music ranging from Beethoven to Brahms and of quotes within a piece and to antecedents in the work of Gustav Mahler. A high modern master whose quoting can be heard as a forerunner of Adams is Alban Berg. At the outset of his Piano Sonata, op. 1, the

first phrase moves from atonal material through an altered transposition of Richard Wagner's Tristan chord/progression down a half step to a dominant-tonic close on B minor. For a comparison between the two passages, see exx. 3 and 4.

In Berg's music, the quote is quite hidden but unmistakable. Wagner's *ascending* half step G♯-A♮ becomes Berg's *descending* half step G♯-G♮; and, of course, Berg transposes the entire Tristan progression down a half step—a pun on Wagner's semitonal voice leading. Berg's wit can

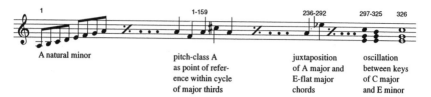

Example 2. John Adams, *Nixon in China,* overview of mm. 1–326.

Example 3. Richard Wagner, "Prelude to *Tristan and Isolde*," piano-vocal arrangement, mm. 1–3.

Example 4. Alban Berg, Piano Sonata, op. 1, mm. 1–3.

also be seen in the example's reversal of its own history: the tonal-chromatic-atonal sequence of music's tonal orientation from the classical period, through the nineteenth century, to the turn of the twentieth century is *reversed,* as if the music were listening back through its own past.[7]

In Western art music written after the high modern period, quoting spans the continuum from minimal quotation at one "end" to saturation quotation at the other. Much of Philip Glass's music is an example of music with minimal explicit or implicit quotation. At the other "end" of the continuum, *everything* in the musical text points to previous styles, previous pieces, or clichés from other eras, as, for example, in much of the music of George Rochberg. In his *Caprice Variations for Violin Solo,* Rochberg juxtaposes fragments of a wide variety of masterpieces, including Beethoven's Fifth Symphony, Brahms's Violin Concerto, and Paganini's solo violin works, along a single "red thread" of continuity—the pitch class A♮. The third movement of Luciano Berio's *Sinfonia* juxtaposes and superimposes a wide variety of direct quotations on a continuum of spoken text from Samuel Beckett. In John Adams's "pseudoquotes," the source rarely comes completely clear; his style of quotation occurs in a gray area in the middle of our continuum in which styles, orchestral colors, orchestration techniques, and harmonic progressions are appropriated without a clear tag pointing to the quote's origin. Like Berg's early altered and transposed Tristan progression, many of John Adams's quotes are indirect. Further on in *Nixon in China,* Adams indirectly quotes the opening of Richard Wagner's *Das Rheingold.* Example 5 shows that the C-major triad (see mm. 297–325 of ex. 2 above) embodies new minimalism's style-specific rhythmic cliché of steady sixteenth notes. An upward arpeggiation of a C-major triad begins in the bass in m. 295 and sounds through m. 308. This upward arpeggiation of a major chord at the beginning of *Nixon in China* is reminiscent of the arpeggiation of an E♭-major triad at the beginning of *Das Rheingold.* See exx. 5 and 6.

Both Adams and Wagner superimpose an ascending arpeggiation of a major triad in dotted rhythm over a static arpeggiation of the same chord in the bass. Both prepare, as well, for vocal entries in their respective operas. In *Nixon in China,* the oceanic, undifferentiated texture of the opening gets charged with musical conventions that gradually pre-

Example 5. John Adams, *Nixon in China*, mm. 294–310. *Nixon in China* Copyright 1987 by Hendon Music, Inc., a Boosey & Hawkes Company. Reprinted by permission.

figure the "quote" from Wagner: the *pitch class* A♮ is a nonfunctional axis of the cycle of major thirds in the bass from mm. 1–159; E♭- and A-major *chords* are juxtaposed from mm. 236–92; the oscillation between the C-major and E-minor chords from mm. 297–325 embodies the style cliché of semitonal voice leading in new minimal music. The moment of our recognition of the quote from Wagner opens the space between John Adams the composer and the listener. We have the illusion that our listening has created an element of musical structure as we hear the difference between being enclosed by the music of the initial measures of the piece and being split from the music as it becomes marked by convention. Such threshold crossing is precisely a representation of the sonorous envelope as fantasy *space*.

But what does "threshold crossing" have to do with developing subjectivity? I have suggested that music as sonorous thing can "remind" us of something we can only imagine; I have suggested that music as sonorous space can connect such fantasies to a wide variety of theoretical, historical, and personal contexts. But there is an additional structure that supports this connection between musical representations of a sonorous fantasy thing and space to other contexts *as an emergence into conventionality.* This is the development of the subject as mapped out in Lacanian and post-Lacanian theory. Although I will expand on this "sequence" of stages of developing subjectivity in the section on the acoustic mirror below and throughout this book, I offer a large-grain version below by way of introduction.

Example 6. Richard Wagner, *Das Rheingold,* mm. 51–60.

As suggested above, the sonorous envelope represents our sense of having been at one with the touch, smell, and voice of the mother in the womb and shortly after birth.[8] In the *acoustic-mirror stage*, the child "plays" with its voice in an attempt to match it to the mother's. The acoustic-mirror stage is the precursor of the visual mirror stage, in which the child "recognizes" itself in the mirror and face of the mother.[9] The acoustic- and visual mirror stages are part of what Lacan calls the Imaginary Order; it is the division of the child's experience into binary oppositions of full/empty, presence/absence, etc.[10] As will be shown below, the acoustic-mirror stage begins shortly after birth; the visual mirror stage occurs between the ages of six months and a year and a half. The child emerges from the mirror stage into language acquisition, or Lacan's Symbolic Order, at very roughly a year and a half. Indications of a clear threshold between the mirror stage and language acquisition will be discussed in subsequent chapters.[11] For now, it is important to realize that, from birth to language acquisition, the subject experiences (and retrospectively represents to itself and others) a series of splits away from phenomenal experience, from the sonorous envelope, through the binaries of the Imaginary Order, and into the plural, dispersing signifiers of the Symbolic Order. Thus, symbolic reconstructions of moments from developing subjectivity in music are supported by threshold-crossing structures within developing subjectivity *itself*. The more blurred the threshold crossing in the music, the more it will sound like a representation of an event that took place early in developing subjectivity; the clearer the threshold crossing, the more it will sound like a representation of crossing the threshold into the Symbolic Order.[12]

The examples above have shown how, in selected works of John Adams, music represents sonorous fantasy thing and space in which the emergence of conventionality reminds the listener of a moment in his/her developing subjectivity to which he/she does not have direct access. Selected examples from the music of Steve Reich represent sonorous space as regressive fantasy in which threshold crossing undermines the (apparent) stability of conventionality.

Reich's early piece "It's Gonna Rain" (1965) is based solely on manipulations of taped speech. The piece uses repetition obsessively to strip meaning just as it is about to take shape.[13] "It's Gonna Rain" is in two parts. Part 1 begins with a thirteen-second taped passage from a street preacher's sermon. After a one-second pause, two tracks of the phrase *it's gonna rain* go out of phase with one another. As the tracks move out of phase, the language sounds as if it were being ripped apart through the violence of phase motion.

From 0:14 to 2:00, words and syllables also fade in and out. This gives sound a spatial impression—as if sounds were moving close (fading in) and receding (fading out).[14] It is as if the listener must brace him/herself against approaching sounds and "let up" as sounds move away.[15] Reich repeats the word *gonna* over and over again, cutting the word down to the syllable *go*. When severed from the other syllable of *gonna*, the syllable *go* becomes a verb in the imperative voice, calling to the listener. This shift in meaning represents a sonorous fantasy space in which the listener feels directly addressed by the music.

With the shift from heard *gonna* to "speaking" *go*, Reich produces what I would like to call a *listening gaze*.[16] The look and the gaze differ as follows. The look is a conventional representation of one person seeing another in real or imagined social and/or personal space. He/she who looks is the sole agent of the look, and he/she who is looked *at* is the sole recipient of the agency. The gaze, on the other hand, always exceeds the look. The gaze carries an additional weight, and its source is often hidden or transposed. Thus, for example, *objects* can be represented as the source of a gaze; in such cases, the gaze represents the introjection of another's look.[17] It is the structure of the gaze, for example, that supports the cliché in horror movies of a portrait gazing at a vulnerable subject through the cutout spaces through which horrifyingly "real" eyes peer. With the shift from the word *gonna* to the imperative syllable become word *go*, the listener can fantasize that he/she has been seen or heard. It is important to realize that this threshold represents a fantasy of sonorous *space*, not *thing*; it is impossible to tell at which repetition of *go* the shift occurs for different listeners; perhaps some listeners would *never* hear *go* repeated several times as the imperative voice of the infinitive *to go*.[18]

Repetition makes such a moment of threshold crossing possible. Repetition multiplies the possible moments for the shift from *gonna* to *go* to take place; it opens the space for this threshold crossing.[19] From 2:01 to 7:44, several tracks go out of and move back into phase in one gesture. Here, the phase process is audibly prefigured in the "unison" phrase with which the piece begins: *it's gonna rain* (2:01 . . .). The phrase *it's gonna* is doubled at the octave, while *rain* sounds like one voice, suddenly closer to the listener.

Part 1 of "It's Gonna Rain" ends abruptly with a line of taped, spoken speech that extends the text by one phrase: *it's gonna rain after awhile.* The piece is contained within the musical equivalent of a frame —the one-second pause of silence between 0:13 and 0:14 that sets off the thirteen seconds of taped speech from the rest of the piece and the return to taped speech at the end with the phrase *it's gonna rain after awhile.*[20]

Part 2 begins with an extended passage of taped speech—0:00– 0:40. The rest of the section fragments and superimposes words and phrases from this excerpt, focusing on *open the door, God, sure enough,* and *Hallelujah.* Repetition tears meaning away from language by the end of this piece to reveal the disordered sounds that support the Symbolic Order.[21] Through the mediated and conventional techniques of tape-recording, splicing, and phase motion, Reich represents the noise within the sonorous envelope.[22]

Different Trains (1988) is a multivalent representation of the sonorous envelope. The piece is for string quartet and tape in three movements entitled "Before the War," "During the War," and "After the War." The piece is a monument both to those who died in the Holocaust and to those who survived.

On an elementary level, *Different Trains* represents a sonorous fantasy thing by having the string quartet play rapid repeated notes that sound like a train. This is a familiar representation of a motif from early modernism; Arthur Honegger's *Pacific 231* is a high modern monument to trains; in addition, the Futurist glorified machinery of all kinds, and Dada films of the 1910s and early 1920s often represent man as machine and machine as man. I hear *Different Trains,* as well, as a musical analogue to Claude Lanzman's film *Shoah.* This movie is pervaded by the sounds and images of trains, as the survivors whom Lanzman interviews recall the Holocaust. It is also through the sound of a train whistle that the recent film *Schindler's List* opens.[23] Reich strengthens the music's thingness by including taped sounds of American and European train whistles that connect the composer (remembering taking trains between New York City and Los Angeles as a child) to the Holocaust victims who traveled on "different trains" to their deaths during the war.

Different Trains represents a sonorous fantasy space through a discrepancy between elementary narrative temporality, on the one hand, and crossing and recrossing the threshold separating language and prelinguistic sound, on the other. The titles of the parts of the music— "Before the War," "During the War," and "After the War"—denote an elementary narrative temporality. Part 1, "Before the War," establishes the connection between Reich's fantasies of his childhood and the Holocaust. In part 2, "During the War," the distinction between immanent American trains and imagined European trains collapses; the tempo quickens, and the voices of survivors describe events leading up to the Holocaust, reinforced by the sounds of European train whistles and air raid sirens. The elementary narrative temporality moves toward the present in "After the War," as the composer remembers survival; the distinction between the trains he had ridden as a child and the different trains of the Holocaust is back in place.

On the other hand, the composition crosses and recrosses the threshold between clear, denotative language and fantasies of prelinguistic sound. For example, intervallic structures in the accompaniment determine the intervallic structure of the language of the taped speech that is a part of the composition in parts 1 and 3. In part 1, a minor third in the viola is taken over by the voice for the phrase *from Chicago* (0:35–0:40). This technique represents in a nutshell the way we first hear language as pure sound, then as words, phrases, and sentences with meaning. In part 2, the instrumental and vocal intervals are synchronized—a representation of a near-perfect fantasy of musical identification with the experience of the victims of the Holocaust.

Also, once speech has been introduced into the piece, it is effaced in two ways. First, it is stripped of meaning through repetition. For example, the phrase *one of the fastest trains* is repeated twenty-one times (1:23–2:37). The meaning-stripping function of repetition is enhanced in this passage through an intermittent additional repetition of the tag phrase *fastest trains*. Second, the voices are often distorted. In part 2, for example, the phrases *lots of cattle wagons there* (4:49–5:17) and *they were loaded with people* (5:18–5:40) are barely comprehensible without the text that Reich provides for the listener. This crossing and recrossing the threshold between language and presymbolic sound pervades all three parts of the composition. In sum, the fantasy space of *Different Trains* is precisely the discrepancy between the nearly complete musical representation of identification with the victims of the Holocaust in part 2's elementary narrative temporality and the ongoing oscillation between language and fantasies of prelinguistic sound.

The music represents a survivor's need to revisit the site of trauma in a way that can never be complete; as in *Shoah,* the site of trauma must be continuously visited, and revisited, without end. *Different Trains* is thus both a monument to those who died in the Holocaust and a musical representation of repetition compulsion within the psyche of a survivor.[24]

The remarks above have shown how representations of the sonorous envelope as fantasy thing and space function in selected works of John Adams and Steve Reich. The phrase *emergence into conventionality* is crucial for this discussion since thresholds are crossed and enunciated to produce listening space. A special structure that "emerges" from the sonorous envelope accounts for a wide variety of phenomena in "nature," public spaces, and music—the acoustic mirror. The fascination with echoing voices across a canyon or under a bridge underpass is made possible by this structure of acoustic redoubling.

It is crucial to remember that these structures in developing subjectivity do not follow one another in discrete temporal spans; rather, they overlap. For example, Anzieu considers the sonorous envelope and the acoustic mirror to be interchangeable: "We would like to demonstrate the existence earlier still [than the visual mirror stage] of a sonorous mirror, or an acoustic-phonetic skin, and its function in the psychic apparatus of the acquisition of the capacity for signifying and symbolizing."[25]

As the acoustic-mirror stage begins, the sense of being bathed in the sounds of the mother's voice is modified as the child imitates the sounds it hears and has the illusion of *producing* those sounds. According to Kaja Silverman: "Since the child's economy is organized around incorporation, and since what is incorporated is the auditory field articulated by the maternal voice, the child could be said to hear itself initially through that voice—to first 'recognize' itself in the vocal 'mirror' supplied by the mother."[26] For Anzieu, the acoustic mirror arises out of communication with the mother through cries that he has studied in terms of their temporal duration, frequency, and acoustic signature. The hunger cry is the basic cry, of which cries of anger, pain, and frustration are variants. In addition to getting what the child needs, the sound of the mother's voice *alone* stops cries better than any other sound after the second week of life. After the third week, the child develops the so-called false cry to gain attention. At five weeks, the child distinguishes the voice of the mother from other voices while still not being able to distinguish visually among faces. Between three and six months, the child clearly plays with the sounds it emits, gradually moving closer to imitating the mother's voice.[27] The sixth crucial "contagious cry" will be introduced toward the end of the next chapter. The acoustic mirror is thus an aural precursor of the visual mirror stage; the child both recognizes itself in and hears itself separated by the sound of the mother's voice.

So far, we have the following "sequence" of experiences basic to developing subjectivity: the child in the womb is bathed in the touch and sound of the mother in the sonorous envelope. Birth separates the child from the mother and the world. Shortly after birth, the child experiences the world as a fragmented flux of body parts and yearns for the mother; he/she "finds" her through a continuation of sonorous (pre)identification through touch, smell, and sound. The child then enters the acoustic mirror as he/she communicates with first the mother, then others, through cries and imitation of the mother's voice. The voice of the mother produces at once the model for communication *with* and separation *from* the external world.[28]

The story of Echo and Narcissus from Ovid's *Metamorphoses* represents an illustration of the acoustic mirror and its relation to the visual mirror stage. In the story, the female Echo has the power to stall the goddess Juno on her search for Jove owing to the loquacity of her speech; Juno punishes Echo by limiting what she says to verbatim repetition of what she hears. Echo is placed into and trapped within an acoustic mirror to match the visual mirror of the male Narcissus.[29]

Echoes and their representation in literature, music, and film remind the listener of an experience to which no one has direct access—the acoustic mirror. More specifically, there are many aspects of music that suggest an acoustic mirror: question/answer structures, statement/counterstatement, unison melodies, melodies doubled at the octave, unison lines that split into two-part counterpoint, inversion, imitation, theme and variation, echo effects in 1950s rock, etc. More specifically still, the acoustic mirror can help us describe the logic of a particular kind of emergence from the sonorous envelope—a splitting of music into two strands that diverge and then converge in Steve Reich's phase pieces.[30]

In *Violin Phase* from 1967, a performer plays first in unison and then moves out of phase with a taped recording. As the violinist moves out of phase with the tape, a space opens in which the listener hears first an acoustic tugging, followed by echo effects, followed by out-of-phase voices. Psychoanalytically, this series of moments (roughly 0:00–1:50) renders how the fantasy of sonorous enclosure can be represented only retrospectively. Only after hearing voices split apart from one another can we imagine their having once sounded together. This is an elementary description of a representation of the acoustic mirror as a fantasy *thing*. *Violin Phase* represents the acoustic mirror as a fantasy *space* through a shift in listening perspectives. As the piece begins, there is a clear binary opposition between the performers who are playing in unison, the violin and tape, and the listener. As the violin and tape split apart, the listener joins the no-longer-binary configuration. The *tape* sounds but is deaf; it cannot hear. The *violinist* plays with the tape while listening to him/herself and the tape. And the *listener* listens as if mute. The tape and listener complement one another—the tape, pure voice with no ear; the listener, pure ear with no voice. The performer mediates between them: he/she is part human like the listener; he/she is part machine like the tape.[31]

The "universality" of fascination with echoing does not mean that echoes or their representation produce only a positive, playful affect. Echoes can also be threatening, such as footsteps resounding in a large, deserted cityscape, for example. Or think of the uneasy way that rooms resound with voices after they have been emptied of personal belongings, furniture, etc. The affective charge produced by a representation of acoustic mirroring as thing or space depends on other contextual considerations. In the following chapter, I discuss one rock song in some detail to probe the acoustic mirror, its representation, its affective potential, and its relation to other registers of listening.

2

Scatting, the Acoustic Mirror,

and the Real in the Beatles'

"I Want You (She's So Heavy)"

This chapter extends the psychoanalytic material introduced previously with an examination of a well-known song by the Beatles.[1] I will discuss the acoustic mirror as fantasy thing and fantasy space in the song and introduce the *Real* to the musical and theoretical issues at hand. "I Want You (She's So Heavy)" is from the album *Abbey Road* of 1969; it follows the apotheosis of album-oriented rock, *Sgt Pepper's Lonely Heart's Club Band* of 1967.[2] *Sgt Pepper* is conceived as a cycle, beginning with, and returning to, a song in which a circus audience applauds a show. The album ends with one additional song/coda—"A Day in a Life." This song concludes with a "wall of noise" followed by a resounding E-major chord—as if to say, the chaos of life (internal and/or external?) can be redeemed or righted again through tonal clarity.[3] Although *Abbey Road* is less cyclic than *Sgt Pepper,* "I Want You (She's So Heavy)" also juxtaposes music and noise, but in a much different way, to be discussed below.

Because I will theorize the significance of the highly constructed fantasy of regression in "I Want You (She's So Heavy)," it is important to realize just how carefully the Beatles and George Martin put together this song. An overview of the song's production follows.

On 29 January 1969, the Beatles recorded a version of "I Want You" —the first recording of material for a song on their new album *Abbey Road.* On 22 February, the Beatles recorded thirty-five takes of an early version of "I Want You." On 23 February, an edited master tape was put together from the material recorded on 22 February. Take 9 became the early part of the song, take 20 the middle part, and take 32 the end. On 24 February, a copy of the master tape from 23 February was made. On 18 April, George Harrison, Paul McCartney, and John Lennon worked on the guitar parts of the finale (4:37–7:44). Jeff Jarratt said of this session: "They wanted a *massive* sound so they kept tracking and tracking over and over."[4] On 20 April, George Martin worked with John Lennon and Ringo Starr, adding synthesized sounds for the finale and drums to the song. On 11 August, the title of the song was changed from "I Want You" to "I Want You (She's So Heavy)." John Lennon, George Harrison, and Paul McCartney re-recorded the chorus of the song and overdubbed this material onto the 18 April master tape. John Lennon then overdubbed this re-recorded chorus onto the 23 February master as well. Of the wall of noise that John Lennon and George Martin constructed on this day, Lewisohn writes: "John had used the Moog synthesizer in conjunction with a white noise generator to produce a swirling, gale-force wind effect for the last three minutes of the song." On 20 August, the song was completed with the first four minutes, thirty-seven seconds from one master tape and the following three minutes, seven seconds from another master tape.[5]

For Lewisohn, the production of "I Want You (She's So Heavy)" is important because, during the first recording session on 29 January, work on *Abbey Road* began and because the Beatles worked together for the last time in a recording studio on 20 August when the song was completed. For me, the production of the song is important because it suggests the highly mediated structure of this apparently simple, regressive fantasy.

The song begins with a six-measure introduction without percussion; see ex. 7.[6] The harmony of the introduction suggests the beginning of a simple progression in D minor: i-V⁹/V-VI (with added seventh). But the VI chord with added seventh (Bb–Db–Fb–[added] Ab) could also be heard as a German augmented-sixth chord (with Ab functioning as a G♯). The chord does "resolve" as an augmented-sixth chord, with the flat sixth scale degree resolving *down* to the root of the dominant chord (Bb-Ab) and the raised fourth scale degree resolving *up* to the doubled root of the dominant (G♯-Ab). But such an interpretation reproduces a fallacy of uncritically applying voice-leading tendencies of classical, tonal music to popular music. A more

Example 7. "I Want You (She's So Heavy)," mm. 1–6. "I Want You (She's So Heavy)" words and music by John Lennon and Paul McCartney. © 1969 Northern Songs Ltd. All rights controlled and administered by EMI Blackwood Music, Inc. under license from Sony/Atv songs, LLC. All rights reserved. International Copyright Secured. Used by permission.

suggestive interpretation is that the E dominant-ninth chord and the B♭ dominant-seventh chord form a variant of a common jazz progression called *tritone substitution*. Both chords *together* function as a large dominant of the dominant (A major). The shared tritone between the two chords (D♮-G♯/A♭) makes the substitution possible. The absent G♯ in the E dominant-ninth chord is furnished by the B♭ dominant-seventh chord that is part of the tritone-substitution complex.[7]

In a way, m. 5 sounds like an ordinary dominant of D minor—a routine resolution of the tritone-substitution complex discussed above. But the harmony of m. 5 is an A *augmented triad* (A♮-C♯-F♮) sustained by a fermata. This chord sounds like a dominant with a sixth (F♮) substituting for the fifth (E♮) that "wants" to resolve to D minor. But, with the resolution to *A minor,* the "dominant" chord in m. 3 is retrospectively heard as an A-minor chord waiting to happen: C♯ and F♮ "resolve" down to C♮ and E♮—the third and fifth of the A-minor chord. The disruptive effect of the augmented triad is strengthened by a change in color and meter for the verse, not shown in the example. At the beginning of the verse, the percussion enters, and the meter changes from the pastoral 6/8 to the classic rock-and-roll 4/4. The augmented triad heard in mm. 5–6 will become important in the song later on, as will be shown below. Before discussing John Lennon's voice, I would like to follow through some of the harmonic issues raised by mm. 1–6 and worked out in the rest of the song.

The verse includes the keys of A minor, F major, and D minor—chords built on the notes of the tonic triad to which mm. 5–6 "wanted"

Example 8. "I Want You (She's So Heavy)," mm. 12–16. "I Want You (She's So Heavy)" words and music by John Lennon and Paul McCartney. © 1969 Northern Songs Ltd. All rights controlled and administered by EMI Blackwood Music, Inc. under license from Sony/Atv songs, LLC. All rights reserved. International Copyright Secured. Used by permission.

to resolve.[8] The text of the verse is extremely minimal and repetitive: "I want you," "I want you so bad, babe," "I want you so bad it's driving me mad." The musical setting of the verse makes a connection between the augmented triad and madness. See ex. 8. The F♮ *note* in the augmented triad becomes an F-major *triad* on the word *mad* in m. 14. Just as the "wrong" F♮ in mm. 5–6 had been followed by A minor as the verse begins, so, too, the F-major chord of m. 14 is followed by an A-minor seventh chord in m. 15.[9] The rising chromatic figure G♮-G♯-A♮ in the bass in m. 15 connects the F-major and A-minor chords with an inversion of the B♭-B♭-A♮ motion in the bass of mm. 3–5.[10] Frustration is intensified in mm. 27–32 by an E dominant-ninth chord reiterated *twenty-one times;* see ex. 9. The harmony of these measures resolves the harmony of the introduction that had been left hanging: the E dominant-ninth chord of mm. 27–32 is a full version of the incomplete E dominant-ninth chord of m. 2 that resolves to A minor at the beginning of the verse. However, the E dominant-ninth chord of mm. 27–32 has a *dramatic* implication as a representation of frustration that cuts against the grain of its harmonic resolution. Musical representation of frustration has been present in the song from the very first vocal entry with "knocking" figures in the percussion that follow the initial lines of the verse "I want you" and "I want you so bad, babe." These knocking figures and their echo in the twenty-one reiterations of the E dominant-ninth chord discussed above suggest a representation of desire that will turn ominous as the song goes on. To hear how the music represents an ambivalent fantasy of desire, let us now turn to the representation of John Lennon's voice in this song.

In the verse, John Lennon sings while accompanying himself on the guitar at the *unison*.[11] This is an adaptation of the jazz technique *scatting*. In jazz scat song, a voice mimics an instrument; after an instrument has played or a section of a piece has concluded, a solo voice improvises, the singer using timbre, articulations, melodic structure, and gestures to suggest the previously heard instrument. In the blues and rock tradition, scatting is *simultaneous:* while an instrument plays, a voice sings the melody at the unison or octave, with subtle variations to indicate the grain of the voices' differences.[12] Lennon sings the entire verse of "I Want You (She's So Heavy)" as blues/rock scatting with the exception of the third repetition of the verse, which is played by the guitar ad lib. I hear a connection in this song between scatting and the song's representation of desire. Simultaneous scatting in the blues/rock tradition represents an ambivalent acoustic-mirror fantasy—a one-to-one correspondence between the sounds of the child and the sounds of the mother.[13] Scatting in "I Want You (She's So Heavy)" is a fantasy of the acoustic mirror as a fantasy *thing*—an ambivalent unison,

Example 9. "I Want You (She's So Heavy)," mm. 27–32. "I Want You (She's So Heavy)," words and music by John Lennon and Paul McCartney. © 1969 Northern Songs Ltd. All rights controlled and administered by EMI Blackwood Music, Inc. under license from Sony/Atv songs, LLC. All rights reserved. International Copyright Secured. Used by permission.

psychoanalytically and musically.[14] Yet it is a fantasy of an impossible thing. Aside from the fact that representations of the acoustic mirror are always necessarily retrospective fantasies, a sonorous union with the mother's voice is broken once it is perceived; matching the child's voice to its "echo" in the mother assumes already differentiated voices. Thus, fantasies of acoustic mirroring are necessarily stained.[15] In the song at hand, one "voice" is a representation of pure sound (the guitar), the other a representation of pure sound overlaid with language (John Lennon's voice).[16] The knocking motives that follow the lines "I want you" and "I want you so bad" in the verse and the reiterations discussed above turn this difference within echoing voices into an extended representation of frustrated desire for a female object—an attempt to break through a barrier.

In the previous chapter, I suggested that it is precisely a piece's familiar quality that lends itself to representations of structures first experienced in early stages of developing subjectivity. Here, too, "I Want You (She's So Heavy)" relies on familiar textual and musical features. The text is a minimal version of romantic love fantasies so common in 1950s rock and roll; most of the words are monosyllabic. As pointed out above, rock-and-roll scatting relies on the jazz and blues techniques that are part of the "common practice" of popular music. The song has a very traditional form (at least until the finale). There are no classical instruments and no intricate harmonies (beyond the introductory ambiguities discussed above).

The song represents an acoustic mirror as *space* through a fantasy of what sounds between the difference "voices" of the acoustic mirror. One threshold is crossed and recrossed over and over again in the song; the scatting of the *verse* disappears in the *chorus* that sets the text "she's so heavy." The change in the song's title from "I Want You" to "I Want You (She's So Heavy)" highlights the crossing of this threshold. The chorus resolves one musical issue and creates a new textual one. Musically, it is a rewritten version of the opening measures with a significant change. The augmented chord built on A♮ (A♮-C♯-F♮) in mm. 5–6 becomes an A dominant-seventh chord. As the chorus repeats, the A dominant-seventh chord resolves to D minor, turning an open-ended progression into a closed one.

While this element of the music resolves, the text distances the "I" in the song even further from his object of desire than in the verse. During the verse, the male "I" addresses an absent or aloof female object of desire. During the chorus, several male voices (John, Paul, and George) sing to each other of that object of desire in the third-person *she*. After the text of the chorus enunciates this shift with the words *she's so,* the male voices sing *heavy* repeatedly like voices echoing into the distance. In addition, crossing and recrossing the threshold from scatting to echoing voices suggests an oscillation between two fantasies that trap the male subject—the acoustic mirror and physical, oppressive presence. Thus, the male subject seems further away from his object (speaking of her as "she") *and* closer to her—"she's so heavy!" On the other hand, crossing and recrossing the threshold between scatting and echoing voices suggests a shift in the fantasy of acoustic mirroring from one of an ambivalent unison (musically and psychoanalytically) between one's own voice and the voice of *another* to hearing one's *own* voice echo into the distance.

This representation of the acoustic mirror as an echoing away into silence of one's own voice is made possible by the "imitative cry" described by Didier Anzieu in early subjectivity: "In his babbling, the baby is imitating the sounds he hears others make as much as his own; at three months, for example, imitative cries appear."[17] This is a qualitatively different cry from those cries that are variants of the hunger cry (cries of anger, pain, frustration, and, later, attention). The contagious cry is caused only by the cry of another *like oneself.* The contagious cry is thus disembodied; the child cries "back" at a cry it mistook as its own. As the child develops, a sense of its own body as the source of its voice must cause the contagious cry to fade as an automatic response. The contagious cry also retrospectively produces misrecognition, as the developing subject "realizes" that he/she mistook the cries of others for his/her own.[18] In the song at hand, the contagious cry signifies the musical narrator's frustration level, as a result of which he hears his voice echoing away, trapped in an acoustic mirror.

At the end of the fourth repetition of the verse, John Lennon emits a searing scream from 4:27 to 4:30.[19] Of this scream, John Lennon said: "When it gets down to it . . . when you're drowning you don't say 'I would be incredibly pleased if someone would have the foresight

to notice me drowning and come and help me,' you just *scream*."[20]
The piano-voice reduction provides the word *Yeah!* for the scream; for
me, it sounds poised between the traditional, affirmative rock-and-roll
Yeah! and a nonlinguistic scream of horror. Lennon's words above suggest more the latter than the former. On one level, the scream suggests
the primal enunciation of communication discussed by Anzieu—the
cry. As such, its representation suggests a sound that binds the child
to its mother.[21] On the other hand, the scream *is* coming from a man
representing in music an ambivalent acoustic-mirror fantasy of unison
with a female object of desire. In *La voix au cinéma,* Michel Chion describes the male scream in cinema as follows: "It is a cry of strength, to
exercise power, to mark a territory, a structuring cry that is expected.
If there is something bestial in this cry, it is like the identification of
the male with the totemic animal. The most famous example is the cry
of Hollywood's Tarzan constructed in the 1930s out of multiple animal
cries: a phallic cry through which the male parades himself and lets his
virile power resonate."[22] Of the female cry, Chion says: "The cry of a
woman is more the cry of a human being who is subjected to language
faced with death. . . . The cry of a man delimits a territory; the cry of
a woman points to the limitless."[23] These rather essentialist character-
izations seem more or less appropriate for classic Hollywood cinema,
but scenes in more recent cinema have blurred Chion's clear binary between male and female screams. Two screams in *The Godfather Part III*
suggest male subjective positions that "point to the limitless"—Sonny's
scream right before he dies, having been pumped full of bullets by enemies of his family, and Michael's scream that takes several seconds to
form on the death of his daughter on the steps of the opera house.[24]
In "I Want You (She's So Heavy)," John's scream belongs to the post–
classic Hollywood male scream of horror at a limit. In *The Godfather
Part III,* the screams of Sonny and Michael are screams of terror at
death; in the song at hand, John Lennon screams at what he is about
to hear within his acoustic-mirror fantasy.[25]

Right after the scream, the chorus begins with *she's so,* and then the
finale repeats the introductory material fourteen times. The silent *heavy*
that the listener provides marks the threshold between the song proper
and its extraordinary finale. The silent *heavy* also silences the echoing
voices of the "contagious cries" generated by earlier versions of the

chorus. The silent *heavy* signifies the limit of the song's representation of the acoustic mirror in which the male subject can no longer hear the echoes of his own voice.

The fourteen repetitions of the introductory material suggest a new representation of the acoustic mirror in the song, as if the music's repeat signs were themselves barriers binding the music; repeat signs have a double bar with two dots on the right representing the limit to the left and a double bar with two dots on the left representing the limit to the right. John Lennon's scream thus represents foreknowledge of this acoustic trap.

At 4:37, the music could have faded out to a repetition of the first three measures. But, where we might hear the music potentially fading *out,* we get a wall of white noise *fading in* between the music's double bars. One often hears rock and roll dismissed because of the common fade-out at the end of many songs.[26] It makes sense, however, that this song can neither resolve nor fade out. The music is all about representing an ambivalent fantasy of acoustic mirroring that turns into a trap. The lack of forward motion is essential to the music, and we can now retrospectively hear the logic of the augmented triad in mm. 5–6. The augmented triad A♮-C♯-F♮ symmetrically divides the octave; the chord can move neither musically nor psychoanalytically.[27]

Fading in popular music makes a temporal art sound spatial. When it fades out (as in most 1950s and 1960s fades), the music sounds as if it were going away; when it fades *in,* the music impinges on the listener's space.[28] This impingement makes the music sound as if it were aware of the listener, as if it were listening to *him/her.* The finale thus represents a listening gaze.[29]

But what about the wall of noise within the acoustic mirror? The wall of noise is a representation of the Lacanian concept of the *Real* as both fantasy thing and space.[30] What exactly *is* the Real? How does it differ from "reality"? How does it differ from "horror"? I will address these questions below using an example from the visual arts.

Around the time of this writing, I saw a large exhibit of the photographs of Cindy Sherman in Hamburg, Germany; for me, her art is all about making the Real appear. Her work focuses on the construction of the female gender through images. Cindy Sherman became well known originally because of her film stills. Since the late 1970s, she has photographed herself in a wide variety of subject positions—object of the male gaze in the fine art tradition, prostitute, housewife, little girl, etc. Her most recent work relies less on her phenomenal body than replicated body parts used for instruction in medical schools. Many of her recent pictures represent extreme violence, often explicitly or implicitly sexual, proximity of the camera to the objects represented, and dismemberment. Consider the picture reproduced as ex. 10.[31] The Real is an inscrutable force or thing beyond the limits of sensory or linguistic representations. It cannot be heard, seen, or named directly since the Real is that which supports but evades signification. Yet, in the fissures of some representations, it can and does appear, as in the "face" in the example. If we subtracted all our experiences from our lives, all our patterns of sensory and linguistic understanding, all social conventions, all cultural memories, all personal and collective identities, all historical contexts, we would be left with the Real.[32]

The photo reproduced here is a Real fantasy *thing* in its representation of the pulp that lies just beneath the surface of the face. The photo is a Real fantasy *space* as the viewer crosses and recrosses the threshold between the face as pulp beneath skin and artificial substance that replicates body parts. For example, there seems to be one pure tear (the noun, not the verb) beneath the eye on the left. An expression of sadness, or a horrid drop of clear fluid oozing out of the Real?

This picture is one of a series (five in all—"Untitled" #314A–E), and, in each variation, the eyes are different, a reference to the fact that the two halves of the human face contain subtle differences? The series is also a comment on the series as a genre itself in the Western art tradition. For example, in Monet's series, the same object is painted at different times of the day to reveal subtle shifts in light, as in *Haystacks* or *Rouen Cathedral*. In Monet's series, the objects are less important than the play of light on them. In Sherman's series, the Real as pulp abides in each picture; it is precisely the inscrutable support of all faces that will not go away.[33]

The image suggests at once inanimate mask and pure human subjectivity. And the expression? At once death, stupor, horror, and complete neutrality. The face is neither recipient nor source of aggression since it is put together out of parts—the nose of two segments, eyes, separate sockets, cheeks, pulp/plastic beneath.

Example 10. Cindy Sherman, Untitled #314E, 1994.

In the video "No One Home but Me," Sherman says that she composes her pictures spontaneously in front of a mirror. She tries on clothes and manipulates her body until she does not recognize herself in the mirror; then the work is ready. Her art is thus supported by a fantasy of mirror misrecognition from which the Real can appear.[34] In this video, she also speaks about horror; she is "addicted" to horror films but does not want her art to be too explicitly terrifying. She does not explain why, but I think it is because she wants the Real to appear, and the Real is clearest when attached to conventional representations in social space.[35]

The photograph represents Real space as it crosses and recrosses the threshold between pulp flesh and the conventional representational form of the *portrait*. And as *self*-portrait (the root form of Cindy Sherman's art), the picture says, "I am that image in the thing; I am that thing in the image." Neither of these clauses can be subordinated to one another; this is the photo's Real.

How, then, is the emergence of the wall of noise between the two double bars at the end of "I Want You (She's So Heavy)" Real?[36] First, as a fantasy *thing*, the wall of noise is an acoustic equivalent of Cindy Sherman's pulp. But, since music is not a spatial but a temporal art, it is crucial that the wall of noise occurs at the end of this highly obsessive representation of an ambivalent acoustic-mirror fantasy of unison with a female object of desire. When put under enough concentrated pressure, the acoustic mirror opens, and the Real emerges. The pressure is created by the fourteen repetitions of the initial measures at the end of the song and the absence of voices after John Lennon's scream. This threshold crossing is the Real as fantasy *space* in the song.

During the entire finale, the wall of noise gets louder and louder, while the guitars remain at one dynamic level. It is as if the guitar parts of the finale were in a different place than the wall of noise; the guitars rearticulate their music over and over again, but they seem unable to hear the wall of sound. On the other hand, the listener hears everything—the guitars' repetitive riff as well as the wall of noise. The wall of noise fades in and holds at a dynamic level equal to the guitars; it is as if the guitar music were being confronted with its reflection in the acoustic mirror. But only the listener can hear both the guitars and the(ir?) noise; this is a representation of the Real in the music as fantasy *listening space.*[37]

Why couldn't one say that the noise *symbolizes* John Lennon's inability to realize his fantasy; why couldn't it represent plain and simple frustration? Because it goes on for too long. In *Looking Awry,* Žižek discusses Hitchcock's film *The Birds,* pointing out that, if the movie had had a more restrained, a more subtle *background* presence of the birds, then their representation could be subordinate to the plot, to the dynamics of what is going on with the characters. One could say that the birds "symbolize" nature's revenge against human destruction, the main character's anxiety about women, etc.[38] But the extremely grotesque and unrealistic element of the birds' attacks, the arbitrary choice of victims, and the inscription of the viewer into the film render the birds Real.

Similarly, "I Want You (She's So Heavy)" is a song seven minutes, forty-four seconds long with over three minutes engulfed by noise. The birds exceed symbolism in Hitchcock's movie; in "I Want You (She's So Heavy)," the three minutes of white noise suggests a nightmarish nothingness within male desire. In *The Birds* and "I Want You (She's So Heavy)," quantity produces a qualitative shift from the symbolic to the Real.[39]

Since the song represents a fantasy of gradually *opening* the acoustic mirror to reveal the Real, the way the song *ends* is crucial. The song ends with a unique gesture—a violent slash.[40] See ex. 11. The tame, written example does not do justice to the sound of the end of this song. Lewisohn reports that, during the 20 August recording session, John Lennon was listening to the finale and said, "There! Cut the tape there" at the moment at which the song ends.[41] Lewisohn points out that the tape would have run out at eight minutes, four seconds, but Lennon had many possibilities for choosing the song's ending. The song could have faded out, or it could have ended with the wall of noise being followed by a chord as in "A Day in a Life." The noise could have faded away and a purely musical conclusion written, or the white noise could have taken over, etc.

The slash is a clear representation of the music's textual and musical premise—being trapped in a fantasy of acoustic mirroring at the threshold of the Real. A cadence, a major chord, any "end" would

Example 11. "I Want You (She's So Heavy)," mm. 70–75. "I Want You (She's So Heavy)," words and music by John Lennon and Paul McCartney. © 1969 Northern Songs Ltd. All rights controlled and administered by EMI Blackwood Music, Inc. under license from Sony/Atv songs, LLC. All rights reserved. International Copyright Secured. Used by permission.

have weakened what this music is all about. But how did John Lennon know at which split second he wanted the slash to occur? Although there are an infinite number of possibilities for locating the slash, there are three *kinds* of possibilities: (1) have the slash cut off the music arbitrarily; (2) have it come on the downbeat of the tonic D minor; (3) cut the music on one of the three other harmonies in D minor: the E dominant-ninth chord, the VI chord (with added seventh), or the augmented triad.

Ending arbitrarily would suggest being overwhelmed by the Real; ending on D minor would suggest closure; ending on the E dominant-ninth chord or the VI chord (with added seventh) would have sounded somewhere between the two. As we know, the piece ends right on the A♮ that stands for the augmented chord at the end at the song's introductory phrase. It is the perfect ending—a slash that is poised at the threshold between the tonality of D minor and the noise of the Real.

"I Want You (She's So Heavy)" represents a fantasy of male desire for a female object. The fantasy takes the form of unison with the voice in the acoustic mirror that opens to reveal the Real. In the next chapter, I examine a similar psychoanalytic structure. In Franz Schubert's song cycle *Winterreise,* the composer constructs a fantasy of a male narrator who wanders in a winter landscape in search of a subjectivity he imagines to have resided in desire for a female object. As his fantasy collapses, the Real appears. This psychoanalytic "plot" connects the material of this chapter with the material of the next, although the works differ in many ways. The Beatles' "I Want You (She's So Heavy)" is a product of the blues, jazz, and rock of the popular music tradition, the 1960s youth culture of the West, and the studio discipline and classical training of the Beatles' producer George Martin. Schubert's song cycle combines folk elements in text and music with a simplicity of form and ensemble to represent male subjectivity in crisis in the early phase of historical modernism. Since *Winterreise* is an acknowledged masterpiece in the canon of classical works, there are precise historical and musical-theoretical approaches available for its study that are less appropriate for popular music study. In the next chapter, I will use these techniques to interrogate a *classical* musical representation of male desire that collapses to reveal the Real.

3

Why Notes Always Reach

Their Destination (at Least Once)

in Schubert's Winterreise

For some time, I have had the feeling that Schubert uses motivic, modal, metrical, textural, and harmonic musical materials to represent both conventional subjective structures and what happens when they come under strain in his song cycle *Winterreise.* A psychoanalytic approach to *destination* provides the means for describing such structures. The first register of destination represents setting up conventional materials; the second register of destination represents conventional structures ruptured by traumatic shock.

Music theory can specify how music embodies a wide variety of listening registers, and it is crucial in describing *Winterreise* as a musical representation of psychoanalytic destination. Music theory ranges from elementary harmonic descriptive labels (as in the previous chapters) to more sophisticated transformational tools such as Schenkerian voice-leading graphs. This chapter relies implicitly on Schenkerian concepts in musical-theoretical analysis; they will be used explicitly in the next chapter on Schubert and the gaze.

Within a movement of Western tonal art music, Schenkerian music theorists speak of notes reaching their destination when pitches in the fundamental melodic line descend to tonic at the final cadence. This teleological approach to pitch structure is based on the works of such common-practice composers as Bach, Haydn, Mozart, and Beethoven, in which the two harmonic motions of tonic to dominant and dominant to tonic support a melodic line that outlines the tonic *key* and ends on the tonic *note* at a deep structural level.[1] Recent theorists have extended Schenker's diatonic notion of musical structure in studies of the works of later composers such as Schubert, Schumann, and Wagner. Despite the fact that ambiguous, chromatic structures trouble the clarity of the tonic-dominant/dominant-tonic structural binary discussed above, these theorists show how local musical materials inform larger aspects of structure. Or, after ambiguous wanderings, notes also reach their destination in Romantic and post-Romantic music.[2]

While much of the material that follows relies on these hermeneutic theories of diatonic and chromatic destination, I will supplement this approach with a psychoanalytic theory of destination to theorize relations among literary texts, Schubert's musical settings of these texts, and psychoanalytic registers. In general, so much nineteenth-century music seems to be about hearing things within the voice, moving in and out of distinct phases of musical representation, blurring formal, subjective, and syntactic boundaries.[3] For me, *Winterreise* is all about such issues. In particular, I am interested in describing the musical representation of conventionality and traumatic shock using Žižek's Lacanian notion of destination.[4]

Schubert's two great song cycles, *Die schöne Müllerin* and *Winterreise,* are works that explore fantasies of love in text and music at both the individual song and the cycle level.[5] Both cycles are musical representations of texts that describe a central male narrator who yearns for an unattainable female object of desire, although the registers of yearning in these cycles are different. *Die schöne Müllerin* (1823) is about a narrator who imagines himself working in a mill and falling in love with the miller's daughter, who, although out of reach, is nevertheless present in a community from which the narrator is not entirely alien. The narrator of *Winterreise,* however, is alienated from both the beloved and her social space before the cycle has even begun.[6]

In *Winterreise* (1827), a male narrator leaves the house of his beloved and wanders a desolate landscape that mirrors the deterioration of his inner landscape as the cycle unfolds.[7] As Susan Youens has pointed out, the cycle has no clear harmonic unifying factors; musically and textually, it drifts.[8] The narrator begins by acknowledging that there has always been something wrong in the relationship between himself and the female object. The first song, "Gute Nacht," begins with the lines "Fremd bin ich eingezogen, / Fremd zieh' ich wieder aus" ("I arrived a stranger, / a stranger I depart").[9] Why *fremd?* What has marked the narrator so irrevocably as an Other? There is some trauma, flaw, or transgression within the narrator's subjectivity that Schubert represents musically. The apparently undermotivated, obscure transgression generates a conflict between desire for and dread of the beloved in the text. The narrator's inability to reconcile these forces contributes to his psychic estrangement from the social conventions that support his subjectivity by the end of the cycle of poems.

In *Winterreise,* Schubert represents the narrator's subjectivity in music in two ways. The first is a structure of representation in which there is an apparently stable discrepancy between the narrator's thoughts and the language and music he uses to represent them. This is the letter reaching its *first* destination. To use another Žižekian formulation, this is "remembering to forget." "Remembering to forget" means that we behave as if there were a connection between what we "know" are arbitrary signifiers and signifieds, the conventions of social space, that red means "stop" and green means "go," for example. In order to function in social space, we need to remember to forget the arbitrary structures that are the underpinnings of language, the law, and social space.[10]

In the second structure of representation, a traumatic kernel that resists symbolization emerges from conventionality and threatens its cohesiveness. To refer to another Žižekian formulation, this is "forgetting to forget."[11]

More specifically, one of the most common signifiers of the letter arriving at its first destination in *Winterreise* is the conventional usage of the major and minor modes to represent the narrator meditating on his past and present. In other words, the narrator "remembers to forget" to use our Žižekian formulation; he constructs and is supported by the fantasy structure of representation, in which, for example, the minor mode denotes "sadness" and the major mode "happy" flight into memory and/or fantasy. The letter arriving at its second destination in the cycle is represented by the narrator experiencing traumatic shock, the collapse of his conventional fantasy support and a sense of being flooded by immediate sensations.

Susan Youens argues that the cycle is informed by a binary oscilla-

tion between fantasy (signified by the major mode) and reality (signified by the minor mode).[12] There are several moments in the cycle in
which a shift from tonic minor to major represents a shift in the text
from meditation on the narrator's present to illusion, memory, fantasy,
such as the shift from D minor to D major in m. 71 of "Gute Nacht."
But the next song, "Die Wetterfahne," has a shift from tonic A minor
to A major (mm. 32–33 and 44–46) that represents the narrator's exas-
peration that his beloved has become a rich bride by marrying another
man—hardly a representation of memory, illusion, dream. In "Auf dem
Flusse," a turn from tonic E minor to E major (m. 23) likewise represents the narrator's coming to terms with the birth and death of his
love as he carves the dates of his love into the frozen surface of a river.[13]
Measure 28 of "Rückblick" illustrates Youens's paradigm as G minor
turns to G major to represent the narrator remembering better times.
The turn from G minor to G major in "Der Wegweiser," as well, illustrates the narrator turning from an obsessive meditation on his journey
(G minor) to a fanciful meditation on the question of the culpability
of his subjectivity (G major).

Shifts from tonic major to tonic minor do often signify a shift in the
text from fantasy to "reality" as in the shift from E major to E minor
in m. 29 of "Der Lindenbaum," the shift from E♭ major to E♭ minor
in mm. 27 and 72 of "Die Post," the shift from A major to A minor in
m. 22 of "Täuschung," and the shift from A major to A minor in m. 16
of "Die Nebensonnen." But what about this major/minor structure
and "Der Leierman" with its open drone fifth B♮-F♯? And why does
Schubert set minor to major mode shifts to texts that represent anger
and frustration ("Die Wetterfahne" and "Auf dem Flusse")? Why does
Schubert use the major mode to signify the flooding of the narrator's
psyche with sensations from his immanent experience in "Einsamkeit"
and "Der greise Kopf"? On the surface, the minor mode seems to signify connection between the narrator's psyche and his experience; the
major mode seems to signify a discrepancy between these registers.
But *Winterreise* is about the musical representation of a different kind
of "immediacy" that is sometimes associated with the major mode,
sometimes with the minor mode. *Winterreise* is a textual and musical
representation of the narrator trying to sustain the illusion of signification and *failing*. When the music moves from a minor key to its parallel

major *or* from a major key to its parallel minor, the conventionality of musical representation is in place precisely because this conventionality is based on affective associations of major signifying happiness and minor signifying sadness in Western art music.[14]

Schubert's "first" *Winterreise* was a cycle of twelve songs set to poems by Wilhelm Müller in February 1827. Schubert set poems that represent a male narrator in crisis with his own desire as a musical representation of conventionality in "Gute Nacht" that "opens" to moments of traumatic shock by the end of the cycle; see, in particular, the discussion of "Einsamkeit" below. After several months, Schubert discovered additional poems in Müller's cycle and wrote twelve more songs that he added on to his original twelve-song cycle in October 1827. In his new settings, Schubert intensified his musical representation of the poetry's representation of a crisis of subjectivity. Schubert's "second" *Winterreise* begins with a song explicitly about writing, sound, and representation at odds with one another ("Die Post," part 2, song 1), and the cycle ends with a near psychotic break in "Der Leiermann" (part 2, song 12).[15]

Part 1 of *Winterreise*

Part 1 of the cycle[16] opens with "Gute Nacht," in which the conventionality of the narrator's self-consciousness is represented in the music through the steady pulse of eighth notes that suggests walking and, by extension, the journey on which he is about to depart. Generally, the expository strophes are set in the tonic minor; at the rhetorical shift to direct address ("Will dich im Traum nicht stören" ["I will not disturb you as you dream"; Wigmore, trans., 365]), the music shifts to tonic major. But the music represents the narrator struggling with an idea that is more complex than this tonic minor/major binary would suggest. The song is all about the narrator trying to contain the "sighing" minor-second interval F♮-E♮.

The dyad F♮^{2}-E♮^{2} opens the vocal melody; it is transferred to the lower octave and reaches its hermeneutic destination as it expands to the third F♮-E♮-D♮ (mm. 10–11, 14–15).[17] The downward motion of the register transfer and the completion of the third reinforce the conventional sighing half step. The F♮-E♮ sigh reverses hopefully as the music tonicizes the submediant B♭ major through the mediant F major (which becomes its dominant). Moving to the submediant harmony of B♭ major lets Schubert give harmonic significance to a motivic detail: the submediant harmony (mm. 20–23, 52–55) is supported by a B♭ in the bass that is connected to the A♮ in the bass in mm. 27 and 31 and mm. 59 and 63; this A♮ will bring the piece back to D minor in mm. 29 and 65. The B♭-A♮ voice leading in this passage echoes the F♮-E♮ sighing motive on a large scale. The "sad" F♮-E♮ motive opens up to the "happy" whole step F♯-E♮ in mm. 71–72, only to collapse to the sighing F♮-E♮ as the music returns to D minor in mm. 97–105.

The sighing motive is also projected on a large scale across the song: the F♮^{2}-E♮^{2} motive is echoed by the F♯^{2} (of D major, mm. 71–96)–F♮^{2} (of D minor, mm. 97–105). Finally, the F♮^{1}-E♮^{1} sigh is troubled at the famous stumbling motive of the piano introduction to the song on the fourth beat of m. 2. Both notes are *consonant* on one level (F♮^{1} is consonant with the bass; E♮^{1} is a chord tone in the C♯ fully diminished-seventh chord); both notes are *dissonant* on another level (F♮^{1} is not a member of the fully diminished-seventh chord; E♮^{1} is dissonant with the D♮ in the bass). E♮ is subordinate to F♮ in mm. 20–21 in the right hand of the accompaniment; F♮ is supported by the submediant harmony. But, in m. 24, F♮ is subordinate to E♮; E♮ is a member of the half-diminished-seventh chord of the dominant. The sighing motive seems to be calling out from the mute accompaniment; it is in open octaves and repeated (mm. 24–25, 26–27 in the accompaniment).

Schubert thus represents far more than a conventional association of minor with sadness and major with fantasy; in the collapse of F♯^{2} to F♮^{2} in m. 97, in the stumble of m. 2, and in the reversal of subordinate roles within the submediant key of B♭ major, he shows how there is an instability *within* conventional musical representations that can cause them to shift meanings back and forth across an inscrutable threshold.

After "Gute Nacht," "Die Wetterfahne" is a musical grimace, as the narrator turns to begin his journey. After the close, four-part texture of "Gute Nacht," the unison opening measures of "Die Wetterfahne" sound not just open, but *empty.* This song is about the anxiety of listening. The low octave trills on B♮ represent the rattling of the weathervane. And the note to which B♮ trills is C♭—a shuddering transposition of the "sigh" from "Gute Nacht."

Example 12. "Die Wetterfahne," mm. 24–28.

Measures 24–28 are a near exact repetition of mm. 5–10, with a crucial difference. In mm. 5–10, the voice doubles the right hand of the
accompaniment, which in turn doubles the same line an octave lower
in the left hand of the accompaniment. The text here is "Der Wind
spielt mit der Wetterfahne auf meines schönen Liebchens Haus" ("The
wind is playing with the weather-vane / On my fair sweetheart's house"
[Wigmore, trans., 365]). In m. 9, there are fermatas on the E♮s in the
accompaniment, while the E♮² in the vocal line dies away. In mm. 24–
28, the text is as follows: "Der Wind spielt drinnen mit den Herzen,
wie auf dem Dach, nur nicht so laut" ("Inside the wind is playing with
hearts, / As on the roof, only less loudly" [Wigmore, trans., 365]). The
text of mm. 5–10 describes the house of his beloved; the text of mm.
24–28 internalizes the image as a metaphor for his vulnerable subjectivity. The vocal line of mm. 24–28 contains the same notes as mm.
5–9, but the accompaniment has been lowered an octave. The unison
texture thus expands from two octaves (mm. 5–10) to three octaves
(mm. 24–28), opening the musical and subjective space of the music.
Also, all three "voices" have a fermata on F♮, as if voice and accompaniment were listening to/remembering the F♮-E♮ sigh of "Gute Nacht."
See ex. 12. This phrase is repeated once again from mm. 34–39, with
the F♮-E♮ sigh emerging even more than in mm. 5–10 and 24–28. In

mm. 35–36, the "rattling motive" is transposed to F♮, bringing out an F♮-E♭-F♮-E♭ motion in the bass from mm. 35–38, and the trill sounds more harsh than earlier. In mm. 4–5, the trill was a close B♮-C♮ half step; in mm. 35–36, it is an augmented second, G♯-F♮. The music returns to a three-octave unison texture in m. 37 with a hard-edge "cut" that brings the F♮-E♮ sigh into relief.

"Der Frühlingstraum" seems to represent the narrator's dreams of better days in the past that are interrupted by the narrator's present pain. His reverie seems to be set by Schubert to the pristine music from mm. 1–14 in A major. Then the narrator's present pain comes back in a succession of minor sonorities culminating in A minor (mm. 22–26). But Schubert connects the two registers in his musical setting of the text. Within the music in A major, Schubert repeats the line "von lustigem Vogelgeschrei" ("And merry bird-calls" [Wigmore, trans., 368]). And it is the idea of sounds of birds that causes the narrator to be flooded by memories of the traumatic expulsion with which the cycle had begun. Schubert sets the following lines to a progression of minor chords in first inversion that lead to A minor: "Und als die Hähne krähten, / Da ward mein Auge wach; / Da war es kalt und finster, / Es schrieen [sic] die Raben vom Dach" ("And when the cocks crowed / My eyes awoke; / It was cold and dark, / Ravens cawed from the roof" [Wigmore, trans., 368]). This is not only a shift from the tonic major of "Der Frühlingstraum" to its parallel minor but a destination at which the narrator is brought back to the key of "Die Wetterfahne" (A minor). At the moment in "Der Frühlingstraum" at which the narrator is brought back to his traumatic memory, the music is poised on the dominant of A minor, and the vocal line in m. 21 erupts with the F♮^{2}-E♮^{2} sighing motive. See ex. 13. The peaceful, conventional fantasy of bird song, "Vogelgeschrei," in A major nightmarishly opens up into a scream: "es schrieen [sic] die Raben vom Dach." The note F♮^{2} in m. 21 is very dissonant; it adds a ninth to the dominant harmony. This sigh turned scream in m. 21 moves into the accompaniment from mm. 22–24. It sounds as if the piano tried to sustain holding the sigh motive down at the pitch level F♮^{1}-E♮^{1} and failed. The piano plays F♮^{2}-E♮^{2} in m. 24 as a premonition of the vocal reiteration of the motive in m. 25.

This (re)emergence of F♮^{2}-E♮^{2} is a cross-referential detail linking "Der Frühlingstraum," "Die Wetterfahne," and "Gute Nacht." The

Example 13. "Der Frühlingstraum," mm. 18–23.

pitch class F♮ is also enharmonically respelled as E♯ in "Der Frühlings-traum" itself. In m. 2, E♯ conventionally points to the submediant F♯ minor. As I have suggested above, it is also the enharmonically re-spelled F♮ of the cross-referential sighing motive.

The verb tenses in "Der Frühlingstraum" are crucial: "Und als die Hähne kräh*ten*, / Da *ward* mein Auge wach, / Da *war* es kalt und fins-ter, / es *schrieen* [sic] die Raben vom Dach" ("And when the cocks *crowed* / My eyes *awoke*; / It *was* cold and dark, / Ravens *cawed* from the roof" [Wigmore, trans., 368]).[18] The text is not saying that the narra-tor's fantasy is brought up short by his present pain because his pain is explicitly located in the past of "Gute Nacht" and "Die Wetterfahne." The triplet octaves in mm. 16, 18, and 20, the climactic A♮s in m. 22, and the A♮ octaves of mm. 42–43 and 86–87 suggest a cross-reference to the musical materials of "Die Wetterfahne." The muddy sound of the final A-minor chord closes the song in m. 88.[19]

"Einsamkeit" follows "Der Frühlingstraum" and ends the cycle as Schubert first conceived it; the piece is in B minor.[20] The text begins with a conventional metaphor that compares the narrator's wandering to the motion of a cloud. Schubert sets the metaphor to B minor with reiterated B♭s in the bass: "Wie eine trübe Wolke / durch heitere Lüfte geht, / wenn in der Tanne Wipfel / ein mattes Lüftchen weht" ("As a dark cloud / Drifts through clear skies, / When a faint breeze blows / In the fir-tops" [Wigmore, trans., 369]). The bass moves to the leading tone A♯ as Schubert sets the text that associates the motion of the cloud to the wanderings of the narrator: "So zieh' ich meine Strasse / Dahin mit trägem Fuss, / Durch helles, frohes Leben, / Einsam und ohne Gruss" ("Thus I go on my way, / With weary steps, through / Bright, joyful life, / Alone, greeted by no one" [Wigmore, trans., 369]). The bass moves away from its tonic pedal on the word *zieh*—a musical pun since the music moves on a word that suggests suspension or tension; the music had been pulling earlier in the song, such as in mm. 3 and 5 with the fully diminished-seventh chord of the dominant, all of whose notes were dissonant ("pulling") with the bass B♭ except the G♮.

For the phrases *trägem Fuss* and *ohne Gruss,* Schubert brings back our E♯ for a guest appearance, with the open octaves that recall "Die Wetterfahne" one last time in the cycle as Schubert first thought of it. The narrator is overwhelmed in the phrases that follow with a world whose brightness horrifies him: "Ach, dass die Luft so ruhig, ach, dass die Welt so licht" ("Alas, that the air is so calm! / Alas, that the world is so bright!" [Wigmore, trans., 369]). These lines are all about the collapse of the narrator's previous metaphor; the world is not like him in any way. Musically, the traumatic split between the narrator and the world is set to reiterated progressions in A major, in which E♯ gets enharmonically respelled (again) as F♮ in the fully diminished-seventh chord of A major. Each progression is followed by an eruption of the half-step sighing motion that we have been tracking throughout the cycle. Here, it sounds less like a conventional sigh than a traumatic kernel of the narrator's experience that resists incorporation into fantasy.[21] The musical representation of resistance is the F-E motive that is embedded within the brief tonicization of A major *and* emerges as the "sigh." See ex. 14.

The text clearly states that inner turmoil reflected in the world offers conventional solace. Schubert sets the line "Als noch die Stürme tobten" ("When storms were still raging" [Wigmore, trans., 369]) with conventional word painting in mm. 28–30. Measures 35–42 repeat mm. 23–30 with one difference. Instead of the reiterated progression of a fully diminished-seventh chord moving to A major (mm. 24–25, 26–27), the harmony of mm. 36–39 is directional; a fully diminished-seventh chord of G major leads to G major, followed by a fully diminished-seventh chord of A major leading to A major.[22] After a prolongation of the dominant, the song closes on B minor. For me, this change drives home the narrator's fate, with the stepwise ascent G major, A major, B *minor*—the nail in the coffin of the narrator's hope. The nail is driven home, so to speak, not on the arrival of B minor but on the downbeat of m. 45. The F♮ in an inner voice is supported by a dominant-seventh chord of the Neapolitan in m. 42 through the first beat and a half of m. 44. In the upbeat to m. 45, F♮ is enharmonically respelled as E♯, the sharp-four scale degree of the German augmented-sixth chord leading to the dominant of B minor. The metaphoric nail is, of course, none other than our guest E♯, which (re)appears from an inner voice. The raised fourth scale degree moves *up* to the fifth scale degree as the flatted sixth moves *down* to the fifth scale degree in mm. 32–33 and 44–45, right between reiterations of the word *elend* (misery) in the text.[23] The E♯ is subtly prepared by the F♮ in an inner voice in m. 43, and the E♮-F♮-E♮ sighing motion binds "Einsamkeit" to "Gute Nacht" with which the cycle had begun. See ex. 15. The example, with its echo of the sighing motive of "Gute Nacht," suggests that Schubert

Example 14. "Einsamkeit," mm. 23–27.

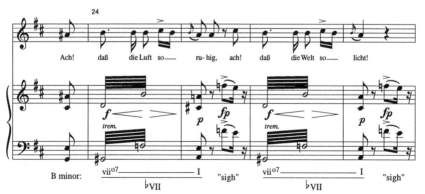

Example 15. "Einsamkeit," mm. 43–48.

has ended part 1 with the letter reaching its first destination. Yes, the second destination is reached in mm. 24–27 and 36–39, but the representation of conventionality is in place at the close of "Einsamkeit" as the narrator is able to represent his suffering. Conventionality is indexed clearly into the music. Notice how the sigh motives in mm. 25 and 27 become internalized by the inner voice preceding the final cadence shown in ex. 15. As we will see below, the ending of part 2 differs in crucial ways from the ending of part 1.

Part 2 of *Winterreise*

Like part 1, part 2[24] opens with a troubled, conventional musical representation of disappointment in "Die Post" that seems to turn on a shift from the "hopeful" tonic major, Eb major, to the "sad" tonic minor, Eb minor, to depict the narrator's disappointment when he realizes that he will not get a letter from his beloved. The song turns, not on this consideration of mode, but on the relation between vocal line and accompaniment in the Eb-major part of the song and on the significance of musical repetition. The song is in two parts (stanzas 1–2 and 3–4) set to exactly the same music; this song represents the paradox of a letter (not) arriving at its destination *twice*. Each part of the text represents one of these (non)arrivals of the letter. Here is the text to the first two stanzas of "Die Post"; I omit Schubert's repetition of phrases:

> Von der Strasse her ein Posthorn klingt.
> Was hat es, dass es so hoch aufspringt,
> Mein Herz?
>
> Die Post bringt keinen Brief für dich.
> Was drängst du denn so wunderlich,
> Mein Herz?
>
> A posthorn sounds from the road.
> Why is it that you leap so high,
> My heart?
>
> The post brings no letter for you.
> Why, then, do you surge so strangely,
> My heart? [Wigmore, trans., 369]

In the first stanza, the narrator hears the sounds of a post horn; the dotted rhythms and dominant-tonic harmonies of the opening measures represent, perhaps, a horse and the simply diatonic sound of a post horn.[25] In the second line, the narrator asks why "it" is springing so high, and the German *es* could refer to the *Posthorn* or *Herz*. The first, declarative sentence that describes what is happening is set by Schubert to plain dominant-tonic harmonies in E♭ major. The second line that sets up the slippage in metaphor among the sound of the horn, the galloping of the postman's horse, and the excitement of the narrator is set to a rapid modulation first to the subdominant (A♭ major), then to the subdominant of the subdominant (D♭ major). See ex. 16. This is a musical "springing up" to dominant-preparation chords that could lead to a decisive dominant-tonic cadence. Instead of this diatonic cadence, Schubert sets a repetition of line 2 to a chromatically descending bass (D♭ in mm. 15–16, C♮ in m. 17, C♭ in m. 18, to B♭ in m. 19) that resolves to tonic in m. 24. The rapid springing up to the subdominant of the subdominant sets the narrator's heart's hope that there is a metaphoric relation between its galloping and the galloping of the postman's horse, between an external image of excitement and

Example 16. "Die Post," mm. 11–15.

Example 17. "Die Post," mm. 16–20.

an internal one. But the accompaniment is "aware" of something of which the vocal line is not; during the vocal rests in mm. 16–18, the space between the tonic and the subdominant of the subdominant that had been opened with leaping fourths (E♭ / A♭ / D♭) deflates to a chromatically descending third in the bass (D♭-C♮-C♭-B♭). See ex. 17. The German augmented-sixth chord of m. 18 moving to the dominant reminds me of the German augmented-sixth chord that had driven the nail into the coffin of the narrator's hopes in m. 44 of "Einsamkeit."

The space in the text between the two stanzas is set by Schubert as a measure of silence—m. 26. This measure silences the heart's desire for a metaphoric relation to the external world; the pulse of the music continues, but it is not connected to notes. The arrival of E♭ minor is connected *rhythmically* to the music in E♭ major; a fermata would have severed such a connection. The connection between E♭ major and E♭ minor is also implicit in Schubert's treatment of E♭ major. During the accompaniment's chromatic descent from the subdominant of the subdominant to the dominant of E♭ via the German augmented-sixth chord, all the accidentals of E♭ minor have been "added" to the key signature (D♭ in m. 12, G♭ in m. 13, and C♭ in m. 18). The diatonic, bright sound of E♭ major that sets the declarative first sentence in the text unravels to represent the moment at which the metaphoric slippage occurs.

Schubert sets the beginning of the second stanza to E♭ minor, which moves down stepwise to D♭ major in m. 30; D♭ had been the subdominant of the subdominant in E♭ major, the signifier of leaping hope of the heart/the sound of the post horn/a desire for a metaphoric connection among these images. Schubert links *Dich* in the first line of the second stanza to *mein Herz* in the first stanza through D♭ major triads that occur in m. 15 and m. 30. I have suggested above that, when the vocal line is singing, the music represents its desire and that, when the vocal line rests, the music represents something more—a slippage in the metaphoric signification suggested above (mm. 16–19) and a rupture in the metaphoric connection between the narrator's heart and external images (m. 26). Thus, D♭ represents the heart that the narrator incessantly questions in the song. This process continues in the setting of the rest of the second stanza as the leaping motion continues to G♭ major (the subdominant of the subdominant of the subdominant of E♭ major). Schubert concludes his setting of the second stanza to an extension of the diatonic dominant-tonic harmony of his setting of the first line of the first stanza.

Schubert sets stanzas 3 and 4 to the exact same music:

> Nun ja, die Post kommt aus der Stadt,
> Wo ich ein liebes Liebchen hat',
> Mein Herz!
>
> Willst wohl einmal hinübersehn,
> Und fragen, wie es dort mag gehn,
> Mein Herz?

But yes, the post comes from the town
Where I once had a beloved sweetheart,
My heart!

Do you want to peep out
And ask how things are there,
My heart? [Wigmore, trans., 369]

These lines represent the second (non)arrival of the beloved's letter. Stanzas 1–2 depict the narrator's hope and disappointment, first that he does not get a letter from his beloved, and that there is a metaphoric slippage between his heart and external images. He seems to hear the postman's horn, doesn't get a letter, and reacts by exploring the discrepancy between the absence of a letter and his pounding heart's driving rhythm. But, in stanzas 3–4, we discover, retrospectively, that stanzas 1–2 had been a fantasy—a textual and musical representation of desire anterior to a potential arrival of a letter. Stanzas 3–4 depict the postman actually coming, and, as he does, the narrator's attention swerves away from the postman and the knowledge that he does not have a letter for the narrator, and the narrator ponders the connection between the postman and his point of origin (not destination). The (non)letter thus arrives in this song for a second time since the letter in "Die Post" is, in fact, "a letter in a bottle." In *Enjoy Your Symptom*, Žižek discusses a letter always reaching its destination as soon as it is placed in circulation; that is, a message in a bottle (*Flaschenpost*) always reaches its destination despite the fact that it is addressed to no one. Its destination is the imagined reader whom the sender imagines him/herself to reach as soon as his/her hand lets it go.

The letter paradoxically bears in its silence the message of the alienation of the narrator from not only his beloved but the social order in which she lives. The poignancy of the second part of the text lies in the narrator's attempt to transform a passive experience of seeing desire unravel into an active experience of going back to the letter's point of origin. Schubert connects these seemingly different registers of experience (passive to active) to the same, exact music, to make the song musically clear about letters reaching their destination twice in apparently different but profoundly similar ways.

The narrator reiterates question after question to his heart concerning desire in the setting of stanzas 1–2. This is the first (non)arrival of the letter in the song; its first (non)arrival is its anticipation within the subjectivity of the narrator. When voice and accompaniment sound together, the music leaps in hope to the subdominant of the subdominant of the subdominant. When the voice rests, the accompaniment slips. In the setting of stanzas 3–4, the narrator reiterates question after question to his heart concerning the letter as something to be *sent,* not received. He wants to reenter the social space from which he has been severed; the letter (which he cannot send, as the unanswered questions attest) is one that he wants to send back to a projection of himself before he was separated from social space. Schubert's exact repetition of the music of stanzas 1–2 in stanzas 3–4 irrevocably grounds the futility of both gestures in the structure of desire that can never reach its object. The first necessary failure of the letter to reach its destination is set by Schubert as the unraveling of conventional musical representation as the voice rests; in the second part, the same vocal rests represent the failure of the narrator even to send out a message in a bottle.

At the outset of "Der greise Kopf," the note A♭ is subordinate to G♮, the fifth scale degree of tonic C minor. The upper neighbor A♭-G♮ is present in m. 1 in the accompaniment; in mm. 1–3, A♭¹ is transferred to A♭², the harmony of mm. 2–3 is a fully diminished-seventh chord of the tonic C minor over a C pedal. In m. 7, Schubert associates the narrator's illusion that he has grown old (as if the snow on his head were white hair) with the note A♭ given the song's first vocal embellishment in m. 7. The misrecognition of the narrator is not just that the snow is snow and his young hair is young hair but that his subjectivity depends on a correspondence between his psyche and the outside world. The misrecognition that asserts the metaphoric relation between snow, his suffering, his desire for death, and the external world is in place precisely because of this traditional A♭-G♮ neighbor motion. The pleasure this misrecognition gives the narrator is represented by Schubert in A♭ being enharmonically respelled as G♯ in mm. 11–16; Schubert tonicizes A minor (the raised submediant of C minor) and then G major (the dominant of C minor). The text to this articulation of the raised submediant and the dominant is "Da glaubt' ich schon ein Greis zu sein, / Und hab mich sehr gefreut" ("I thought I was already an old man, / And I rejoiced" [Wigmore, trans., 369]). See ex. 18. In the example,

Example 18. "Der greise Kopf," mm. 6–14.

the connection between A♭ and G♯ is clear; the B♮ fully diminished-seventh chord (dominant substitute in C minor) is respelled as a G♯ fully diminished-seventh chord (dominant substitute of the raised submediant in C minor).

A♭ pulls away from its conventional neighbor motion as Schubert sets the lines "Doch bald ist er hinweggetaut, / Hab wieder schwarze Haare, / Dass mir's vor meiner Jugend graut" ("But soon it melted away; / Once again I have black hair, / So that I shudder at my youth" [Wigmore, trans., 369]). The text represents the metaphoric relation collapsing; the narrator simply has black, young hair; and the lack of a correspondence between the narrator and his environment is horrifying to him. A passage in octaves reminiscent of "Die Wetterfahne"

Example 19. "Der greise Kopf," mm. 20–29.

opens up the space between the A♭ of m. 20 and the G♮ of C minor in m. 29. See ex. 19.

Notice that the unison line shown in ex. 19 shows rhetorical and musically metrical accents on C♮ in m. 25 setting *weit,* A♭ in m. 27 setting a reiteration of *weit,* and G♮ in m. 29—the dominant of tonic C minor. The music is an excruciating setting of the text; the yearning for the grave in the text is set to a large-scale descending major third. The silence of the text as the music sounds the dominant in m. 29 represents the horror that the half step A♭-G♮ brings the narrator not forward to the grave but right back where he started. Notice how the C♮-A♭-G♮ motion suggests a slow motion in two-measure groupings—a representation of the narrator's funereal desire. The return to tonic in m. 30 comes one measure "too soon"—a representation of the shock of the return to his present suffering.

Measure 40 is crucial for the representation of A♭'s conventional moorings. At the beginning of m. 40, A♭ emerges from an inner voice of a half-diminished-seventh chord to move to the bass by the end of the measure. This is the first and last time in the song that the A♭-G♮ motion governs the *bass.*

"Täuschung" is structured similarly; it is a song about the support that conventional representation provides the narrator. In the first part of the text, the narrator acknowledges that he is following an illusory light on his wanderings; the lilting A major sonorities seem an ironic contrast to this recognition of illusion. But, as soon as the music turns to A minor in m. 22, we see that, underneath the illusion that the song represents, there is unbearable pain—represented by the collapse of C♯ to C♮. Schubert not only moves back to A major, but he fills in the third A♭-A♯-B♭-B♯-C♯ from mm. 28–31, respelling C♮ as B♯ and subordinating it to A major. The violence of this rising line of half steps that (re)assert tonic A major is reflected in the accompaniment; the lilting accompaniment figures disappear for the first and last time in the song in mm. 28–30. A major then completes the song with the line "Nur Täuschung ist für mich Gewinn" ("Even mere illusion is a boon to me!" [Wigmore, trans., 371]). The meaning of this line is crucial for the narrator's subjectivity as I understand Schubert's representation of it; *Täuchung* is not illusion or disappointment but a self-conscious mastery of conventional means of representation. In the musical language of this song, illusion is the narrator's reward because he is able to re-inscribe C♮ as B♯ into the orbit of the song's major mode.[26]

"Die Nebensonnen" is the last song in the cycle in which conventionality is securely in place.[27] The E♮-F♮ motive of "Gute Nacht" (re)appears once more in the cycle. The pitch class E♯ appears in the bass in m. 12, a local leading tone to the submediant harmony (F♯ minor) later in the measure. Notice that, at the precise moment the music sounds E♯, the text refers to desire: "Als *wollten* sie [die Nebensonnen] nicht weg von mir" ("As if unwilling to leave me" [Wigmore, trans., 372]). See ex. 20.

After the song turns to the parallel minor in m. 16, E♯ is enharmonically respelled as F♮; the sigh F♮-E♭ in m. 21 is reminiscent of "Gute Nacht," and the text explicitly reinforces this look back to the expulsion that initiated the cycle; the words *auch wohl* are set to the F♮-E♭

Example 20. "Die Nebensonnen," mm. 9–13.

Example 21. "Die Nebensonnen," mm. 20–23.

sigh: "Ja, neulich hatt' ich auch wohl drei, / Nun sind hinab die besten zwei" ("Yes, not long ago I, too, had three suns; / Now the two best have set" [Wigmore, trans., 372]). See ex. 21. To the phrase *besten zwei,* Schubert transfers the sigh motive to the bass for a tonicization of the submediant of A minor—F major. F♮ turns back to E♯ in m. 28, and the conventional cycle of enharmonic respellings is closed.

Throughout this analysis of *Winterreise,* I have been arguing that Schubert sets musical representations of notes reaching their first, conventional destination and notes reaching their second destination when the musical materials of the first arrival show signs of strain or collapse. But musical representations of the second destination have always been stained by the conventionality of the first destination. All representations of the second destination are logical impossibilities; it is not possible for any signifying system to represent that which evades its signification.[28] But, to vary the title of one of Žižek's books, it is possible to represent the arrival of notes at their second destination by

listening awry. "Der Leiermann" is a song that "listens awry"; it represents that which lies within yet beyond signification.[29] The text of the
song is as follows:

> Drüben hinter'm Dorfe
> Steht ein Leiermann,
> Und mit starren Fingern
> Dreht er was er kann.
>
> Barfuss auf dem Eise
> Schwankt er hin und her;
> Und sein kleiner Teller
> Bleibt ihm immer leer.
>
> Keiner mag ihn hören,
> Keiner sieht ihn an;
> Und die Hunde knurren
> Um den alten Mann.
>
> Und er lässt es gehen
> Alles, wie es will,
> Dreht, und seine Leier
> Steht ihm nimmer still.
>
> Wunderlicher Alter,
> Soll ich mit dir gehen?
> Willst zu meinen Liedern
> Deine Leier drehen?
>
> There, beyond the village,
> Stands an organ-grinder;
> With numb fingers
> He plays as best he can.
>
> Barefoot on the ice
> He totters to and fro,
> And his little plate
> Remains forever empty.
>
> No one wants to listen,
> No one looks at him,

> And the dogs growl
> Around the old man.
>
> And he lets everything go on
> As it will;
> He plays, and his hurdy-gurdy
> Never stops.
>
> Strange old man,
> Shall I go with you?
> Will you grind your hurdy-gurdy
> To my songs? [Wigmore, trans., 372–73]

The song opens with an eight-measure introduction as shown in ex. 22.[30] The first sonority of the song is a vestige of the F♮-E♮ sigh. "Gute Nacht" had opened with F♮-E♮, and F♮ has been enharmonically respelled as E♯ in a variety of contexts throughout the cycle. The E♯ grace note in the bass at the outset of "Der Leiermann" represents, on the surface, trying to get the hurdy-gurdy going. Psychoanalytically, it suggests repetition compulsion—a force that moves again and again to a site of trauma. In m. 3, E♯ reaches its second destination and stays there as it is absorbed by the B♮-F♯ drone.

In the text, the narrator mistakes his fantasy for reality; he forgets to forget not only that subjectivity is supported by an arbitrary network of signifiers but that he has been interested throughout the cycle in maintaining the binary, metaphoric relation between himself and the external world. In "Der Leiermann," this binary almost totally collapses. The subjective crisis in the text is conveyed by overuse of the conjunction *and*, suggesting an endless series without subordination.

After an eight-measure introduction in the piano, the setting of stanzas 1–2 is identical to the setting of stanzas 3–4. This music, repeated

Example 22. "Der Leiermann," mm. 1–8.

Table 1

mm. 1–8	introduction	
mm. 9–10 = mm. 31–32	piano left hand and voice	unit a
mm. 11–12 = mm. 33–34	piano	unit b
mm. 13–14 = mm. 35–36	piano left hand and voice	unit a
mm. 15–16 = mm. 37–38	piano	unit b
mm. 17–18 = mm. 39–40	piano left hand and voice; new idea	unit c
mm. 19–20 = mm. 41–42	piano; new idea	unit d
mm. 21–22 = mm. 43–44	piano left hand and voice	unit c
mm. 23–24 = mm. 45–46	piano	unit d + v.e.[a]
mm. 25–26 = mm. 47–48	piano left hand and voice; new idea	unit e
mm. 27–30 = mm. 49–52	piano; extended material	unit f

[a] Voice exchange.

once exactly, is composed of twenty-two measures of two-measure alternating fragments, with one exception at the end, the four-measure fragments mm. 27–30 and 49–52. The precision of this large-scale repetition is illustrated in table 1 with musical ideas given motivic tags represented by lowercase letters.[31] The extraordinary regularity of this music, its mechanical alternation of two-measure phrases between the voice and the accompaniment, as well as the large-scale repetition of the music to set both stanzas of poetry represent musically the narrator's lack of connection to his own consciousness.[32]

Stanzas 1–4 are in third-person narration; the narrator is describing what he sees. In the fifth stanza, the voice shifts to the second person; the narrator addresses the *Leiermann* directly. For me, the narrator has been addressing a projection of himself all along without knowing it. The music's psychotic "forgetting to forget" is signified not only by the mechanically repetitive structures above but by the drone fifth that pervades the music.

Schubert sets the fifth stanza as an incomplete fragment in terms of phrase and pitch structure. After the obsessive two-measure units of the previous fifty-two measures, the piece ends with a single six-measure vocal phrase. The four-measure postlude in the piano is very fragmentary as well. Measure 58 is like m. 49 with one rhythmic and one dynamic change. The dotted rhythm of m. 49 has been eliminated,

Example 23. "Der Leiermann," overview of the vocal part.

and the dynamic level rises suddenly from *pianissimo* throughout to *forte*—a sudden and dramatic shift. Measures 59–60 are unit b from the setting of the first two stanzas with a dynamic marking that brings the music back to *pianissimo.* The song ends with cadences we have heard at mm. 13 and 17 with middle D♮ added for tonal clarity.

The texture of the setting of the fifth stanza shifts subtly. No longer is there a clear alternation of two-measure phrases between the voice and the piano; from mm. 53–58, the voice and piano play *together.* This musical togetherness pulls at the text that ends with an unanswered question. The relation between the unanswered question in the text and the music that sets the unanswered question represents the psychosis of the song. We hear what the narrator cannot understand; he has been accompanying himself all along.

A crucial shift in the pitch structure of the vocal part represents the narrator not knowing that his question cannot be answered. Example 23 provides an overview of the vocal part; the example shows that the vocal part clearly outlines the key of B minor and stays within the octave F♯^{1}-F♯^{2}. The example shows that the harmonic implication of the vocal phrases is i-V in mm. 9–10, 13–14, 17–18, 21–22; the vocal line closes on i in B minor for the first time in m. 26 right before the four-measure extension closes out the setting of the first stanza. Note the musical irony of the voice closing on tonic for the first time on the word *leer* (empty).[33] The vocal line in the setting of the fifth stanza disrupts this clear tonal structure. The vocal line in the setting of stanzas 1–4 had plenty of D♮s to make the tonal focus clear, and the melodic and harmonic close on B minor clear in mm. 26 and 48. In the vocal setting of the fifth stanza, there is only one $D\natural$, a passing sixteenth note, and the vocal part hauntingly stresses $F\sharp$ at $F\sharp^1$ and $F\sharp^2$ pitch levels. The $F\sharp^1$-$F\sharp^2$ octave had been the limits of the voice for the settings of the first four stanzas; for the setting of the fifth stanza, the limit is strained. The deep structure of the vocal part from mm. 9–48 is a B-minor scale or a B-minor triad; the deep structure of the vocal part from mm. 53–58 is an open $F\sharp^1$-$F\sharp^2$ octave suggesting the dominant. And, of course, the dominant represents the harmonic correlate of the unanswerable question in the text. Furthermore, the octave limit is breached by two upper neighbors in mm. 56–57. The repetition of the $G\natural^2$-$F\sharp^2$ neighbor fuses what the narrator can never know. The text asks whether the Leiermann would like to play *"my* songs" ($G\natural^2$-$F\sharp^2$) on *"your* hurdy-gurdy" ($G\natural^2$-$F\sharp^2$). They are one and the same.

Schubert ends the cycle with the letter having reached its second destination—not death as the narrator so desires throughout the cycle, but something much worse, contact with a piece of the inscrutable Real.[34]

Having taken a rather large-grain approach to issues of music theory, musicology, and psychoanalysis in *Winterreise* in this chapter, the next chapter probes in much greater detail how two late Schubert songs index their psychoanalytic features into precise details of musical-theoretical analysis. The psychoanalysis will probe mirror fantasies, doubles, and the gaze in music; the music theory will focus on Schenkerian voice-leading graphs of the songs.

4

Music and the Gaze:

Schubert's "Der Doppelgänger"

and "Ihr Bild"

Schubert wrote *Schwanengesang* between August and October 1828. The Heine settings in particular have attracted interest because of the beauty and simplicity of both their texts and Schubert's extraordinary musical settings.[1] Two of Heine's poems are particularly suggestive for an exploration of music and psychoanalysis—"Der Doppelgänger"[2] and "Ihr Bild."[3] Both poems represent a male narrator whose subjectivity depends on the gaze.[4] Recent psychoanalytic criticism has explored the different structures in the *look* and the *gaze*. As discussed in the chapter on music as sonorous envelope and acoustic mirror, the look facilitates communication; it divides social relations into clear subject/object binaries; it helps distinguish speakers from listeners. The gaze, on the other hand, is an overdetermined look; it often bears an uncanny sense of looking and *being looked at;* subject/object relations are confused; the gaze often suggests judgment or being exposed to the whim of a threatening superego. The gaze is more than just "staring"; the gaze is the representation of a transposed look onto an object that "objectively" cannot look.

In "Der Doppelgänger" and "Ihr Bild," a male subject gazes at an object from which he has been barred; in each poem, the gaze then shifts to an external position to reveal to the subject the emptiness at the heart of his fantasy support.[5] In "Der Doppelgänger," the subject stares first at the empty house where his beloved had lived for the first four lines of the poem. His gaze then slips to another male subject that the narrator realizes is himself in the next four lines. At the moment of revelation, the subject thus sees himself twice, simultaneously: first, he sees himself from the same subject position from which he had gazed at the beloved's house; and, second, he sees *that* subject position as if from the position of a detached observer. For the last four lines, the narrator addresses his double as if (an)other; the poem ends on a cru- cially unanswered/unanswerable question, reminiscent, perhaps, of the question that closes *Winterreise*:

> Still ist die Nacht, es ruhen die Gassen,
> In diesem Hause wohnte mein Schatz;
> Sie hat schon längst die Stadt verlassen,
> Doch steht noch das Haus auf dem selben Platz.
>
> Da steht auch ein Mensch und starrt in die Höhe,
> Und ringt die Hände vor Schmerzensgewalt;
> Mir graust es, wenn ich sein Antlitz sehe—
> Der Mond zeigt mir meine eigne Gestalt.
>
> Du Doppelgänger! du bleicher Geselle!
> Was äffst du nach mein Liebesleid,
> Das mich gequält auf dieser Stelle,
> So manche Nacht in alter Zeit?[6]
>
> The night is still, the streets are dumb,
> This is the house where dwelt my dear;
> Long since she's left the city's hum
> But the house stands in the same place here.
>
> Another man stands where the moonbeams lace,
> He wrings his hands, eyes turned to the sky,
> A shudder runs through me—I see his face:
> The man who stands in the moonlight is I.
>
> Pale ghost, twin phantom, hell-begot!
> Why do you ape the pain and woe
> That racked my heart on this same spot
> So many nights, so long ago?[7]

The music represents the narrator gazing at his beloved's house by the obsessive four-measure motive at the outset of the song, with its muddy texture, and an incomplete neighbor note C♯ that moves to B♮.

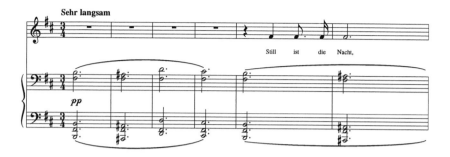

Example 24. "Der Doppelgänger," mm. 1–6.

Example 25. "Der Doppelgänger," a reduction of the vocal line.

See ex. 24.[8] The musical signifier of the gaze is the pitch class F♯, which is ubiquitous in the music; it is even prolonged through the tonicization of D♯ minor from mm. 47–50.[9] Schubert sets the turn of the narrator's gaze back on himself as a gradual process of revelation. The musical signifier of *recognition* is the pitch class G♮ as upper neighbor to F♯. The vocal line begins on F♯[1] and moves slowly up an octave to F♯[2]. G♮s creep into the vocal line slowly as upper neighbor notes to F♯s; the climactic G♮ in mm. 41–42 is resolved in its register only in m. 52. See ex. 25.

Once this shock of recognition has been registered, the narrator addresses the double with an unanswerable question, and the vocal line has no more G♮s in the song—a musical representation of the unique status of this shock. The music in B minor with G♮ as an upper neighbor to F♯ represents the fantasy of the gaze in place as a representation of the narrator first gazing at the house of the beloved and then at the narrator's other. After the G♮^{2} of mm. 41–42, the vocal line retraces its ascent from F♯^{1} to F♯^{2} in phrases that sound like recitatives, and the final line sinks down from F♯^{2} to B♮^{1} with a clear sense of melodic resolution. The absence of G♮ upper neighbors to the gazing F♯ signifies the slip in the gaze of the other as other to a gaze of the other as *self*. And here is the real double of the poem represented in Schubert's music. The G♮-F♯ neighbor signifies the narrator's (mis)recognition of the other as other; the collapse of the G♮ signifies the perception of *that* gaze both from its "original" subject position and from the position of the double himself—from public space.

What kind of musical fantasy of doubling is this? And how does the double function for the narrator driven again and again to a site of trauma? In his essay "The Uncanny," Freud points out that there are *two* kinds of doubles in literature, each corresponding to a distinct stage of development. The first moment of psychic doubling "was originally an insurance against destruction of the ego." And, for Freud, forms of the double "are a harking-back to particular phases in the evolution of the self-regarding feeling, a regression to a time when the ego was not yet sharply differentiated from the external world and from other persons."[10] Freud points out that the positive doubling that is a product of primary narcissism is replaced by a more threatening double—that part of the self that monitors—the superego. The double that first multiplies and therefore protects the self begins to look back at the ego from (a fantasy of) social space.

Schubert's setting of Heine's double is a mute, threatening double—a remnant of the double that had once protected the ego of the narrator. Lawrence Kramer points out that Schubert sets Heine's lines of direct address to the double with a nostalgic recitative; and the music does melodically and harmonically resolve, bringing the music to its hermeneutic conclusion.[11] See ex. 26.

This double is a bad double abjected from developing subjectivity since he/it is radically split from the narrator's ego (like Freud's second kind of double as agent of the superego). And he/it continuously draws

Example 26. "Der Doppelgänger," mm. 52–56.

the narrator back to a site of trauma. For Lawrence Kramer, "The spare repetitiveness that Schubert associates with the spectral double has a generic basis. The speakers in the Heine poems that Schubert set in 1828 are victims of compulsive repetition who return endlessly to the scene of their worst loss. Similar compulsives, haunted by sexuality or guilt, are frequent in the music and literature of the Romantic period."[12]

In *Beyond the Pleasure Principle,* Freud discusses repetition compulsion as the structure that enables developing subjects to master separation from the mother in early infancy. For Freud, pleasure is produced by a reduction in tension. When, for example, a child plays the famous fort-da game, he/she is both repeating and mastering his/her separation from the mother. For Freud, the game transforms a passive experience into an active one, and unpleasure is thereby changed into pleasure as the absence is symbolically mastered through play.[13] But Freud discovers that certain forms of trauma (such as those experienced during the First World War and self-destructive acts) produce symptoms of repetition compulsion that go beyond the pleasure principle. Freud characterizes the activity of the psyche as a tension between life and death instincts. Traumatic dreams, memories, and self-destructive acts are representations of repetition compulsion in the service of the death instincts; fort-da games, the symbolic, active mastery of trauma experienced passively, are representations of repetition compulsion in the service of the life instincts.[14]

For Lacan, the subject is always split, and traumatic loss is central to subjectivity. The subject can only return again and again to an impossible lack—the *objet a,* the (always necessarily) lost object. Lacan describes the psychic apparatus as a circle that cannot close; in the space of blocked closure is the *objet a.* See ex. 27.[15]

For Žižek, "It is important to grasp this inherent impediment [the *objet a*] in its *positive* dimension: true, the *objet a* prevents the circle of pleasure from closing, it introduces an irreducible displeasure, but the psychic apparatus finds a sort of perverse pleasure *in this displeasure itself,* in the never-ending, repeated circulation around the unattainable, always missed object. The Lacanian name for this 'pleasure in pain' is of course enjoyment (*jouissance*), and the circular movement which finds satisfaction in failing again and again to attain the object . . . is the Freudian *drive.*"[16] The remarks below will show how "Der Doppelgänger" is a musical representation of this Lacanian enjoyment.[17]

The pitch class G♮ seems to disappear after it vanishes from *the vocal line* from m. 43 to the end of the song; but the note swerves into an E-minor chord that sounds in the *accompaniment's* postlude after the voice's F♯s have reached their hermeneutic destination. The key of E minor has been hovering just out of earshot throughout the song. There are three augmented-sixth chords at crucial and climactic moments in the song; the first two of these chords are spelled as if the song were in E minor; only the third brings the climactic moments of the music clearly into the orbit of the tonic B minor. See ex. 28.

The F♯-G♮ neighbor that had articulated the narrator's horror of recognition in the vocal line gets reversed in the bass of mm. 51–52 to ground the music in B minor; G♮ sounds again in the accompaniment as a ninth in the enormous dominant that brings the fundamental line down to its hermeneutic destination (see mm. 54–55 in ex. 26). And

Example 27. Lacan's structure of the drive according to Žižek.

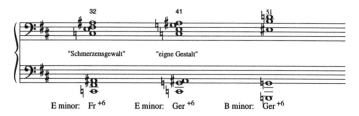

Example 28. "Der Doppelgänger," augmented-sixth chords.

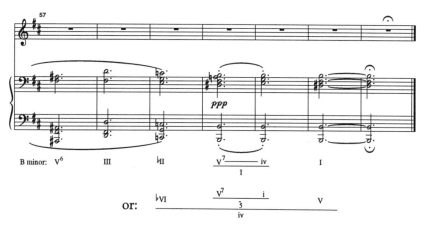

Example 29. "Der Doppelgänger," mm. 57–63.

the piece ends pointing toward but crucially withholding E minor in the accompaniment's postlude; see ex. 29.

Lawrence Kramer suggests that the Picardy-third B-major chord at the end of "Der Doppelgänger" echoes the "dissonant D♯ tonality" of mm. 47–50;[18] but I hear a more intimate, harmonic connection among the last four chords of the song. These chords form the progression (E minor) ♭VI, V⁷, i, V, as noted in the example. The music thus ends on an unresolved harmonic progression. The unresolved dominant of E minor seems to represent the text's unanswered/unanswerable question. But, more than this, E minor is the music's *objet a,* the signifier of the music's irreducible alterity. The pitch class G♮ swerves from the voice into the accompaniment to suggest that, at the moment of the narrator's revelation, self-conscious knowledge of the *objet a* slips away. A Schenkerian sketch of the entire song is given in ex. 30.

From mm. 5–31, the music tries to achieve a large-scale register transfer from F#¹ to F#². In mm. 31 and 40, the pitch is reached, with diatonic mediant harmonic support; the arpeggiations from mm. 26–31 and 35–41 are supported by dominant harmonies, and F#² is supported by an augmented-sixth chord in m. 32 and the diatonic mediant in m. 40. Only after the shock of recognition has been psychoanalytically

Example 30. A middleground sketch of "Der Doppelgänger."

registered in mm. 41–42 can the music achieve its musical register transfer. From mm. 47–52, the arpeggiation of D♯ minor leads to F♯^{2} as the head tone $\hat{5}$. The head tone $\hat{5}$ (F♯^{2}) descends tentatively without support for $\hat{4}$, as shown in the example. Schubert subtracts G♮s from the vocal line after the climactic augmented-sixth chord of mm. 41–42 to signify the narrator's recognition that the double is a part of his own split subjectivity. It seems that the music represents mastery of trauma by having the horror of recognition (the neighbor motion in the vocal line F♯-G♮) mastered by the register transfer from the initial F♯^{1} to the F♯^{2} of m. 52. But I think that Schubert hides, but cannot entirely do without, G♮s in the rest of the song. The note is a dissonant ninth in an inner voice in m. 54, and the music evokes E minor (with G♮ as the third) in the song's postlude. And the $\hat{5}$ at the end is a representation of the music's irreducible drive.

In "Ihr Bild," the subject constructs and meditates on an image of his beloved in the first two lines of the poem; in the rest of the poem, the image comes to life, the subject is frozen in terror, and the image vanishes to reveal his own reflection:

> Ich stand in dunkeln Träumen
> Und starrt' ihr Bildnis an,
> Und das geliebte Antlitz
> Heimlich zu leben begann.
>
> Um ihre Lippen zog sich
> Ein Lächeln wunderbar,
> Und wie von Wehmutstränen
> Erglänzte ihr Augenpaar.
>
> Auch meine Tränen flossen
> Mir von den Wangen herab—
> Und ach, ich kann es nicht glauben,
> Dass ich dich verloren hab'![19]
>
> I stood there, lost in dreaming,
> Before her picture—and oh,
> Her dear belovèd image
> Began to live and glow!

> Her lovely lips were parted,
> I saw a smile arise,
> And, as through tears of sorrow,
> A splendor lit her eyes.
>
> My tears burst out overbrimming,
> Brimming bitterly—
> And still I cannot believe it
> That you are lost to me![20]

On the surface, the poem is about a frustrated male yearning for a female object of desire. On a subtler level, the poem is about a musical representation of mirror misrecognition. The beginning of the poem tells a story in the simple past tense of the narrator looking at a picture of his beloved. Two things are noteworthy: (1) the narrator is looking at a representation of his beloved, and (2) he is talking about a moment in the past. The image of the beloved's face begins to "live," and a delightful smile appears on her face; her eyes gleam as if from melancholy pain. So far, the mode of address has been third person; the beloved has been referred to as *she*. With the *ach* of the final two lines of the poem, the narrator's voice shifts in two essential ways: (1) he uses the present tense, and (2) he addresses the beloved directly.[21]

The poem presents fragments of impressions and links them as if they formed a logical, diachronic narrative. The narrator remembers a dream, *and* the face of his beloved began to become animated. *And,* as if from melancholy, her eyes glistened with tears; *also,* his tears fell on his cheeks; *and, ach,* he can't believe that he lost her. These conjunctions signify narrative coherence. The poem expresses, however, a nightmare of mirror misrecognition that makes these conjunctions sound forced.

Schubert sets this text in an ABA Lied form. The A section sets the text "Ich stand in dunkeln Träumen und starrt' ihr Bildnis an, und das geliebte Antlitz heimlich zu leben began." The music opens with reiterated B♭ octaves in the piano; see ex. 31. Joseph Kerman suggests that this is an example of Schubert's late practice of having songs begin with a piano introduction that is enigmatic; he cites the beginning of "Das Meer" as another example of an ambiguous opener.[22] In an early essay, Heinrich Schenker hears these B♭s embodying the staring idea in the text to be discussed below. For Schenker, the repeated B♭s make

Example 31. "Ihr Bild," mm. 1–2.

Example 32. "Ihr Bild," mm. 1–6.

the listener "stare" acoustically at the music as the narrator in the poem stares at the image of his beloved.[23]

The voice enters on Bb, and on *stand* the doubling that characterizes the relation between voice and piano begins; see ex. 32. The obsessive sound of these opening measures derives in part from the fact that the first eight notes one hears in the music are all Bbs. Measures 3 and 4 fill in the Bb octave with the key Bb minor as the voice is doubled by the piano in two octaves. As can be seen in the example, the melodic structure of this four-measure phrase outlines two double neighbor notes—the first around the note Bb, the key of the A section, and the second around the note Gb, the key of the B section. Three things are noteworthy here. First, each of these phrases is melodically static; one moves around the note Bb, the other around the note Gb. Second, Schubert musically emphasizes the horror of looking in the text through the descending leap of a diminished fifth from the C♮ *und* to the Gb of *starrt* on the downbeat of m. 5.[24] Third, this jolt from C♮ to Gb seems to generate an intensification of the dotted rhythm of m. 3. Not only does a dotted quarter note followed by an eighth note become a *double* dotted eighth note followed by a sixteenth note, but there are *two* dotted figures in m. 5—a musical depiction, not only of a gaze, but of the paralysis that the German word *starr* denotes. The German word *starr* has a semantic field that is larger than the English word *stare*. The verb *starren* means "to stare, to look in a fixed manner"; the adjective *starr,* however, denotes stiffness and petrification as well. Thus, the German *starrt' ihr Bildnis an* suggests the narrator's petrifying gaze.[25]

The accompaniment in mm. 6–8 prolongs the dominant of Bb minor. The text "und das geliebte Antlitz heimlich zu leben begann" suggests that there is a reversal in the text between the fantasy of the narrator looking at an image of his beloved and the image of the beloved *looking at him*.[26] Schubert does remarkable things with this text. First, as the narrator immerses himself in the fantasy of the "living" image of the beloved, the music both turns to Bb *major* and resolves to tonic with full four-part harmony in m. 12.[27] See ex. 33. As opposed to the two static melodic fragments of mm. 2–6 (the double neighbor-note figures on Bb and Gb), the upper voice from mm. 8–12 ascends stepwise to D♮2 and descends stepwise to Bb1.[28] The major mode and full, four-part harmonies represent the illusion of the coming to life of a representation of the beloved.[29]

As in the Beatles' song discussed earlier, unison and doubling at the octave are musical representations of the acoustic mirror. Schubert's acoustic mirror undergoes a transformation in "Ihr Bild." For mm. 2–6, the voice is doubled in the accompaniment two octaves below. The octaves suggest a musical fantasy of the acoustic mirror in which the narrator's voice is at one with the voice of the mother, the other, the object of desire. As the narrator has the illusion that the face of the beloved starts to "live," the acoustic mirror becomes at once more perfect (the voice is doubled *at the unison* by the upper voice of the piano) and distorted. The acoustic mirror vanishes and is replaced by a full four-part harmony culminating in a perfect authentic cadence in Bb major on the downbeat of m. 12.

The highest note in the piece is the Eb2 on the downbeat of m. 11. It

Example 33. "Ihr Bild," mm. 8–14.

is marked for memory in three ways: (1) it is the highest pitch so far, (2) it occurs on the downbeat of the measure that fills in the above-mentioned structural gap between the pitch classes C and G♭ (compare the vocal line, mm. 4–5, and the tenor voice in the piano part, mm. 10–11), and (3) the pitch is the upper neighbor of D♮².

The word in the text that this E♭² sets is *heimlich,* and the connection between a psychoanalytic theory of the uncanny merges precisely at this point in Heine's poetry and Schubert's music. In his essay "The Uncanny," Freud defines the uncanny as "all that arouses dread and creeping horror." But there are many kinds of terror and anxiety that are not uncanny, and Freud narrows his definition as follows: "The 'uncanny' is that class of the terrifying which leads back to something long known to us, once very familiar." Freud's inquiry leads him to explore the space within what he had considered a clear binary opposition, *heimlich/unheimlich:* "What interests us most . . . is to find that among its different shades of meaning the word *heimlich* exhibits one which is identical with its opposite, *unheimlich.* . . . In general we are reminded that the word *heimlich* is not unambiguous, but belongs to two sets of ideas, which without being contradictory are yet very different: on the one hand, it means that which is familiar and congenial, and on the other, that which is concealed and kept out of sight. The word *unheimlich* is only used customarily . . . as the contrary of the first signification, and not of the second."[30]

Through an exploration of the etymology of the word *heimlich,* Freud realized that its meaning began as "familiar, friendly, intimate" and acquired connotations of "fearful and secret." There is a direct relation between etymology and the mind for Freud; what was once familiar (*heimlich*) can become charged with secrecy and fear: "Thus *heimlich* is a word the meaning of which develops towards an ambivalence, until it finally coincides with its opposite, *unheimlich. Unheimlich* is in some way or other a sub-species of *heimlich.*"[31] Heine captures the ambivalence of *heimlich* in this poem. Although the narrator feels in touch with the familiar image of the beloved, these lines are also grotesque; they describe a return of the living dead, a *beginning to live,* a *secretly beginning to live,* a tremor of life. Schubert's music does everything to focus on the word *heimlich* in Heine's text. *Heimlich* is set to the first voice exchange in the piece (marked with a large X in ex. 33; the line "und das geliebte Antlitz heimlich zu leben begann" is set in full four-part harmony cadencing in Bb major after the octaves of mm. 3–6; the voice is doubled at the unison for this line, having been doubled two octaves below from mm. 3–6; the melodic line of mm. 8–12 is conjunct after the static and disjunct melodic line of mm. 2–6; the word *heimlich* articulates the (structurally crucial) note D♮^{2}; the first *crescendo* in the piece emphasizes the word *heimlich;* and the texture thickens gradually from the Bb in mm. 1–2 to the six voices of the perfect authentic cadence on the downbeat of m. 12.[32]

On first hearing, mm. 12–13 sound like a repetition of mm. 10–11 one octave lower, echoing the way mm. 7–8 repeat mm. 5–6 one octave lower. But there is a difference; the C-minor harmony of *heimlich* in m. 11 becomes an Eb-major harmony in m. 13. The accompaniment knows how uncanny the Eb^2 is; it harmonizes the pitch with a C-minor sonority in m. 11 that is supported by the voice exchange that leads to the cadence in Bb *major* in m. 12. The uncanny association of Eb^2 and the major mode is made more explicit in m. 13 as the voice exchange echoes in the accompaniment, transposed to support a major subdominant chord, Eb major; what was a *note* in m. 11 becomes a *chord* in m. 13.

The line "Um ihre Lippen zog sich ein Lächeln wunderbar" is set by Schubert in music that modulates from Bb major to Gb major. See ex. 34. Right before the modulation to Gb major, Schubert reminds us of Bb minor with the Ab^1 in m. 15—a delicate instance of word painting as the eighth note Ab^1 of the syllable *pen* in m. 15 sounds after the Abs in the accompaniment. It is as if the music were slipping to suggest the smile pulling gently around the lips of the beloved. The idea of pulling

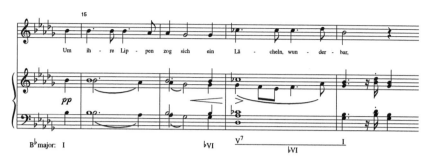

Example 34. "Ihr Bild," mm. 14–18.

in the text is also musically intensified through the 2-3 suspension in the bass on the words *zog sich* in m. 16.[33] The Gbs in m. 16 confirm the modal shift back to Bb minor, remind the listener of the prominence of Gbs earlier in the piece (the downbeats of mm. 5 and 7), and point forward to the key Gb major.

The texture of mm. 14–18 synthesizes the unison doubling of the voice and the accompaniment of mm. 8–12 and the octave doubling of mm. 1–6. It is crucial that the harmonic rhythm slows down so much in this middle section of the song. The harmonic rhythm in mm. 11–12 is two beats of dominant preparation (ii in m. 11 with the voice exchange), two beats of the dominant, and two beats of tonic Bb major in m. 12.[34] In m. 17, there is a full *measure* of a dominant-seventh chord in Gb major with four voices playing whole notes; in m. 18, the chord resolves to one full measure of Gb major. The slow harmonic rhythm draws attention to two crucial ideas in the text. First, the slight *wie* set by the Bb of m. 19 points to the crucial semantic slippage in the poem from objective description to subjective interpretation "*as if* from tears of pain." The Cbs of m. 20 prepare for the whole note Cb of m. 21 (supported by the same dominant-seventh chord that had set the phrase "Lächeln wunderbar"), drawing attention to tears that gleam. It will be with this image that Heine shifts from images suggesting a representation of the beloved to images suggesting contemplation of the self, to be discussed below. See ex. 35.

The imagery of the beloved is getting more precise, or, better, it is getting closer to her *eyes: ihr Bildnis, Antlitz, Lippen, Augen.* As the narrator's eyes meet the eyes of the beloved, the music "stares" as well;

it stares and becomes stiff, capturing both aspects of the earlier *starr* in German. And the sixteenth notes in mm. 18 and 22 echo the only other sixteenth notes in the piece—those following the music that sets the phrase "und starrt' ihr Bildnis an."

The only ornament in the vocal line is on the key word *Augen,* in m. 21 the organ of specularity.[35] This ornament also contains in microcosm the double neighbor notes of mm. 2–6. The music from mm. 10–22 also articulates a motivic concern of the music that cannot be linked to word painting or a musical depiction of the acoustic mirror: a chromatic descent from a *minor third* (Bb, A♮, Ab, G♮ in mm. 10–11, piano, inner voice), to a *perfect fifth* (Bb, A♮, Ab, G♮, F♮, Eb in mm. 12–13 piano, lowest voice), to a *major sixth* (Bb, Ab, Gb, F♮, Eb, Ebb, Db in mm. 19–21 piano, lowest voice). In a piece in which the vocal part so closely acoustically mirrors the piano part, this descending chromatic fragment is an extra, a supplement, something that is not inscribed within the experience of the narrator. Psychoanalytically, the descending line is a musical signifier of abject secretion; the line begins as the music sets the first word in the text that depicts the image of the beloved: *Antlitz* in m. 10.

The music had modulated smoothly *to* Gb major from mm. 14–18; it jolts *back* to Bb in mm. 23–24. See ex. 36. The Italian augmented-sixth chord of m. 23 gives us the first E♮ in the piece; the augmented-sixth interval resolves outward to an F♮ octave in Bb minor. Schenker hears the progression in mm. 22–24 bringing the narrator back to himself; while he had stared at the image at the outset of the song (musically

Example 35. "Ihr Bild," mm. 19–23.

Example 36. "Ihr Bild," mm. 19–24.

signified by the reiterated B♭s), the narrator is brought back to his own suffering and stares at it in mm. 22–24.[36] For me, mm. 22–24 are a horrific echo of the psychotic curtsey motive of m. 18 in which the narrator hallucinates that he is interacting with an image of the beloved; in m. 24, the narrator sees himself in the mirror.

This move back to B♭ is, of course, quite organic and typical of Romantic harmony. As Robert Bailey has pointed out, a chromatic key is often in a third relation to tonic, as the B♭-G♭ opposition of this piece would suggest.[37] Also, the pitch class G♭ is clearly a structural upper neighbor to pitch class F♮ (the fifth scale degree of B♭ major/minor) in mm. 5 and 6. The tonicization of G♭ major in the middle section of the music represents a large-scale working out of this local detail. And the G♭-F♮ voice leading is crystal clear in mm. 23–24 in an inner voice.

The music from m. 25 to the end repeats with some differences the music of mm. 3–14. The music returns us to the octaves of the beginning as the text shifts to a perception of the narrator's own suffering: "Auch meine Tränen flossen mir von den Wangen herab." The *auch* is a desperate attempt to give connection to an experience that really involves rupture.[38] The word *auch* and the fact that moist eyes characterize the image of the beloved *and* the narrator suggest, as mentioned earlier, that the text is a fantasy in which the image of the beloved becomes a mirror reflection of the narrator himself. The final lines "und ach! ich kann es nicht glauben, dass ich dich verloren hab" refer first to a general sense in which the entire poem represents an attempt that will fail to regain access to his lost beloved through fantasy, dream, art. The lines also suggest that the narrator has lost the *image* of the beloved just after the lines "und wie von Wehmutstränen erglänzte ihr Augenpaar." Schubert represents the consequences of "as if" in an erasure of fantasy—a jolt back to B♭ in mm. 23–24. Although the voice leading is clear and close, we expect a dominant chord to connect the dominant-preparation augmented-sixth chord to the tonic B♭ chord that initiates the repeat of the A section.[39]

Two additional details suggest that the narrator is fantasizing about looking at an image of his beloved that becomes an image of himself. First, the nouns in the poem that describe what is seen track one trajectory: *Bildnis, Antlitz, Lippen, Lächeln, Augenpaar, Tränen, Wangen.* The narrator says that the eyes of the beloved gleam as if from tears of pain; then he says that his tears, too (!), are flowing from his cheeks. The narrator tries to hold on to the hallucination of seeing his beloved, but he cannot. Her image begins to live; a smile rises from around her lips; but, *as if* from suffering, her eyes gleam. The spell is broken, and he returns to his own reflection in the mirror. It is poignantly ironic that the music to the earlier line "und das geliebte Antlitz heimlich zu leben begann" is also used for the shift to the horror of the narrator's *present tense:* "und ach! ich kann es nicht glauben, dass ich dich verloren hab'!" See ex. 37.

Heine saturates the text with "ah" sounds: "und d*a*s geliebte *A*ntlitz heimlich zu leben beg*a*nn" (mm. 8–12) and "und *a*ch Ich k*a*nn es nicht glauben, d*a*ss ich dich verloren h*a*b" (mm. 30–34). Schubert sets all these linguistic "ah"s to B♭-major chords (except "k*a*nn"); the "ah"s prefigure the exclamation *ach* that pinpoints the narrator's revelation of his mirror misrecognition; Schubert's "ah" is the B♭-major chord that first sets up, then collapses, the narrator's fantasy support.

Example 37. "Ihr Bild," mm. 30–36.

The poignancy consists in music that had set the eerie coming to life of the beloved "und das geliebte Antlitz heimlich zu leben begann" returning in the setting of the text "und ach, ich kann es nicht glauben, dass ich dich verloren hab." The music is in four-part chorale style, as if a phrase from a Bach chorale. There is an incredible discrepancy between the Steven King-esque return of the living dead image in the text and Schubert's conventionally voiced harmonies.[40]

The Bb-*major* sonority at the close of the phrase that sets both "und das geliebte Antlitz heimlich zu leben begann" and "und ach, ich kann es nicht glauben, dass ich dich verloren hab" represents Lacanian misrecognition. The word *verloren* suggests both literal and Lacanian loss. On the surface, the phrase "Ich kann es nicht glauben . . ." is routine, rhetorical, and melodramatic. More crucially, the narrator really cannot confront the lost object of desire (". . . dass ich dich verloren hab"). Why? Because knowledge has an ambivalent charge in the structure of his gaze. For the first phrase of the text, the narrator looks at his representation of the beloved as the gaze shifts to *her* or *it*. For the second phrase of the text, the narrator seems to know that he has lost the representation of "her" or "it," but he has lost a fantasy of his own mirror reflection. He has lost, in short, what he could never have had—the object cause of desire.

Schubert makes five changes with the music from mm. 12–14 for the end of the song from mm. 34–36. See ex. 37. (1) Pitch class Gb is clearly inscribed within the key of Bb minor with the Eb-minor chord on the downbeat of m. 35; (2) the music has no *crescendo-diminuendo* as it had in m. 13 (this would have emphasized a clear echo of the melodic rise to *heimlich* in m. 11); (3) the passage is played *forte* as if slamming the door shut on a song that had had *pianissimo* markings before m. 34; (4) the four-part harmony of mm. 13–14 becomes darker with five, six, and seven voices; and (5) while the dominant harmony has four voices in m. 13 (see ex. 33), six voices of the dominant in m. 35 bear witness to the final cadence.

What about doubling, playing in unison, and the acoustic mirror as the song ends? The song is a musical representation of a fantasy of reliving a moment in the acoustic-mirror stage poised right between complete union with the voice of the mother and a recognition of acoustic difference between one's own voice and the voices of the mother and the *father*.

The text is a concise and complete visual mirror fantasy. The (visual) mirror stage in Lacan is that phase governed by the visual identification of the child with its own reflection in a mirror or in the mother's face. The mirror phase is the quintessential experience of Lacan's Imaginary Order; it is ruled by binary oppositions in which the child feels at one with, or lost without, the (m)other's reflection in a mirror. Motor incapacity and the fantasy of capturing a perfect image of oneself are crucially interdependent: "The event [the mirror stage] can take place . . . from the age of six months. . . . Unable as yet to walk, or even stand up, and held tightly as he is by some support, human or artificial . . . , he nevertheless overcomes, in a flutter of jubilant activity, the obstructions of his support, and, fixing his attitude in a slightly leaning-forward position, in order to hold it in his gaze, brings back an instantaneous aspect of the image."[41]

As the child's motor capacity grows, he/she realizes that the mirror image is not full, but empty. This retrospective "realization" propels the child toward the Symbolic Order, the realm of language, the mediated deferral of signification, and social conventions: "This moment in which the mirror-stage comes to an end inaugurates, by the identification with the *imago* of the counterpart and the drama of primordial jealousy . . . , the dialectic that will henceforth link the *I* to socially elaborated situations. . . . It is this moment that decisively tips the whole of human knowledge into mediatization through the desire of the Other."[42] "Ihr Bild" represents a single large-scale crossing of this imaginary/symbolic threshold.

The line "und ach! ich kann es nicht glauben, dass ich dich verloren hab'!" is a fantasy of just having crossed from the Imaginary to the Symbolic Order; the narrator uses language to name absence. The *music* represents this separation from the lost object of desire through *register* and *texture*. The five, six, and seven-voice texture in mm. 35–36 represents the voice of the father—another phase within the acoustic mirror. Rosolato discusses the role of the voice of the father in the following extended passage from "La voix":

The revitalization of the voice always implies a swerve, an irreversible trajectory with regard to the lost object. And within that distance, the very agent of that separation, the father has his vocal guarantor. The child thus distinguishes the voice that comes between the mother and him and electively picks up her interest and desire. There is there a difference of register otherwise strictly connected to sexual difference, being the first mark with which he familiarizes himself. If one conceives this loss, this primary abandonment taken up again and remembered as distance by the voice itself, a subtle play of sacrificial evocation arises that will engage itself between that of the man and that of the woman. Because of this separation of the child and the mother, assured by the father, must be added a redoubling with the death of the father, this time to the very principle of the symbolic system: which has the effect of overstepping and at the same time maintaining—the relief—for the lack.[43]

Measures 34–36 represent the voice of the father that inaugurates entry into the Symbolic Order. The apparently routine repetition of the A section of the music is a musical representation of the horror that lies within the narrator's fantasy construction as he emerges from the mirror stage. Musically, another detail represents the narrator's horrified gaze at his own lost reflection. In m. 11 a voice exchange prolongs a supertonic harmony in B♭ major signifying the narrator's conventional fantasy support. In m. 13 the voice exchange moves into a lower register to prolong the (major) subdominant. In m. 33 the voice exchange of m. 11 returns with hideous irony as the narrator registers his loss. In m. 35 the voice exchange moves (again) to a lower register and incorporates in the (minor) subdominant the pitch class G♭ that had signified the gaze throughout the song.

Example 38 shows a Schenkerian sketch for the entire song. The sketch clarifies the analyses above. The middle section tonicizes G♭ major, the harmonic version of the pitch class G♭, Schubert's gazing note; the middle section also prolongs the note B♭ of the fundamental line (what had been scale degree î in B♭ major becomes scale degree ĵ in G♭, articulated with its upper neighbor C♭). Thus, Schenker shows us how the note that had stressed the coming into focus of the image of the beloved ("heimlich zu leben begann") is projected through the middle portion of the work and connected to the revelation signified by "ach, ich kann es nicht glauben, dass ich dich verloren hab."

Example 38. A middleground sketch of "Ihr Bild."

Concluding Remarks

What is the relation between psychoanalysis and Schenkerian voice-leading techniques in these analyses? In the introduction, I suggested that listening as a thing is produced when a piece of music is described and analyzed as if from a stable perspective. Listening as a space is produced when a piece of music enunciates a crossing of thresholds between or among music theory, history, psychoanalysis, and personal experience(s).

Combining Schenkerian voice leading and psychoanalysis to listen to "Der Doppelgänger" and "Ihr Bild" can produce fantasies of the music as *thing* or *space,* depending on whether the two registers are *subordinated* or *coordinated* to one another. Subordination tends to produce a representation of thingness; it denotes a stable relation between a basic, primary structure and a dependent, secondary structure or feature. If I assert, for example, that the psychoanalytic material of this chapter is subordinated to the Schenkerian voice-leading analyses, then I produce a representation of the music as if a thing. Coordination, on the other hand, tends to produce fantasies of space, more a signifying structure that is open than a signified structure that is closed. This is how Schenker and psychoanalysis relate in these songs—as coordinated structures of listening space.

In this chapter, I have examined the structure of the gaze in two of Schubert's late songs; in the next chapter, I turn back to popular music to interrogate the structure of the gaze in two recent versions of a rock song. This turn takes the rest of the chapters of the book into issues of music, representation, gender, and violence; in the next chapter, this violence will be understood as residing in the structure of the male gaze represented first in a high-tech, then thrash-funk version of "Intruder."

5

Peter Gabriel's "Intruder,"

a Cover, and the Gaze

Peter Gabriel's "Intruder" is the first song on his third solo album entitled *Peter Gabriel* issued after his departure from Genesis. The sound of the album is more austere than his earlier work—an influence of the "new wave" producer Steve Lillywhite.[1] The song opens with a one-measure theme played by the snare drum and bass drum; it pervades most of the song: see ex. 39.[2]

The theme is clearly rooted in 1950s and 1960s rock and roll with the signature backbeat in the snare and the eighth notes in the bass drum. There are no cymbals, however, and this omission hardens the sound, makes the song sound threatening.[3] There is a *sforzando* on the bass drum's upbeat to the third beat. The third beat sounds too early; it impinges on the second beat, leaving a brief but haunting silence. Also, Gabriel did something to the fourth beat of the theme to make it sound as if the music were holding its breath. The real time pulse of the music continues to drive the theme along from measure to measure, while, immediately after the snare's backbeat on the fourth beat, the surface of the sound seems to vanish for a split second. It sounds like a sucking in of breath in anticipation of a loud noise, the sound of your breath right before a dish that you've dropped hits the floor.

In m. 3, a sound like a guitar pick being drawn very slowly along a very tight guitar string under heavy amplification emerges. I will call this the "pulling metal" sound. On the surface, it seems to signify literal intrusion into someone's space as if a screen were being forced. The sound is close to the listener, at once very real and very artificial.[4]

Example 39. Peter Gabriel's "Intruder," the opening percussion theme.

Example 40. Peter Gabriel's "Intruder," the "jolt" theme begun in m. 5.

Gabriel subtly prepares the listener for this "pulling metal" sound. If one listens very carefully to the first two measures of the piece (the two measures that immediately precede the entry of "pulling metal"), one can hear the "pulling metal" sound behind, as it were, the second beat (the first snare backbeat).

This is an acoustic intrusion into the listener's space because what we subliminally hear as secondary sound on the second beats of the opening percussion theme becomes primary sound shortly thereafter. In film theory, this is called "sneaking." Sounds, motives, and themes with which the viewer identifies come (as if from a position beyond our control) out of noise or ambient sound.[5] This example of musical sneaking and its intrusion into our listening space binds the listener to the intruder because of the above-mentioned closeness of the "pulling metal" sound. The link between the secondary sound of the second beat of the percussion theme and the emergence of the "pulling metal" sound in m. 3 is secured by Gabriel's choice of the moment at which the "pulling metal" emerges into full acoustic "view": it happens on the second beat of m. 3, the beat of the backbeat behind which it had been hiding. The "pulling metal" sound continues intermittently throughout the first sixteen measures.

In m. 5, Gabriel gives us two new sounds: a "jolt" and a synthesizer "riff." The jolt is shown in ex. 40; it continues for every measure from mm. 5–16. The jolt is a harmonic interval of a perfect fifth; it is overlaid on the opening percussion theme, articulating the first beat and the

sforzando upbeat to the third beat. The open fifth could suggest either
B♭ major or B♭ minor.[6] The synthesizer "riff" sounds first in m. 5, as
shown in ex. 41. This riff both clarifies and obscures the tonality of the
song. The G♭ on the upbeat to the third beat suggests B♭ minor. Taken
together (which is how we hear the two themes), the riff and the jolt
produce a dissonance of a minor second on the upbeat to beat 3. The
G♭ clashes with the F♮. The effect is one of a noise—a representation
of a sound with meaning that is charged with ambiguity.[7]

The riff sounds only once in full in m. 5; from mm. 5–16, the performer improvises minimal "echoes" outlining the minor third of B♭
minor. To me, mm. 5–16 sound like a fantasy of the intruder having
entered a woman's space; the riff echoes minimally and hauntingly for
eleven measures, as if poised and listening.

A theme in B♭ major/minor sounds in mm. 16–19, as shown in ex.
42. The first measure of the theme expands the syncopated sound of
the initial percussion theme; the second measure solidifies the riff's improvised echo described above. The first measure suggests B♭ *major,*
the second measure B♭ *minor.* The note D♭ defines the minor mode
of the second measure of this theme, and Gabriel brings in distorted
voices for the first time in the song right on the D♭. I hear the high,
contorted voice as a male impersonation of a female voice.

There is a long tradition in rock and roll of male singers imitating female voices.[8] Sometimes this suggests an erotic or playful an-
drogyny (Little Richard, Michael Jackson); sometimes it suggests a
fantasy of presymbolic aggression, as if one could get in touch with

Example 41. Peter Gabriel's "Intruder," the synthesizer "riff."

Example 42. Peter Gabriel's "Intruder," the B♭ major/minor theme.

Example 43. Peter Gabriel's "Intruder," the "chant."

Example 44. Peter Gabriel's "Intruder," the major/minor
theme with secondary articulations.

one's anal/sadistic "origins" before sexual difference.[9] There are two
measures of "chant" from mm. 20–22, shown in ex. 43. Here, we get
a choir of distant, distorted male voices. They chant in unpitched syllables on quarter notes that accompany the pitched notes in the example. The notes G♭-A♭-B♭ suggest at once the key of B♭ minor and
the blues scale on which much rock and roll is based. The chant suddenly falls to the low B♭ as if fatigued. In this chant, there is a discrepancy in dynamics between the male, chanting voices and the pitched
instrument. The pitched instrument *crescendos* through the A♭s, while
the male voices maintain a moderate dynamic level throughout.

From mm. 23–24, one clear and close note struck on a small metal
object (a crotale? a triangle?) echoes for eight beats. With the vocal
entry in m. 25, we retrospectively hear the "ringing" of mm. 23–24
as the announcement of vocal entry. And the "ringing" is another example of sneaking in the song. In the major/minor theme discussed
above, there is a secondary sound of a crotale or triangle on crucial
pitches of the theme, as shown by question marks in ex. 44.

We can now clearly link Gabriel's thematic sneaking with the representation of the intruder in the song; the crotale/triangle sound
emerges from its hiding place in the major/minor theme to announce
the solo entry that begins by asserting, taunting, affirming knowledge
("I know"). In m. 25, Peter Gabriel's voice enters. Here is the text as
printed in the CD liner notes:

I know something about opening windows and   doors
I know how to move quietly—to creep across   creaky wooden floors
I know where to find precious things in all   your cupboards and drawers

  Slipping the clippers
  Slipping the clippers through the   telephone wires
  The sense of isolation inspires
  Inspires me

I like to feel the suspense when I'm certain you   know I am there
I like you lying awake, your bated breath   charging the air
I like the touch and the smell of all the   pretty dresses you wear

  Intruder's happy in the dark
  Intruder come
  Intruder come and he leave his mark
       leave his mark

Peter Gabriel's voice as he sings the verse is very close to the microphone; he sings purely, quietly, as if right into the ear of the listener. For me, it sounds as if Gabriel were putting his arm around the male listener's shoulders and sharing with him the narrator's fantasy of intruding into the space of a woman. But how can a listener "identify" with a voice in a song, and how does the proximity of the voice determine listening identification?

In *La voix au cinéma*, Michel Chion discusses voices in film for which the viewer has not seen the source. He calls this voice the *voix acousmatique*.[10] The acousmatic voice in film is made possible by the binary on screen/off screen. In music, such a binary is replaced by a continuum of proximity to the listener's space. Many factors facilitate listening identification with a sung voice—clarity of register, closeness of recording, and minimum of distortion. Peter Gabriel's voice is clear, unstrained, close, acoustically pure, and quiet, singing to us from just the other side of the speaker.

Gabriel's voice changes as he sings the chorus; it becomes tighter, more distorted, more distant.[11] The intrusion fantasy undergoes a shift in these lines from rhetorical exposition ("I know," "I like"—coherent parallel structures sung clear and close to the listener) to a representation of action ("slipping the clippers," "slipping the clippers," "Intruder come and leave his mark"—reiterated fragments sung tighter and fur-

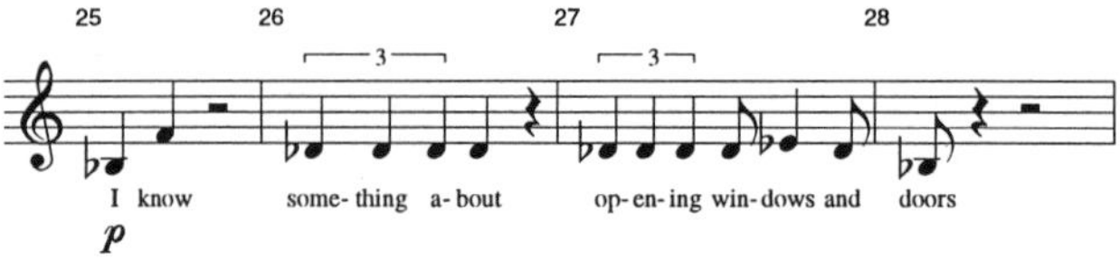

Example 45. Musical setting of each line in the verses of Peter Gabriel's "Intruder."

ther away from the listener). In the penultimate line of each chorus, there is an acoustic realignment. With the line "the sound of it inspires me / inspires me," Gabriel's voice returns to clear, close, and pure singing. This realignment suggests that the music is all about male impotence. The narrator can tell the fantasy (homoerotically to a male listener, sadistically to a female listener) as long as there is rhetorical distance. The music to each line is shown in ex. 45.

The opening perfect fifth of the voice is remarkable. I can think of very few songs that open with this interval.[12] In "Intruder," its emergence signifies sneaking; the text and the music "know." We first heard the B♭-F♮ fifth played harmonically at the "jolt" idea first heard in m. 5. The harmonic perfect fifth that elaborates the characteristic accents of the opening percussion theme becomes the melodic fifth that sets "I know." The open fifth gets filled in with the *minor* third D♭ that we had heard in the major/minor theme. There is a larger-scale example of musical sneaking going on here as well. We first hear the pitches B♭, D♭, and E♭ in the major/minor theme; the addition of the F♮ on the vocal entry allows Gabriel to inscribe the space of these pitches into a pure, open, hollow fifth. There is something horrifying about the triplets on the pitch D♭; the D♭s signify the minor mode associated with women for centuries. A triplet adds a note where two are expected; it suggests a quickening of motion, an excess overlaid with self-assured mastery.

At the bridge, Gabriel offers a xylophone solo that moves back and forth between the right and the left channels—a common technique in rock-and-roll recording since the British Invasion. This bridge says, "This is just a song." It gives the listener an alibi; it is a virtuoso studio construction, innocent, expressive, and sophisticated.[13]

After the words are over, an odd, distant whistle sounds. It is pure, like Gabriel's voice throughout most of the song, yet it is very far away—echoing into the distance away from the listener. Whistles have been a part of popular culture for a long time. The wolf whistle, so common in classic Hollywood cinema and 1950s television, draws lines around the sexuality of women's bodies, around their breasts, around their hips, and down to their ankles. Whistles are also common substitutes for calls; they are thus pure signifiers of interpellation. Whistles come from behind; they stand for "you!" Whistles can also signify male bonding, as in the unison chorus of men whistling in *Bridge over the River Kwai*. Whistles often signify careless abandon, satisfaction, and mastery.[14] See ex. 46.

The melody expands the initial percussion theme's syncopation onto both beat 2 and beat 4. This melody represents the narrator's fantasy of mastery in the song. The "chant" had outlined an ascending minor (or blues) scale rising from G♭ to A♭ before a fatigued collapse to the low B♭. The whistle melody obsessively encloses the A♭ that had collapsed in the "chant" idea between the perfect fourth F♮-B♭. The A♭-F♮ glissando emphasizes the melody's representation of mastery. Throughout the whistle melody, the accompaniment sounds extraordinarily drained: the percussion theme that had been pounding throughout the song becomes a faint and irregular throb.

At the arrow on the A♭ in ex. 46, the whistle cuts off, and Peter Gabriel sings "I am the Intruder" on a low B♭. This is another example of large-scale sneaking in the song: the collapse in the "chant" becomes associated with the climax of intrusion later in the song. On the one hand, the line "I am the Intruder" is trite and ridiculous. Yet it is not the obvious denotative value of the utterance that matters. As in the alternation of vocal distance within the song itself in which Gabriel can master only what he "tells," so, too, at the end of the song, his fantasy of power is complete, not with the whistle, but with the speech act that connects him to his listener. The music represents this language-bound

Example 46. The whistle at the end of Peter Gabriel's "Intruder."

I am the Intruder

fantasy of power by a shift in the percussion from the limp "throb" idea that suddenly stiffens after the line "I am the Intruder" to a return of the initial pounding percussion theme with which the song ends.[15]

For me, this song is all about castration anxiety. In *The Acoustic Mirror*, Kaja Silverman discusses "discursive interiority" and "castration" as central to representations of gender. "Discursive interiority" represents the fact that all subjects are, in part, "feminine" since we are born into language and other structures of the Symbolic Order that both determine our subjectivity and are always already in place before we are born. In order to deal with this "feminine" part of their nature, men disavow and then displace their castration anxiety outward onto active, potent, visionary/fantasy representations of men who elicit the real or foreclosed scream of a woman.[16] Of the scream, Silverman says: "Hollywood is at the greatest pains to extract from the female voice, i.e., the cry. (One thinks here of *Psycho* . . . which enshrines a musically simulated version of that sound, or of the more recent *Blow-Out* [1981], which turns upon the search for a 'realistic' female scream)."[17] In Peter Gabriel's "Intruder," the male listener is encouraged to displace his castration anxiety onto the narrator, who elicits the scream of a woman—elegantly covered by the xylophone solo.

"Intruder" by Primus

Primus is a three-man band in the thrash-funk scene that is a product of blue-collar communities outside San Francisco. The band consists of Larry Lalonde, guitar; Tim Alexander, drums; and Les Claypool, six-string, fretless bass guitar, and kazoo, and vocals. "Intruder" is the first song on *Miscellaneous Debris*.

The Primus version of "Intruder" opens with the percussion theme shown above; the music is so similar it need not be notated again. The Primus percussion theme, however, is much more aggressive than in Peter Gabriel's version; some of the backbeats (especially at the outset of the song) are struck on or very close to the rim of the snare drum. The theme is also very close to our ears; it is relentless. While the Gabriel percussion theme leans heavily on the upbeat to the third beat in the bass drum, the Primus version pounds each beat evenly.

The jolt theme begins in m. 5; it is answered by a laconic minor third D♮-F♮ (the F♮ sounds flat to me) in the bass guitar.[18] The jolt continues

Example 47. "Intruder" by Primus, the stalking theme.

for eight measures, doubling the phrase length of the opening percussion theme. The major/minor theme is at once more tight and more loose than in Gabriel's version. The tightness is produced by the careful rhythmic precision of the theme. The looseness is produced by the laconic bass guitar theme, whose dead-slow harmonic rhythm is intensified by an improvisatory decoration of B♭ minor for the repeat of the two-measure theme.

The chant theme doubles the G♭s and A♭s an octave lower; the voices are so distorted it is hard to tell male voice from guitar from a synthesizer from noise.[19] While Gabriel announces the vocal entry with a pure sound of a bell, the Primus version empties out for two measures (mm. 19–20) to the percussion theme alone. With the vocal entry, Primus gives us two new details of the song at the same time—a "stalking" theme in the bass guitar and a voice that is extremely distorted.

What I find so powerful in Primus's sense of rhythm is the way that all beats are accented. As in the opening percussion theme, the bass stalking theme accents each and every note, making each note an attack that will not be subordinated to any other. See ex. 47.

This theme stresses the flat seventh—A♭ from the B♭ major/minor blues scale, which is also prominent in the chant theme. What makes it so electrifying is its proximity. Peter Gabriel's voice is close, as if whispering/singing in the listener's ears right at the speakers. The bass "stalking theme" seems even closer, as if on *our* side of the speakers. By *the speaker,* I mean an acoustic equivalent to a concept that is common in art criticism—the picture plane. The picture plane is a fantasy of a threshold between the space of the viewer and the space of a representation.[20] I would like to name a similar phenomenon in music the *listening plane*—an impression of a threshold at the surface of a speaker that divides our listening space from a fantasy of performance space. By breaching the listening plane, the bass stalking theme impedes identification with the narrator's fantasy of intrusion.

As a complement to the proximity of the bass, the *voice* enters very far away and wired tight. The proximity of the bass and the distance of the voice persist for the entire song; it is this structure and the subjectivities that it produces that differentiate the Peter Gabriel from the Primus version of "Intruder."[21]

Les Claypool's voice is difficult to locate. On the one hand, it sounds *in front* of the listener (if one imagines listening to music coming out of speakers placed in front); on the other hand, it sounds "dark," as if hiding. For me, Les Claypool's voice is a representation of a listening gaze. Like the visual gaze in which something that cannot "see" seems to "see" (the house of Norman's mother at Lilah's approach in the famous scene from *Psycho*), the voice in the Primus cover of "Intruder" seems to come out of a darkened space ahead. The unsettling effect of this darkness is made possible by the structure of the ear and how we learn to locate sounds, voices, and music in early subjectivity.

Film theorists have discussed the semiotic structure of film music as being based on the "all-around" quality of acoustic perception. And this theory can be supplemented by theorizing relations among directionality, acoustic representation, and subjectivity.[22] In a nutshell, the "all-around" theory asserts that we *hear* "all-around" and *see* in one direction only. The idea is theoretically appealing; it links representations of sound to the presymbolic realm of sonorous enclosure; it places visual signs clearly within the binary of the Imaginary Order.

But we hear both all-around *and* in front and in back. The *front* of the ear has little hair, and the molding spirals of tissue amplify sounds in the mid-range—making it more possible for us to hear language. The minimum of hair makes sounds heard in front of the body "bright." Sounds heard from the front enter the ear canal.

The *back* of the ear, however, has much more hair, and sounds do not enter the ear canal through it; thus, sounds are more diffuse, "darker." The ear thus enables sounds and representations of sound to be at once unified, allover sensations *and* carriers of signals and signs from the binary world of the Imaginary Order. We hear and see ahead; we hear what is behind in an acoustic penumbra.

In general, the fact that the structure of the ear has both an allover and a binary quality is crucial to the psychoanalytic argument of this book. The *allover* field of acoustic perception links sounds and their representations to the sonorous envelope; the binary *behind/in front* of acoustic perception links representations of the sonorous envelope to the acoustic- and later visual mirror stage. More specifically, the structures described above account for the uncanny listening gaze of Les Claypool's voice in the Primus cover of "Intruder."

Peter Gabriel's "Intruder" is all about representing the castration anxiety of the male listener. Gabriel's voice is close as he shares his secret fantasy that soon becomes the listener's; the musical motives that accompany the fantasy soon take over as the driving forces of intrusion once themes sneak out from their musical and psychoanalytic hiding places. Gabriel evokes but tastefully spares the listener the woman's scream.

The Primus version of "Intruder" represents in sound a listening gaze that blocks a transparent identification between the listener and the narrator's fantasy of intrusion.

But what are listening equivalents of Lacan's eye/gaze binary? There are no given acoustic equivalents to the eye/gaze structure, so I call the acoustic equivalent of eye the *listening look* and the listening equivalent of the gaze the *listening gaze*.[23] The listening look is produced by the ear of the listener that maintains the binary distinction between the listener's subjective position and a music's object position. This binary is clear throughout the Peter Gabriel version of "Intruder." We listen clearly on our side of the acoustic plane described above as Peter Gabriel, close, but always just on the other side, tells his fantasy.

The listening gaze, on the other hand, is the music listening to *us*. How can music listen to us if we are silent listeners? By pinning us down. The Primus version of "Intruder" pins the listener through the pounding bass guitar and percussion that accompanies the text throughout, sounding just on *our* side of the listening plane. The voice pins us as well by singing in a space that curiously echoes *behind* the bass guitar and percussion. In order of proximity to our ears, the Primus version of "Intruder" pins us to the following layers of the music: (1) the bass guitar and percussion, (2) the listening plane, (3) the lead singer's voice, and (4) a space into which his voice echoes.

While both versions of "Intruder" rely on gender-specific violent scenarios, Peter Gabriel's version confirms a traditional male subject position at the expense of female object specularity. The Primus cover of "Intruder" forces the listener to confront the horror of his castration anxiety by refusing to cover up the fantasy scream and by pinning the listener as described above. This pinning threatens to violate the listener's space, threatening to make the music sound like a representation of the text's fantasy. In short, the music holds up to the male listener an acoustic mirror in which he hears his own horrid desire.[24]

This chapter examined structures of the gaze and male aggression in two versions of a rock song; in the next chapter, the musical representation of male violence is extended in two ways. First, the next chapter looks at a large-scale social and historical context for the violence associated with German Oi Musik. Second, the chapter describes a general style of music and the ideological structures that support it, as opposed to individual songs or the works of one composer.

The next chapter moves as well into the musical and theoretical area of postrock. It is extremely problematic to use the prefix *post-* in connection with popular music. Andreas Huyssen has described postmodernism in art, history, politics, and discourse as intimately related to *modernism*. He views postmodernism as a revitalization of modernism itself, appropriating, while at the same time critiquing, modernism's allegiance to modernization, monumentalism, and an aesthetic of progress.[25]

Rock and roll came together in the mid-1950s as a synthesis of the blues, country western, and Tin Pan Alley musical traditions — a very different past from the modernity of avant-garde Western culture.

For me, there is something quintessentially *modern* about post–World War II rock and roll in the West — the increasing glorification of technology in musical instruments and sound systems that reproduce rock and roll, the urge to find increasingly "new" sounds, forms of expression that surpass antecedents, the massive, public spectacle, an increasing monumentality of compositions, and glorification and commodification of individual subjectivity. At the same time, there is something *postmodern* underlying the entire phenomenon of post–World War II rock and roll in the West: its appropriation by worldwide advertising, its rootlessness, its increasing emphasis on multiple media, its multivalent textuality (covers marking and remarking songs), and the rock star as a simulacrum of a rock star. Rock and a postmodern critique of modernism come together, not in academic discourse, but in the practice of the music of the 1960s and its critique in the West of the "establishment" and the war in Vietnam.

Postrock describes an impression that a body of rock has been set aside, not as a set of procedures, traditions, forms, to be extended into the future along a red thread of continuity, but rather as a store of materials from which to put together "new" music from "old" bits and pieces.[26] The next chapter will explore what bits and pieces of rock and roll are put together in contemporary German Oi Musik.

6

Oi: Music,

Politics, and

Violence

Introduction

Oi Musik has been produced and consumed predominantly by socially and economically marginal white men in First World countries over the past twelve years.[1] Post–World War II immigration of foreigners to industrialized Western countries, more recent shifts of geographic boundaries in Europe, and social, economic, and sexual pressures are among the conditions that have led to increasing acts of terror such as the burning of homes and places of business of foreigners, particularly in Germany. While a variety of works have appeared in Germany and other countries that track the history of Oi Musik and its connection to violent acts, this chapter will unpack the musical, social, and psychoanalytic elements that have made Oi possible.[2] I will conclude with an examination of how the delicate balance in more conventional forms of interpellation (between conscious acts in social space and the unconscious structures on which they depend) gets reorganized in Oi into a volatile combination of simultaneous *affirmation* and *denial* of history.

Even though relatively few people outside the German skin scene have heard this music, a publicly acknowledged subculture has arisen around skins and German Oi Musik. German officials estimate that there are around forty-five hundred active skins and around twenty thousand people who sympathize with skins, their music, and their activities.[3] The main reason that few people have listened to this music is that it is never played on the radio, rarely sold in record stores, and never advertised in public space. The records, clothing, and CDs are sold under the counter at skin boutiques and mail-order stores throughout Germany.[4] And, when the music is described in magazine articles and newspapers, some German journalists again and again dismiss Oi as "bad." This negative aesthetic judgment is wrongheaded for three reasons. First, it inhibits an examination of a music that powerfully affects its listeners. Second, leftist denial of right-wing threats echoes social liberal dismissals of Hitler in the 1920s. And, finally, the aesthetics of rock have been consistently pushed into forbidden areas as an expression of rebellion against not only conservative but also liberal pedagogy, parental authority, and the law.

I will show below that one of Oi's long-term effects on its listeners is the production of a sense of community for skins in Germany. Its most common short-term effect is that it is sometimes used to incite acts of terror against foreigners, reported, for example, in the summer of 1993 in Germany.[5]

A Brief History of Oi

Farin and Seidel-Pielen locate the origins of the skin phenomenon in post–World War II England. The uniformity of white, working-class neighborhoods began to break up after the war owing to two political/social forces. Foreign workers came to England during the 1950s and 1960s from the Caribbean, Pakistan, India, and West Africa to support the postwar boom. According to Farin and Seidel-Pielen, the British government did very little to assimilate these immigrants.[6] In addition, white working-class neighborhoods became gentrified; hot water and central heating were the cornerstones of postwar British improvements that resulted in poor white workers being displaced to new social housing units in the suburbs of large cities and middle-class people moving into improved and expensive urban housing.[7]

The splintering of British working-class social space in the postwar years is reflected in a series of movements that position marginalized (mostly male) groups against dominant politics; these movements mark their identity through clothes and music. The Teddyboys of the 1950s wore expensive clothes and listened to the rock and roll from the United States that was being broadcast from Radio Luxembourg. Jon Savage points out that the ambivalent relation that British mar-

ginal, male groups have to the social order can be seen in Teddyboys'
clothes; they are expensive, and they self-consciously acknowledge the
power of Britain's class system (they wore clothes from the Edwardian
era).[8] The rough affect of the Teddys was replaced by the more cool
Mods at the end of the 1950s. According to Farin and Seidel-Pielen,
"To be mod meant expensive clothes, ska and northern soul, Vespas
with chrome siding, speed, fights, and a job as a bank courier."[9] The
mods fought battles that were heavily covered in the British press with
so-called Rockers—the first generation of skins; as the mods were ad-
justing their hair to just the right length, the Rockers or "hard-mods"
were shaving it closer and closer to the scalp.

Farin and Seidel-Pielen point out that shaving the scalp originated in
"working houses" of the nineteenth century. Workers who disobeyed
"God-given" rules were punished by having their heads shaved. This
form of punishment was also common in early twentieth-century re-
formatories and prisons.[10] The self-infliction of this act among men of
the same class as those who were punished in the nineteenth century
is one of the keys to understanding what I call "Oi subjectivity." One
takes over the negative judgment of the social order in order to form
an identity at its margins.

Parallel with these developments, black gangs called Rude Boys were
being formed. Here is the same dynamic described above applied to
names: one takes over the negative judgment of the dominant social
order in order to carve out an oppositional subjective position. This
has both a normative and a marginalizing quality. Many movements
in the arts that have become canonized began by naming themselves
in precisely this way: the impressionists and the fauves, for example.[11]
Particularly in skin, punk, and Oi Musik, the names of performers and
groups are insults that become appropriated: Sid Vicious's name came
from the name of Johnny Rotten's hamster; Johnny Rotten's name
came from Sid Vicious pointing out how rotten his teeth were; the
German Oi band Die böhse Onkelz got their name from a group of
kids pointing to the band members as they were walking across a lot
and saying: "Guck mal, die böhse Onkelz da!" (Look at those bad guys
over there!).[12]

These gangs brought a kind of music to England that would influence the music of skins: ska. Since I will focus in the musical-analytic

portion of this chapter on the "white" and "black" elements of Oi, it is important to realize how Britain's first skin movement took over this "black" music from Jamaica.[13] Ska came together around 1960; one of its first songs was Laurel Aitken's single "Little Sheila." Ska is heterogeneous; radio transmissions from the United States to Jamaica in the late 1950s and early 1960s gave ska sounds from jazz (particularly the common saxophone solos and complex percussion parts), the twelve-bar blues from rock and roll, the vocal style of Fats Domino, and the energetic music of Little Richard. Ska also used an instrumental ensemble including metal drums, brass choirs (trombone with two trumpets), and a common emphasis on the upbeat that became the crucial musical signifier of reggae.[14]

In 1969 the word *skins* began to circulate in the British press; it referred to the *black* skin groups—the Rude Boys, who shaved their heads, listened to ska, and defended their territories. Whites joined black gangs, and the norm of skin appearance was formed: shaved heads, heavy black boots, leather jackets. The clothes, the music, and the (violent) expression of marginal existence marked Britain's first skin movement; *class* was primary. Farin and Seidel-Pielen point out that the birth of reggae in the late 1960s corresponds to a development among immigrant intellectuals and artists in Britain—a growing consciousness that Jamaicans, blacks, and other minorities were being systematically discriminated against by the white British government. Thus, an increase in ethnic consciousness among blacks and increased social pressures caused skin groups to break apart along lines of color.[15]

White skins had begun to be seen in Britain as the right-wing politician Enoch Powell gave a speech in 1968 laying the groundwork for white racial anxiety and hatred of the colored Other. White skin groups went on "Paki bashings," wrote racist graffiti in public spaces, and carried out spontaneous acts of violence against foreigners until the movement faded out in the early 1970s.[16]

Punk

Punk appeared in the mid-1970s and lasted only a few years.[17] Like other marginal movements, punk is visible through clothes and audible through music. Jon Savage makes it clear that punk was made possible by a variety of factors ranging from the personality and taste of Malcolm McClaren and Vivienne Westwood, deteriorating social conditions for working-class whites in British cities, the decline of the first skin generation, and the influence of American punk—particularly the Ramones and the New York Dolls.[18] By the mid-1970s, unemployment was higher than it had been since 1940, and there was "a full fledged capitalist recession, with extremely high rates of inflation, a toppling currency, a savaging of living standards, and a sacrificing of the working class to capital."[19] Punk emerged from the same social conditions as the stagnating and fragmented skin movement had only a few years before.

Malcolm McClaren went to New York in the early 1970s and heard the Ramones and the New York Dolls; their music was apolitical, nihilistic, fast, loud, and repetitive. The Sex Pistols and other bands such as the Clash took this music and made it British. British punk of the 1970s is often referred to as "leftist"; but, like most skins before and after punk, the Sex Pistols distanced themselves from any established political movement.[20] Like skins before and after, the Sex Pistols emphasized the present, life on the streets, the oppression of public institutions, the meaninglessness of mainstream life, and the emptiness of culture.

Musically, the Sex Pistols were a typical rock band with four musicians: Paul Cook, drums; Steve Jones, guitar; Johnny Rotten, singer; and Glen Matlock, bass (later replaced by Sid Vicious).[21] The songs tend to reflect rock-and-roll formal norms, with an introductory riff and verse/chorus alternation; they emphasize the fourth scale degree— a stripped-down but clearly *black* sound that links the liturgical plagal cadence with the early slave hollers and early blues.[22] The voice is rough—a heritage from the vocal style of the blues (to be discussed more fully below in connection with German Oi Musik). The meter is $\frac{4}{4}$; there is almost always a backbeat in the snare, and the tempo is fast.[23] Although a product of the enormous social pressure being experienced by working-class whites, the music of the Sex Pistols freely steals from the black tradition of blues (the wounded voice, the plagal emphasis on the fourth scale degree), rhythm and blues (steady streams of eighth notes), and white rock and roll (the signature backbeat of 1950s rock). This musical style is capable of parody, however. I hear a clear reference to the Doors' "I Love You" in "Sub-mission," with the harmony moving from $\hat{1}$ to $\flat\hat{7}$ to $\flat\hat{3}$ back to $\hat{1}$. And Sid Vicious's "My Way" is a clear parody of Frank Sinatra's version of the same song. This song is beautifully rendered in the film *Sid and Nancy*. It is an example of punk making a clear ideological statement about its own roots in rock and roll. One of the three musical styles that came together in rock and roll of the 1950s was popular music, or Tin Pan Alley. Sid Vicious's version of "My Way" thus at once reenacts and parodies this quintessentially popular music. I will contrast punk's ability/willingness to comment explicitly on its roots with German Oi Musik's quite different treatment of the history of rock and roll below.

In addition to the musical aspects discussed above, punk's self-destructiveness is reflected in punk bodies: hair takes on the colors of mass-produced objects; bodies are seen as vulnerable surfaces of skin that must be protected from a hostile world by black leather; bodies are scarred, marked, wounded. These wounds are at once signifiers of the white working class under siege and self-inflicted wounds.[24]

The self-destructive nature of punk is reflected in the difficulty the Sex Pistols had working together on their one album, *Never Mind the Bollocks: Here's the Sex Pistols;* the group lasted only a couple of years, and Sid Vicious died of a drug overdose. "God Save the Queen" and "Anarchy in the UK" are completely negative songs that hold out no hope for a place within British social space. Even as they became famous, or perhaps because they became famous, their tenuous cohesion imploded on the group. Even the relationship between performers and audience was negative; it was common at Sex Pistols concerts for the musicians to spit at the audience and for the audience to spit back. Savage reports that this practice (called "gobbing") frequently got out of hand: "The very English phlegm which had served as a powerful physiological metaphor for denial and needless stoicism was now, literally, expelled in torrents as . . . punk audiences covered their objects of desire with sheets of saliva."[25] Punk represents the body as *abjection;* as we will see and hear below, German Oi subjectivity fine-tunes this abjection into a precarious synthesis between self-loathing and loathing of the Other.

British Oi Music

With the commercialization of punk into new wave, the second phase of the skin movement began to emerge as former skins and the remains of the (still marginal) punk movement joined hands. This music was called "Street Punk," "Real Punk," or "Working-class Punk."[26] It is in this music that the sound *oi* can be heard in songs by the Cockney Rejects (begun in 1979) and the Angelic Upstarts (begun in 1977).[27] And Jon Savage locates one of the earliest appearances of the sound *oi* in a song called "Career Opportunities" by the punk band the Clash.[28] The sound *oi* covers a broad and resonant semantic field. It is British, white working-class dialect for "hey!"[29] *Oi* is also a skin call to action, as in this line from a song by the Cockney Rejects: "I run down a side street, Oi! Oi! Oi! / and I run and I am free Oi! Oi! Oi!"[30] *Oi* also became a more neutral signal for the beginning of a song; Farin and Seidel-Pielen point out that the Cockney Rejects replaced their characteristic "1, 2, 3" at the outset of a song with "Oi! Oi! Oi!" The audience would then echo "Oi! Oi! Oi!" back, and the song would begin.[31] *Oi* is also a more aggressive attack sound that derives from "zickezacke zickezacke zickezacke Oi! Oi! Oi!"—a shortened form of the phrase "einem Skin-Oikalyptus."[32] *Oi* also reminds me of the Yiddish interjection *Oy!* as in "Oy weh ist mir!"[33]

The year 1981 was crucial for skin music. Apolitical/leftist second-generation skin bands planned a tour that would make it clear to the British public that Oi was nonviolent. The National Front used the occasion to orchestrate violent disruptions at skin concerts that turned second-generation skin music into the domain of the right wing. Farin and Seidel-Pielen point out that the National Front (founded in 1967) won more than 200,000 votes in the election of 1977 with the slogan "If they're black, send them back!"[34] Although skin bands strenuously avoided explicit political affiliation, the National Front was able to recruit enough right-wing skins to disrupt a concert at Southall on 3 July 1981. The resulting injuries and press coverage caused the recall of Gary Bushell's just-released album *Strength through Oi!* and the bands the 4-skins and the Business lost their recording contracts.[35]

German Oi

In both England and Germany, right-wing skin music arose out of the punk scene, which had become fragmented after the mid-1970s with the disintegration of the Sex Pistols, the commercialization of new wave music, and the emergence of white, working-class rock and roll that expressed right-wing ideologies. One of the first German Oi[36] bands continues to play concerts and to record CDs; it plays a key role in the history of Oi and in current debates on its music, texts, and legal status—Die böhse Onkelz, founded in 1979.[37] As opposed to the Sex Pistols, who self-destructed after only a few years, the members of this band based in Frankfurt have remained together since 1979; they continue to produce an average of one album per year since 1984.[38] Like many rock groups since the 1950s, the band consists of four per-formers: Kevin Russell, singer; Peter "Pe" Schorowsky, percussion; Matthias "Gonzo" Roehr, guitar; and Stephan Weidner, bass. The British-German cross-fertilization of Oi is represented by the fact that the lead singer of this German Oi band that often calls for the preserva-tion of the German state against foreigners is *British*.[39] In an interview with the magazine *Emma*, Stephan Weidner recalls that one of his first powerful influences was the Sex Pistols and that, before taking on the name Die böhse Onkelz, his band was a no-name punk band.[40]

Der nette Mann

Der nette Mann (1984) is Die böhse Onkelz's first album. The title song, "Der nette Mann," has become for many a symbol of the brutality of German Oi Musik.[41] The song has been placed on the infamous "index" since 1986.[42] One problem with indexing is that it intensifies the Oi lis-tener's desire for the music. A second problem is that, when recording, musicians can work around the danger of being placed on the index by changing words or phrases that are well known through concerts.[43]

"Deutschland" by Die böhse Onkelz

"Deutschland," first released on *Der nette Mann*, is structured like much German Oi Musik: (1) intro, (2) verse/chorus/verse/chorus, (3) guitar solo, (4) verse/chorus/verse/chorus, and (5) coda. Here is the text of the song:[44]

> (Zwölf?) Jahre in deiner Geschichte
> wird unsere Verbundenheit zu dir nicht zu nichte
> es gibt kein Land frei von Dreck und Scherben

wir sind hier geboren wir wollen nicht sterben
Deutschland Deutschland Vaterland
Deutschland Deutschland mein Heimatland

Wir freuen uns deutsch zu sein, wollen hier leben
das Land in den Dreck ziehen, die Fahne verhöhnen
doch wir sind stolz in dir geboren zu sein
wir sind stolz drauf deutsche zu sein

Deutschland Deutschland Vaterland
Deutschland Deutschland mein Heimatland

[guitar solo]

wir sind stolz in dir geboren zu sein
wir sind stolz drauf deutsch zu sein
deutsche Frauen deutsches Bier
schwarz und rot wir stehen zu dir

Deutschland Deutschland Vaterland
Deutschland Deutschland mein Heimatland

Es gibt kein Land frei von Dreck und Scherben
wir sind hier geboren, wir wollen nicht sterben
deutsche Frauen deutsches Bier
schwarz und rot wir stehen zu dir

Deutschland Deutschland Vaterland
Deutschland Deutschland mein Heimatland

Deutschland Deutschland Vaterland
Deutschland Deutschland mein Heimatland
Deutschland Deutschland Vaterland
Deutschland Deutschland wir reichen dir die Hand

[guitar repeats chorus without voice]

[end with sustain on tonic note]

[12?] Years in your history
our loyalty to you will not be destroyed
there's no land free of filth and splinters
we were born here we don't want to die

Germany Germany Fatherland
Germany Germany my home country

We are happy to be Germans and want to live here
to pull the country through the filth and spoil the flag
yes! we're proud to have been born in you
we're proud to be Germans

Germany Germany Fatherland
Germany Germany my home country

[guitar solo]

we're proud to have been born in you
we're proud to be Germans
German women and German beer
black and red we'll stand by you

Germany Germany Fatherland
Germany Germany my home country

There is no land free of filth and splinters
we were born here we don't want to die
German women German beer
black and red we'll stand by you
Germany Germany Fatherland
Germany Germany my home country

Germany Germany Fatherland
Germany Germany my home country
Germany Germany Fatherland
Germany Germany we reach out our hand to you

In addition to the social, economic, and political issues in Oi, gender is particularly troubling for the Oi subject. In this song, women are paradoxically praised and dreaded by the male narrator of the text. The essential dynamic of Oi subjectivity is the structuring and maintaining of a clear binary between the self and the Other. The Other is usually the foreigner, less often the leftist, women, occasionally the external world as an entirety. Klaus Theweleit has discussed the role of women in fascist ideology in *Male Fantasies*. Theweleit argues that the

quintessential German soldier was a member of the *Freikorps*—soldiers
from World War I who refused to disband after the war and became the
kernel of the Nazi SA, SD, and SS in the 1920s. Through a detailed examination of letters, diaries, and novels, Theweleit discovered that the
male fascist subject had three absolute categories for women: the white,
pure nurse; the wife who kept the family together back home; and dangerous, red women. He focuses much of the analysis of *Male Fantasies*
on these men's fantasies of red women; she can be a Communist, a
whore, a female of the enemy, and the men describe fantasy red women
in terms of a swamp, a flood, a space that threatens to engulf the male
subject. He describes a desire for destruction, a "burning" for war without end, that informs the language of these men, and the urge for destruction is always closely linked to a desire to obliterate red women.[45]

In German Oi Musik as well, women are often identified with a "red
flood," an oceanic force that threatens to engulf the male Oi subject.
Most German Oi texts assume an external threat of foreigners and leftist politics in Germany. Against this flood a defense must be erected:
a shield is constructed and put in place; it defines the pure race inter-
nally and protects the male subject. The complement to this placement
of the shield is the active and phallic destruction of the Other: striking
out with the sword.[46] "Deutschland" is, as it were, a shield song; the
song yearns for a clear binary between the self and the Other, between
Germany and the rest of the world. Within this fantasy binary, women
are objects to be consumed: "deutsche Frauen/deutsches Bier." The
equation of women and beer is at once an obvious and a horridly
clear objectification of the female body and an indication that, as in
other German Oi lyrics, the objectification of women marks woman
as organic Other. To return briefly to the punk/skin comparison developed earlier, here is one clear and significant difference between the
two subjectivities and musics: there were female punk bands; a female
German Oi band is hard to imagine.[47]

One thing that is so obvious that it can be overlooked is the national
identity that the song obsessively repeats. What is curious about this
song and much German Oi Musik is the nature of the allegiance of Oi
subjectivity to the nation Germany. Most of these bands are all marginalized, and the German government seems to be doing all it can
to curb the dissemination of this music. There are three paragraphs

of the German *Grundgesetz* that more aggressively and explicitly limit freedom of speech than in the United States. Paragraph 130 forbids "Volksverhetzung" (inciting the people) and provides for a punishment of up to five years in prison for infractions. Paragraph 131 forbids "Aufstachelung zum Rassenhass" (promoting racial hatred); paragraph 86 forbids the distribution of propaganda of illegal organizations; and paragraph 86a forbids the use of illegal symbols such as the swastika.[48]

German Oi subjectivity is thus allied to a fantasy of "Deutschland"— a pure Germany at once *present* (as in "Get rid of the foreigners so that our Germany can be pure") and *absent* (a fantasy of the return of a lost and once pure state). The phrase "die Fahne verhöhnen" is curious. There is a parallel structure in the text: subject and verb *we want,* followed by infinitive phrases: *to live here, to pull the country through the filth, to spoil the flag.* What sense does it make for a German Oi band to construct and represent a fantasy of spoiling the flag? There are two possibilities. On the one hand, the agency could be displaced from the singers to the liberal politicians of the postwar Bundesrepublik Deutschland who are "spoiling" the real German flag of the Nazis. Recall that the song begins with a reference to twelve years—presumably those between 1933 and 1945. Or the agency remains with the singers; the flag that they fantasize ruining is the flag of the Bundesrepublik Deutschland—a false nation imposed on Germans from without. German Oi subjectivity is marked with a desire to return—here to the German nation prior to 1945.

The phrase "Wir sind wieder da!" at the outset of "Imperator der G." by Störkraft suggests this sense of return, of repetition. Yet German Oi is supposedly apolitical; German Oi bands have never allied themselves with the established right-wing parties and never participated in party functions. The center of German Oi national fantasy is thus curiously abstract, curiously unstable. One can begin to unpack this instability in the music itself. German Oi is supposed to be pure, German music. In the words of one song by Endstufe, "Wir spielen keinen Punk / Wir spielen Skinhead Rock and Roll!" (from "Skinhead Rock and Roll" on Endstufe's album of the same title). For an introduction to how "Deutschland" sounds, see ex. 48.[49]

The steady stream of eighth notes embodies the punk influence that pervades much German Oi Musik—an extension of the steady eighth

Example 48. The opening riff of "Deutschland" by Die böhse Onkelz.

notes of 1950s rhythm and blues. There is a pungent 2-3 suspension as the minor second between the bass B♭ and the C♮ in the upper system resolves with the stepwise descent in the bass to A♭. More important, the bass motion emphasizes the flatted seventh scale degree—a clear element of the musical language of the blues. A common misconception in some German journalism is that German Oi Musik involves a mindless use of "three-chord minimalism."[50] Most Oi Musik is monophonic and not chordal at all. Within the monophonic style, Oi uses the scale degrees I, ♭II, ii, iii, III, iv, IV, V, ♭VI, vi, ♭VII, and VII and guitar solos that show a mastery of the instrument in a variety of styles. There are Oi ballads, slow songs, fast songs, unique uses of the voice (particularly in songs by Störkraft), electronic manipulations such as echo effects, intentional use of distortion and feedback, noises from the environment, etc. This music is dangerous, but it is not mindless. The harmony of the chorus alternates between ♭VI and V. Again, ♭VII and ♭VI are sounds taken directly from the blues. The chorus of the song expands on the half-step motion between ♭VI and V.

The song "Singen und Tanzen" from Die böhse Onkelz is an example of a skin dance song. The lyrics suggest the subversiveness of Bill Haley and the Comets' "Rock around the Clock," and this song is very close to a self-conscious update of that 1950s classic. The barely disguised appropriation of 1950s rock in this song can be heard in the bass, shown in ex. 49.

The 1950s sound is even clearer in the music right after the first eight measures. The music suddenly stops, and there are eight quiet taps before the first verse begins. This sounds like a reminiscence of the "ticky-tacky" drum sound of Bill Haley before the more aggressive sound of

Elvis and other 1950s rock-and-roll musicians began to dominate. The guitar plays chords off the beat, as shown in ex. 50.

This is characteristic of ska (a forerunner of reggae), and quite a bit of German Oi Musik has this ska influence—particularly guitar chords played *off the beat*. Ska chords played on upbeats sound so good in this music because they sound at the eighth-note level the structure of the backbeat at the quarter-note level. While the backbeat emphasizes beats 1 and 3 by slamming beats 2 and 4, ska chords emphasize the *downbeat* by always sounding on the *upbeat*.

"Stolz" also involves blues-influenced harmonies and ska off-beat accompaniment. The text is as follows:[51]

> Einer von vielen mit rasiertem Kopf,
> du steckst nicht zurück, denn du hast keine Angst,
> Shermans, Braces, Boots, and Jeans [Jeans and Boots]
> Deutschlandfahne, denn darauf bin ich stolz [bist du Stolz]
> man lacht über dich, weil du Arbeiter bist,
> doch darauf bin ich stolz, ich hör nicht auf den Mist!
>
> Du bist Skinhead, du bist Stolz,
> du bist Skinhead, schrei's heraus,
> du bist Skinhead, du bist stolz,
> du bist Skinhead, schrei's heraus!

Example 49. The bass line to "Singen und Tanzen" by Die böhse Onkelz.

Example 50. Off-the-beat guitar chords in "Singen und Tanzen" by Die böhse Onkelz.

Du hörst Onkelz, wenn du zu Hause bist,
du bist einer von vielen, denn du bist nicht allein,
du bist tätowiert auf deiner Brust,
denn du weisst, welcher Kult für dich am besten ist,
die Leute schauen auf dich mit Hass in den Augen,
sie schimpfen dir nach und erzählen Lügen über dich!

Du bist. . . .

One among many with shaved head
you don't stay behind 'cause you're not afraid
Shermans, Braces, Jeans, and Boots,
Flag of Germany, 'cause you're proud of it,
people laugh at you 'cause you're a worker,
but I'm proud of that, I ignore such crap!

You're a skinhead, you are proud
you're a skinhead, scream it out loud
you're a skinhead, you are proud
you're a skinhead, scream it out loud

You listen to the Uncles at home
you're one among many, you're not alone
you're tattooed on your chest
you know which cult is the best for you
people look at you with hate in their eyes
they swear at you and tell lies about you.

You're a skinhead. . . .

The last two lines of the last verse suggest an essential component of Oi subjectivity—anxiety produced by the gaze of the Other. The shield aspect of Oi subjectivity discussed above can always be penetrated by a gaze bearing identity-threatening negative judgment from the outside. The pride that is at the center of skinhead identity seems to be fueled in this song by defending oneself against the Other's gaze through companionship. But I think that no amount of solidarity with other threatened subjects can produce a defense against the castrating gaze of the Other. The music of "Stolz" begins with a riff in the bass that descends stepwise from tonic to the dominant, as shown in ex. 51.

Example 51. Opening riff of "Stolz" by Die böhse Onkelz.

This bass line is accompanied by the guitar playing a ska motive like the one shown in "Singen und Tanzen" (see ex. 50 above). The power of the chorus derives from its musical stripping of ornamentation of the opening riff; the voices are shouting, not singing, as the guitars play a simple descending perfect fourth from tonic to the dominant (F♮ "Du bist Skinhead!" [You are a skinhead!]–E♭ "Du bist Stolz!" [You are proud!]–D♭ "Du bist Skinhead! [You are a skinhead!]"–C♮ "Schrei's heraus!" [Scream it out loud!]). In this and a few other songs, there is a "dive-bomber" effect taken from Jimi Hendrix. Also, there is a consciously massive wall of noise, feedback, and distortion that accompanies the final "heraus!" of this song.[52]

"Wieder mal'n Tag verschenkt" is a pastiche of sounds from the slow rock ballad repertoire. The text is an adolescent fantasy of the meaninglessness of life tightened up a notch to extreme self-pity. The text is as follows:

> Ein neuer Tag beginnt
> auf der Suche nach dem Sinn
> den Sinn in meinem Leben
> doch ich kann ihn nicht finden
>
> was kann das alles sein
> was kommt danach dann ist's vorbei
> wer kennt die Antwort auf diese Fragen?
> Die Zeit vergeht nichts passiert
> nichts ist geschehen und es rebelliert
>
> in den Falten meiner Seelen
> in den Ecken meiner Seele meiner Seele
> Wieder mal'n Tag verschenkt
> wieder mal'n Tag verschenkt

Tage vergehen nichts passiert
nichts ist geschehen und es rebelliert
in den Falten meiner Seelen
in den Ecken meiner Seele

ich hab' nächtelang gezecht
mich ins Coma gesoffen
oft gezielt doch nie getroffen
ich weiss wie es ist der Arsch zu sein

wieder mal'n Tag verschenkt
wieder mal'n Tag verschenkt

A new day begins
with a search for meaning
the meaning of my life
but I can't find it yet

was that it, can that be all there is
what comes afterward, is it all over
who knows the answers to these questions?
Time passes nothing happens
nothing happens and I feel rebellious
in the folds of my soul
in the corners of the soul
once again a day is gone
once again a day is gone

Days pass nothing happens
nothing happens and I feel rebellious
in the folds of my soul
in the corners of my soul

I've raised hell all night
drunk myself into a coma
aimed many times but never hit the mark
I know very well what it feel like to be an asshole

once again a day is gone
once again a day is gone

It is important to remember that both fascist subjectivity and Oi subjectivity emerge not from pathological exceptions to the normalcy of everyday life but precisely *out of* everyday life. Qualitatively, the text is nothing more than a conventional male adolescent fantasy taken a bit into delinquency in the lines "I've raised hell all night / drunk myself into a coma." The music does two things that are reserved for self-pitying German Oi ballads: (1) there is humming right before the vocal entry, and (2) phrases are repeated, such as "meiner Seele." The piece opens with a guitar riff of very heavy bottleneck sliding that sounds like a cheesy imitation of Ry Cooder; there is a strummed acoustic guitar throughout, no percussion, and fragments of melodies played on a piano in cocktail bar ballad style. The harmonic rhythm is slow—one change per measure.[53]

The song "Heilige Lieder" is crucial to a study of German Oi Musik for several reasons. First, it represents the "new" böhse Onkelz, the clean, reformed bunch of bad guys. The first stanza of the verse has been transcribed by Klaus Walter: "Hier sind die süssesten Noten jenseits des Himmels / heilige Lieder aus berufenem Mund / wahre Worte im Dschungel der Lüge / das Licht im Dunkel ein heiliger Bund" (Here are the sweetest notes this side of heaven / holy songs from appointed mouths / true words in a jungle of lies / a light in the darkness, a holy offering).[54] Several newspaper articles have questioned whether this "Wendung" (change) is a ruse, part of the deeper mission of Oi to penetrate mainstream culture using texts that seem less offensive than their earlier material, texts that are irrevocably coded nonetheless.[55] The song has become very well known in Germany, taking Oi Musik out of the exclusive domain of hard-core skins. As of June 1993, *Heilige Lieder* sold over 500,000 copies and occupied the position of number 5 on the German pop charts.[56]

The song is a self-reflexive hymn of praise dedicated to German Oi Musik. It opens with a guitar riff that is fuzzy and distant, shown in ex. 52. This riff is repeated a few times, and then the music shifts channels in a moment of hesitation, as if circling around the head of the listener; then it "snaps into place," and the verse begins in A. The introduction to "Heilige Lieder" is fuzzy and distant; with one hit on the snare drum, the verse is clear, up close, fast, and tight. The music seems to go faster once it snaps into place, but it doesn't—an example of how music can produce acoustic illusion.

Example 52. Opening riff of "Heilige Lieder" by Die böhse Onkelz.

The musical structure of the opening riff is ingenious; it has three components that follow one another diachronically in the melody. The first is the major-second alternation between A♮ and B♮; this is a quickened-up version of the major second that so often signifies the "walking blues." This example blurs our ability to be consciously aware of the blues-like sound of the gesture. But we are aware unconsciously, however, and the riff immediately inscribes us in/hides us from the musical tradition of the blues. The second element of the riff is the chromatic filling in of the major third from the high A♮ to the F♮. The gesture shifts from rhythm (the repeated alternation between A♮ and B♮) to pitch structure (the filled-in major third that moves *down* from A♮, as the initial gesture had stepped *up* from the same note). The third element of the riff is the move down to and pause on B♮. This generates enormous energy for two reasons. First, the rapid motion of sixteenth notes suddenly slows to eighth and dotted quarter notes. Second, the halt on the B♮ frustrates the descent of the melodic line down to the melodic goal—A♮. And it is precisely right after this rhythmically, gesturally, and melodically charged note that the music snaps into place. The harmonic rhythm of the verse is excruciatingly slow, as shown in ex. 53. The aching feeling that something needs to happen to the slow harmonic rhythm of the verse is released with the leisurely unfolding pop harmonies of the chorus, which softens the hard blues progression I-IV-I-V-IV-I with an added minor submediant, as shown in ex. 54.[57]

As the verse returns, it becomes clear that a hint of the A-major/G-major motion of the verse is contained in the vocal part that obsessively works over the double neighbor figure B♭-A♮-G♮-A♮. The B♭-A♮ half step signifies heavy metal. "Heilige Lieder" ends with an unusual sound—two-part vocal harmony—an affectation of commercial pop scoring. While Oi subjectivity is indirectly evoked by a song like "Heilige Lieder," it is explicitly evoked in many songs by Störkraft.

Example 53. Harmonic rhythm of verse of "Heilige Lieder" by Die böhse Onkelz.

Example 54. Harmony of the chorus of "Heilige Lieder" by Die böhse Onkelz.

Störkraft

According to a government report from Lower Saxony, the band Störkraft from Andernach is one of the most important German Oi Musik bands for inspiring listeners with German nationalist feelings.[58] The lead singer of this band is being tried in the German courts (as of the summer of 1993), and government officials have raided apartments in search of material in violation of paragraphs 130, 131, 86, and 86a mentioned above.[59] The text of the band's "In ein paar Jahren" is as follows:

> Früh in der Bildung, da fing es schon an,
> ein Land voller Dreck, genannt Deutschland.
> Sie nahmen dir den Stolz, verhöhnten das Land,
> Doch das hast du damals noch nicht erkannt.
>
> In ein paar Jahren haben wir keine Rechte mehr.
> Unsere Gefühle existieren nicht mehr.
> Doch wir sind geboren in Deutschland.
> Wir kämpfen für das deutsche Vaterland.
>
> Überall wohin du siehst, siehst du wie dein Land überfliesst,
> Fremde Völker mischen sich ein und behaupten auch
> noch deutsch zu sein

In ein paar Jahren. . . .

Ja eines Tages, da wacht ihr alle auf.
Rettet die Rasse, die man einst verkauft.
Ich weiss, in jedem Deutschen, da steckt ein Mann,
der das Verderben noch verhindern kann.

In ein paar Jahren . . .
. . . doch wir sind zum Kampf bereit!

Early in school, it began already,
A land full of waste, a land called Germany.
They took your pride away, mocked the land,
But they never really knew you.

In a few years, we'll have no more rights
Our feelings don't exist any more.
But we have been born in Germany.
We will fight for the German fatherland.

Everywhere you look
you see how your land is flowing over.
Foreign peoples mix themselves in
and claim to be Germans.

In a few years, we'll have no more rights.
Our feelings don't exist any more.
But we have been born in Germany.
We will fight for the German fatherland.

Yes, one day, you will all wake up.
Save the race that one used to sell.
I know that inside every German, there is a man
who can prevent this decay.
In a few years, we'll have no more rights.
Our feelings don't exist any more,
But we have been born in Germany.
We will fight for the German fatherland.

We are ready for the fight!

The word *aufwachen* from "In ein paar Jahren" has clear Nazi over-tones, as from the line "Deutschland erwache!" And much of the song is a fantasy of boundary trauma described by Klaus Theweleit in *Male Fantasies*. The Oi subject behind this text feels as if he has no skin and the external world is flooding into the vacant spot where his person-ality is tenuously holding on for life. This fear pervades many of Stör-kraft's texts. It is dangerous to overpsychologize the subjectivity of a few thousand German skins and to suggest that others, perhaps *many* others, qualitatively share in the structures that clearly mark "the tip of the iceberg," the four to five-thousand hard-core German skins. But the obsessive rituals of tattooing and shaving heads, and lyrics such as this song suggest an extreme version of a trauma in early childhood de-velopment that we all go through, according to Ester Bick: the sense that our bodies have not been incorporated into any space immediately after birth, that we are born into an uncontrollable flux of body parts, surfaces, sounds, smells.[60] Didier Anzieu argues that the perception that one's body is enclosed by skin marks a crucial phase in very early childhood development. He shows that, for infants, the skin has three functions: (1) it contains the various parts of the body, (2) it shields the body from the world from which it has become separate, and (3) it facilitates communication with the outside world. Anzieu argues that all three of these functions must be securely in place before psychic de-velopment can continue to the acoustic-mirror stage, the visual mirror stage, the triangulation of desire, and language acquisition.[61] A wide variety of psychic and/or cultural pressures can cause people to mark their skin as the site of trauma. In addition to the right-wing appropria-tion of neutral punk ideology (with the piercing of skin so common in punk style), extreme social marginalization in German social space of the late 1980s and 1990s caused youths drawn to Oi to scar their skin in an active attempt to master the experience that we all have experienced passively—the perception that our bodies are enclosed, protected by delicate membranes of skin.

The song "Söldner" has received much attention in the German media during the early 1990s. The text is as follows:

> Er ist ein Söldner und Faschist
> Er ist ein Mörder und Sadist.
> Er hat keine Freunde, er liebt nur sich.

Ein Menschenleben interessiert ihn nicht.
Er hat keine Sinne und keinen Verstand.
Er hat keine Herrkunft, man hat ihn verbannt.

oh . . . er ist Söldner

Er ist ein Skinhead und Faschist.
Er hat 'ne Glatze und ist Rassist.
Moral und Herz besitzt er nicht.
Hass und Gewalt zeichnen sein Gesicht.
Er liebt den Krieg, und liebt die Gewalt.
Und bist du sein Feind, dann mach ich dich kalt.

oh . . . er ist Söldner

He is a soldier and a fascist
He is a murderer and a sadist
He has no friends, he loves only himself
A human life doesn't interest him at all
He has no conscience and no brains
He has no ancestry, he's been banned.

O . . . he is a soldier

He is a skinhead and fascist
He has a bald head and is a racist
He doesn't possess a heart or a sense of morality
Hate and violence mark his face
He loves only war and loves only violence
And if you're his enemy, then I will kill you.

O . . . he is a soldier.

In an interview with the German magazine *Der Spiegel,* the band's lead singer, Jörg Petritsch, asserts that this song was written and first performed by a punk band named Target.[62] If this is true, then the boundaries between punk and skin music may be quite blurry indeed.[63] There is a twist in the text that produces an uncanny sense that the text gazes out at the listener, and this shift has been overlooked as often as it has been correctly perceived in transcriptions of the words in articles; the next to the last line is correctly written "Und bist du sein Feind,

Example 55. Opening riff of "Söldner" by Störkraft.

dann mach' ich dich kalt." It is often given as "Und bist du sein Feind, dann macht er dich kalt." The emergence of *ich* in the text suddenly collapses two binaries: the soldier and the singer, on the one hand, and the victim and the listener, on the other. Until the last line of the last verse, we are listening to a horrifying description of a pure killer in the third person: *er,* whose victims are unnamed. With the shift from *er* to *ich,* the listener is addressed, and the musician is identified in an instant as the voice of the soldier. The song combines a sense of the listener as victim of the soldier's violence and *perpetrator* of that violence. A crucial element of Oi subjectivity is precisely this confusion of violence from without and violence from within.

The music sounds like punk (musical evidence to back up Jörg Petritsch's assertion of the song's pedigree); for the opening riff and the musical basis of the verse, see ex. 55. The motion between i and bVII sounds particularly powerful in this song that isolates and obsessively reworks the major second between F♯ (tonic) and E♮ (bVII). The "O . . ." of the chorus is set to a rising line (F♯-G♯-A♮-B♮) that suggests F♯ *minor.* Two aspects of Störkraft's music seem very powerful to me. First, the music often cuts to silence. In "Söldner," there is a cut to total silence after the introductory riff given in ex. 55, accompanied by a dry cymbal sound and *mezzo forte* bass drum notes on each quarter note of each measure. Sudden drops to silence occur in 1950s rock, ska, and much music by Störkraft. Such silences articulate the control the band has over each other and the *listener.* Their unpredictability and very short duration bring the listener up short as if the music were gazing at the listener. Slavoj Žižek discusses silence as gaze in the following: "Lacan determines the *objet small a* as the bone which got stuck in the subject's throat: if the exemplary case of the gaze *qua* object is a blind man's eyes, i.e., eyes which *do not see* . . . then the exemplary case of the voice *qua* object is a voice which remains silent, i.e., which we *do not hear.*"[64] Second, Jörg Petritsch's voice is at once very rough like gravel and very clear—an extraordinary example of a rock *Sprechstimme*.[65] The complete isolation of the subject in the lyrics marks the song as more punk than German Oi Musik. One of the key features of Oi subjectivity is male bonding, and this song produces a fantasy of the totally isolated individual male warrior.

"Mann für Mann" Störkraft

The verses of this song express the boundary anxiety that is common in much German Oi Musik. The following line sounds right out of Theweleit: "die Rote Masse nimmt drastisch ihren Lauf" (the red mass swells drastically). And then, after another line: "dann ist es viel lieber Tod als rot!" (then it's much better to be dead than red"; translations mine). This last line resonates with middle-class rhetoric of 1950s Bundesrepublik discourse that has been reinscribed into an 1980s Oi song. The verses of this song express the fantasy of German Oi subjectivity being flooded from without by women, Communists, and foreigners. The song opens with a slow solo in the guitar that is a whining hymn of self-pity; there are luxurious smears notated by lines between notes in ex. 56, and the meter is free.[66]

The chorus represents the phallic assertion of drawing the boundary between the self and the other through male bonding: "Doch für uns gibt es keine Weiche / wir stehen Mann für Mann / stark wie deutsche Eisen / den niemand mehr flexen kann" (No weaklings for us / we stand man for man / strong as German iron / that no one can bend). The phrase "stark wie deutsches Eisen" clearly was made possible by Hitler's description of the German soldier: "stark wie Kruppstahl." The alternation between anxious fantasies of being flooded and phallic fantasies of assertion is represented in the music by a quickened tempo (nothing specific to this song) and by a shift in the percussion (something that *is* unique to this song). Example 57 shows that in the verse there is no snare drum and the bass drum articulates a syncopated pulse; in the chorus, the backbeat returns in the snare, and the bass plays again on the beat; this is a musical locking into place, a stiffening response to the self-pitying opening solo and the weak, syncopated drum beat of the verse.

Example 56. Opening guitar solo in "Mann für Mann" by Störkraft.

Example 57. Shift in percussion between verse and chorus
in "Mann für Mann" by Störkraft.

One of the song's later verses expresses a rarely explicit link between
Oi subjectivity and flight from women: "Jetzt stehst du da voller Tränen und Leid / dennoch deine Frau wird das niemals mehr verzeihen /
komm zu uns und dann bist du nicht mehr allein / dafür hörst du uns;
ein Leben darf dankbar sein" (Now you stand all alone full of tears and
pain / yet your wife will never forgive you / come to us, then you'll not
be alone anymore / that's why you listen to us / a life can be grateful!).
The musical representation of the last line is like an erection, in this
case, a homophobically constructed homoeroticism.[67] The song ends
with a fade-out, a very rare sound at the end of a German Oi song.
Most Oi songs end with an aggressive close, usually a single note. Fade-
out seems particularly appropriate here, given the whiny solo at the beginning of the song. German Oi Musik actively confronts the listener,
and this is part of its phallic nature; thus, a fade-out is antithetical to
its aesthetic. Recall how the verse of "Heilige Lieder" snaps into place
after its fuzzy opener by having the music briefly oscillate between
the left and the right channels. It is as if the music found the listener
in its musical sights, as it were, aimed, and fired. An additional note
to "Söldner" discussed above: the song begins with a helicopter approaching from the distance, beginning to fire overhead, then receding
into the distance; here again, the listener is sighted and fired on.[68]
   Despite the fact that one can describe characteristics that several Oi
songs share, the category *Oi* also includes some unusual songs, such as

"Mickie" by Störkraft. It opens with an anthem-like solo played by the guitar. The anthem announces a song in which the verses are in a clear twelve-bar blues form in A major. The bass plays both the minor and the major third in a fast $\frac{4}{4}$ that sounds like 1950s rock and roll. The song gets close to acknowledging its musical roots in the black tradition of the twelve-bar blues and 1950s mainstream rock and roll. What differentiates this tip-of-the-hat from punk is that in punk there are specific references to specific songs and in Oi Musik there is unacknowledged appropriation of musical material—a radical disavowal of a musical debt. Punk more openly acknowledges its history; German Oi Musik takes the history of rock and roll, strips it of its affect, and cathects it onto a protofascist subjectivity. A direct quote to a direct song would destroy this ideological-musical mechanism. A direct quote in punk makes the listener consciously aware of a musical debt; Sid Vicious sings "My Way," and most listeners competent in the mainstream popular repertoire of the postwar decades will process the song as a parodistic representation of complacent middle-class individualism. When an Oi band such as Störkraft plays a song like "Söldner," the listener who is competent in punk style recognizes stylistic markers *unconsciously,* aware of the phobic denial on which the song depends, but consciously processes the song as Oi. While it is difficult to mark a clear threshold between conscious and unconscious structures that place a listener within an ideological field, I think that *general* stylistic references trigger unconscious structures while *specific* references trigger conscious structures. The perception of general style depends on a listening competence that is produced by many hearings of many pieces. In an unconscious response to music, one forgets individual pieces and specific references and still responds to the general features of a style.

Another song by the band Endstufe, "Skinhead Rock and Roll," both acknowledges and denies its roots. The denial is in such lyrics as "Wir spielen keinen Punk / Wir spielen Skinhead Rock and Roll" (We don't play punk / we play skinhead rock and roll) and "Sheiss auf die Hippie-Musik" (shit on hippie music). The acknowledgment is in the music; the piece is pure blues with the walking blues major second discussed above in the outset of "Heilige Lieder." Also, the music has a steady stream of eighth notes that would not have been possible without punk, and the ♭VII harmony is out of the blues scale and is ubiquitous in "Hippie-Musik" from the 1960s.

German Oi Musik is anything but fast, three-chord, primitive music. My transcriptions of several hours of Oi Musik yield tempi ranging from sixty-nine to two hundred beats per minute; Oi monophony articulates every scale degree within the blues minor scale (and even a diminished triad in "Singen und Tanzen"); its dynamics (an admittedly very fluid category) range from *piano* to *fortissimo*. Verse and chorus tempi are different from one another in "Mann für Mann" by Störkraft and "Stolz" by Die böhse Onkelz. Even though many Americans and even German intellectuals, teachers, and journalists may never hear German Oi Musik, it is very important music because it has been linked (as suggested above) to the violence of the right-wing skin scene in Germany and to activities that directly precede burning places of residence and businesses owned by foreigners and people seeking political asylum in Germany. This chapter has intended to show how one kind of post–rock and roll can function.[69]

It is also crucial to remember that, appearances to the contrary, the Right is not stupid, or, to put it more accurately, calling the Right stupid lets the Left dismiss it as primitive. I hope this chapter has shown that this music is anything but primitive, anything but stupid. Of course, German Oi musicians respond to questions in interviews with German journalists in ways that resemble stupidity. But the way German Oi musicians talk suggests a carefully polished rhetorical structure that parallels deeper aspects of Oi subjectivity that I have been exploring—particularly the fear of flooding and the need to protect oneself from dissolution. In interviews, and in other statements, Oi band members do not argue; they pursue points until a wall needs to be drawn between "us" and "them."[70] These walls make Oi musicians sound stupid, as if they were unable to draw a logical conclusion from a premise. But these walls have a structure. One common device for excusing the playing of songs at concerts that have been forbidden is that the crowd forces them to do it. A way for Oi musicians to avoid responsibility for acts of violence that were preceded by listening to Oi is the claim that what people do with their music is out of the control of the musicians themselves. The idea that Oi is *nur Musik* (only music) often signifies this alibi. One of the most common rhetorical devices in these articles is the statement that "we are constantly being misunderstood." Stephan Weidner asserts that his music is "Musik aus dem Bauch" (music from the gut)—an appeal to the purely emotional nature of rock. It is a delicious irony to me that Oi musicians assert that they are misunderstood by the public. I think that the essence of Oi subjectivity *is* misrecognition; one both hates and needs the Other; one both rejects and fully cannibalizes the history of rock and roll.

This rhetoric of Oi subjectivity in interviews is represented in the music; turn everything into a brutal attack from without so that the self can protect itself from aggression by bonding with other males and purging social space of the Other. But personal space can never be purged of the Other; the abject is with us in our own body fluids and the vulnerability of own's own *skin*. This is the deadly mixture that makes German Oi Musik burn so powerfully. No matter how many people one kills, one will never be able (one will never really *want*) to eliminate the abjection of one's own body and the Other that fuels one's rage.

Since this chapter was first conceived and written, a new development has occurred in Oi Musik: two central bands have produced new CDs that openly criticize right-wing violence. The double CD *Schwarz/Weiss* by Die böhse Onkelz is an example.[71] German scholars and journalists are divided as to whether this explicit turn away from right-wing ideology is genuine or a screen for continuing the right-wing politics that lie behind the music. I believe that, although the lyrics of the songs of *Schwarz/Weiss* suggest a turn away from right-wing ideology, this ideology is present nevertheless. Suppression of certain taboo representations has been characteristic of German Oi Musik since the 1980s; bands could sing "Türken frei" in a concert and "wirklich frei" on a recording. Thus, one can have it both ways; fans know what the euphemism seems to efface but in fact *underlines*.[72] Rather than a binary opposition between early explicitly dangerous Oi Musik and recent "changed" Oi Musik, I hear a continuum in which lyrics move from explicit to implicit representations of Oi subjectivity. Songs like "Heilige Lieder" and most of the songs from *Schwarz/Weiss* do not explicitly call for acts of violence against others; yet their affect is based on extreme self-pity, especially when the songs seem to criticize acts of violence perpetrated by Oi subjects. Oi self-pity is internalized guilt from mainstream social institutions that is represented in music such as "Das Messer und die Wunde" from *Schwarz:* "Kennst du die Trauer einer Mutter / die ihr Kind verliert / Kennst du das Herz eines Freundes / das Leere spürt und stirbt" (Do you know the mourning of a mother / who has lost her child / Do you know the heart of a friend / who senses emptiness and dies). The rhetorical ambiguity of the pronoun *you* signifies the hinge between the voice of the law (the big Other) and its internalized transposition. Thus, when the narrator of the song berates the "you" who has killed, the source of the voice is multiple. It is at once the law condemning the Oi subject for his act of violence and the Oi subject berating himself in self-pity for having lost a brother—signifier at once of self, actual family member, member of the Oi community, and victim. The structure of this song suggests hidden aggression behind its surface mourning: "Kennst du die Wut, den Schmerz / das Brennen tief in mir / die grenzenlose Ohnmacht / einen Bruder, einen Bruder zu verlieren" (Do you know the anger, the pain / the burning deep in me / the boundless impotence / to have lost a brother). The tempo of the verse is 192 beats per minute (the fastest Oi song I know is "Söldner" by Störkraft at 200 beats per minute). There is also a tempo shift for the chorus—96 beats per minute. The music snaps back in place at 192 beats per minute for the rest of the song; the guitar line stresses the flatted second scale degree, a clear signifier of heavy metal. The self-pitying sadism of this song is signified by text that mourns and music that propels aggression.

On the one hand, the Oi subject lives and sings at the margins of society; on the other hand, he evokes German nationalism explicitly (in Oi's early phase of the 1980s) or implicitly (in Oi's late phase of the 1990s). Žižek offers an explanation for the curious interplay between the law and transgressions of the law that can illuminate the sense of alienation from and allegiance to the nation Germany in Oi subjectivity. Žižek writes: "As numerous analyses from Bakhtin onwards have shown, periodic transgressions are inherent to the social order; they function as a condition of the latter's stability. . . . The deepest identification which 'holds a community together' is not so much identification with the Law which regulates 'normal' everyday circuit as, rather, *identification with the specific form of transgression of the Law, of its suspension* (in psychoanalytic terms, with the specific form of enjoyment)."[73] Oi subjectivity explicitly transgresses the law; it threatens the social fabric by calling for a reappearance of fascist Germany, for the persecution of foreigners, for the celebration of the purity of the

German race. Implicitly, it *affirms* the law in the process of its transgression; the law protects society from the Oi threat while stopping short of silencing it altogether, betraying a bond that connects the Oi subject with the law. Žižek calls this the "common transgression."[74]

Oi's loathing is also complicated; it is introjected from the big Other (although this loathing is mitigated by the "common transgression" described above) and from the self. Loathing is projected onto foreigners and the big Other (recall the phrase "die Fahne verhönen" from "Deutschland" by Die böhse Onkelz). In a nutshell, the musical signifier of sadism in Oi Musik is the textual disavowal of its musical, black roots. In addition, the complexity of Oi loathing can be understood according to Žižek's description of the structure of sadism. The Oi subject is sadistic through an identification with representations in music and text that displace his own boundary trauma onto the bodies of victims making him feel, for a moment, full. Such displacement can never make the sadist full since, if he needed something external to his subjectivity, there must be an abiding lack *within*. This lack in part explains how and why the second structure of sadism is necessary. For Lacan, a more *latent* structure of sadism lies underneath the *manifest* structure. In this second, latent structure of sadism, "the sadist does not act for his own enjoyment; his stratagem is, rather, to elude the split constitutive of the subject by means of assuming the role of the object-instrument in service of the big Other."[75] The Oi subject is allied to the big Other and acts as an instrument of its enjoyment; the Oi subject introjects the transgressive loathing of the big Other and then projects his loathing outward onto the bodies and representations of bodies of others (lowercase *o*)—foreigners, women, Jews, punks, etc. Loathing flows from the big Other to the Oi subject and back out to the little other in a perpetual circulation, like the drive.

Žižek characterizes the structure of the drive as follows: "[The drive] is *always-already satisfied:* contained in its closed circuit, it 'encircles' its object . . . and finds satisfaction in its own pulsation, in its repeated failure to attain the object. In this precise sense, drive . . . appertains to the Real-Impossible, defined by Lacan as that which 'always returns to its place.' And it is precisely for this reason that identification with it is not possible."[76] This is precisely the structure of Oi subjectivity, which is drawn toward a space that evades one's grasp.[77]

Oi is a problem for mainstream culture; it is suppressed/repressed, not because it is dark, brutal, and unacceptable, but because it too clearly uncovers the violence lurking just beneath the surface of Western social space.[78] This music is, after all, being played, not just in Germany, but in the United States, England, France, Italy, and Sweden—the heart of the affluent West. This music is the West's symptom.[79]

Having fleshed out how Oi texts and music work, I would like to conclude by examining Oi Musik as hailing, how Oi listening subjects are produced and sustained. Althusserian interpellation is made possible by a delicate balance between conscious acts produced in social space and unconscious structures into which the subject is born and socialized.[80] This balance is reorganized in Oi interpellation. In Oi, the focus is less on a balance between conscious and unconscious forms of knowledge than on a paradoxical, simultaneity of *affirmation* and *denial* of history. Oi texts are historical since they call the subject to join in a collective project to reclaim national and/or racial public space based on a paradigm from the Teutonic past. Oi Musik is historical in its use of familiar musical materials from the history of rock and roll. And Oi Musik is also *ahistorical,* erasing the contours of specific musical pieces, erasing the music's blackness, and erasing its progressive/expressive roots. I suggest above that Oi Musik must be repressed because it reveals the violence at the heart of the West's Symbolic Order. This obtains for democratic public policy of nations that produce Oi Musik at their margins. But why is the ahistorical nature of Oi necessary for the sustaining of its own subjectivity? The answer is that psychoanalytically and historically, two mechanisms must be held in place for Oi subjectivity to be sustained, and *each* involves a delicate balance between knowledge that is repressed and knowledge that is expressed.

Psychoanalytically, the Oi subject must let himself be convinced that his boundary trauma has been caused by the other—often expressed as the abject *out there* in social space: leftists, women, foreigners, etc. This other must be obliterated by acts of violence (expulsion, burnings, beatings), and the community can be kept pure by erecting phenomenal and symbolic shields against future incursions. In terms of his own body, the Oi subject must repress the knowledge of the vulnerability of his own skin, his biological link to the body of a woman, and the fact that his body in fact produces the kinds of fluids he identifies as the abject. Historically, the Oi subject must let himself be convinced that the black sounds of the blues, reggae, punk, and metal with which he is familiar are incomplete, anonymous materials destined to be named and (re)christened by the white, the Right, the here and now of Oi Musik. He must not remember that his music *needs* blackness and could never have come into being without the history of blacks in America, Jamaica, and England, without the progressive political music of the 1960s and 1970s. And he must not let himself know that he is grafting Oi ideology onto an essentially black music in a cannibalistic act of musical violence.[81]

7

Lamentation, Abjection,

and the Music

of Diamanda Galás

During the summer of 1992, I heard a concert by Diamanda Galás in Hamburg, Germany. The performance took place from 1:00 to 2:30 A.M. in an ornate theater in downtown Hamburg. The initial seconds of the concert shocked me visually and acoustically. Galás sang at the front of the stage, naked from the waist up; behind her, the stage looked like the ruins of a bombed-out building; the stage and Galás were soaked in a bright red light that made Galás's sweat look like blood several minutes into the visceral performance.[1] The dynamic level of the sound was incredibly high, and I heard static in my ears— the telltale sign of sound having crossed the pain threshold. I found the music first repellent and then curiously beautiful; friends who were with me shared these ambivalent responses. In the pages that follow, I will ponder the structures that could have produced these responses culturally and psychoanalytically.[2]

Diamanda Galás is an American of Greek (Maniot) heritage. Her great-grandparents emigrated to the United States around 1912. She studied the piano with her father and played jazz, gospel, and classical music in public at an early age.[3] Having studied avant-garde music with Xenakis, she began creating performance art in the mid-1970s, although, as she says, "I never use that word [*performance artist*] for myself. I use the word *auteur,* as Hitchcock would. Yes, I compose the music and I perform the music and I compose the libretto and I design the lights until I turn it over to a professional lighting designer. But Wagner did that, too! People who call this performance art do it out of sexism—any woman who organizes a *Gesamtkunstwerk* is condemned to this territory."[4] Galás describes her vocal technique as follows: "In 1975 I decided upon the creation of a new vocal music which employs an unmatrixed production of vocal sounds as the most immediate representation of thought. The primary concern is with the execution, chordally, or contrapuntally—of different processes of severe concentration, 'mental' or 'sentient' states, for which vocal sound is used as the fundamental physical coordinate."[5] Having explored the possibilities of manipulating her voice as unmatrixed sound, Galás turned in subsequent years to the study of bel canto singing techniques; her teachers include Frank Kelly, Vicki Hall (in Berlin), and Barbara Meier.[6]

The issue that galvanized her work in the early 1980s was AIDS.[7] She lost her brother to AIDS in 1986, and much of her subsequent work has been dedicated to people infected with HIV: "There are people who will not go hear something confrontational when they are confronting it daily. Perhaps they would rather see Madonna or something they can dance to. I'm not saying there's not a place for that because there certainly is. But as an artist I have to create what I see and what I hear—what's grounded in reality."[8]

Galás plays the piano in jazz, gospel, blues, and classical styles; she has a powerful voice with an enormous range; she has been influenced by American, commercial television, the avant-garde, and feminist performance art. What holds such heterogeneous elements together in Diamanda Galás's art? In part, it is the lament of her Greek, Maniot heritage. I begin my discussion of Galás's art with an investigation of the history, form, style, and gender specificity of lament.

Lamentation

Women occupy a contradictory position in Greek society. On the one hand, they are central to the family and to the complex and crucial rituals of mourning the dead.[9] Holst-Warhaft confirms the centrality of women in lament and broadens the assertion to cover several cultures: "One point on which those who have studied lament in cultures as diverse as those of China, New Guinea, India, Greece, Saudi Arabia and Ireland agree is that laments are generally performed by women."[10]

Yet, on the other hand, women's lives are restricted during the mourning process. A reason for the marginalization of women, particularly during mourning, has to do with the structure of the Greek notion of death and women's relation to it. Danforth describes the Greek notion of death as a gradual transformation of the deceased from the world of the living to the world of the dead that progresses through three phases that are represented in funerary rites: (1) the phase of separation; (2) the liminal, or transition, phase; and (3) the phase of incorporation. Separation begins with phenomenal death and ends with the completion of the burial; the transition period is the time after burial and before exhumation in which the deceased is neither wholly dead nor alive; the incorporation phase begins with the exhumation and inspection of the bones of the deceased. If the bones are clean and white, they are brought to the village ossuary, and the grave is destroyed. If decomposition is not complete, they are reburied, and exhumation is repeated at a later date. During each of these phases, women sing laments and tend the grave, ensuring a successful transition of the body and soul of the deceased from life to death. Since women communicate with the not-yet-wholly dead during the liminal phase, they are linked to the danger that can arise if the corpse of the deceased only partially decomposes. The deceased can return to the realm of the living as a revenant and haunt the living.[11]

Holst-Warhaft argues that male fear of women's power in mourning in ancient Greece had profound consequences for Western culture. She argues that male classical Greek culture appropriated the female role in lament and transformed it into two new literary genres that were the province of men: the encomium or funeral elegy and the tragedy. Holst-Warhaft suggests that, as women's roles in rites of mourning were being *restricted* in Athens, Delphi, and Keos from the sixth to the fifth century B.C., the funeral elegy and tragedy *emerged* as male-dominated forms of literature. At Athens, for example, women's participation in ritual offerings was limited, and the laws at Keos and Delphi legislated women's silence at crucial phases of death rites. Holst-Warhaft suggests that preclassical lamentation may well have continued in classical Greece, owing to repeated forms of legislation that aimed again and again at limiting women's roles.[12] If Holst-Warhaft is right, then there is a gender-specific tension between a woman's lamenting voice and the institutions of the modern state. *Antigone* works out this problem in ancient Greek drama. While the specificity of Galás's political commitment suggests contemporary issues such as AIDS, in part at least the affective intensity of her art rests on this ancient antagonism that pits the voice of women against the law of the state.

Although there are many differences among laments even within certain regions of contemporary rural Greece, laments share paradoxical elements. For example, the lament is at once very expressive (with sharp cries and acts of self-mutilation) and very carefully constructed. The singer of lament is usually a close relative of the deceased, but not *too* close a relative; she is often a professional lamenter/artist whose skill is evaluated by the community.[13] Mourning and performance were linked in ancient Greece, a feature that Diamanda Galás transposes to her contemporary art.

Danforth points out that the same lament can be sung (with changes as appropriate) at weddings, funerals, or occasions that mourn relatives in exile.[14] The essence of lamentation is thus not the representation of an event in itself but the structure of *separation* that marriages, death, and exile produce and that rituals of mourning represent. Within specific laments, as well, even the affective charge can shift from one of mourning to one of ridicule and satire.[15]

Laments often shift perspective, with the narrator addressing the deceased, the deceased addressing his/her survivors, the singer addressing the cause of death, the priest, members of the community, forces of nature that are omens, Christian elements, herself, etc.

In general, everything that has been described above obtains for Maniot lament, with two crucial classes of differences: (1) the style, tone, and imagery of Maniot lament are unique in the Greek tradition; and (2) Maniot lament often blurs the distinction between the emotive expression of loss and a *call to avenge* an unjust death. Maniot laments are often long narratives that recount both the manner of the death of the deceased and the reaction of those who survive the death, often the story of revenge (in the case of revenge laments). They often have stories within stories.[16] They have a flat, understated tone and an intense concern with recording the minute details of death.

Maniot laments are punctuated by sharp cries that express pain, address the cause of death, and/or call for revenge. Holst-Warhaft describes them as follows: "It is clear that these women know the power of their cries. In the revenge laments, they are put to immediate use, but even when there is no possibility for translating anger into action, the outbursts in the controlled body of a narrative are so persistent a feature of the Maniot laments, their position within the text sufficiently regular (almost always preceded by a calm introduction . . . followed by a return to practical detail) to suggest that they are a conscious device of the lamenter."[17]

Like cries, "sobs, sighs and sudden intakes of breath are integral to the performance of Maniot lament." Holst-Warhaft locates the importance of the breath in lament in the meanings of one word: "The soul and breath are synonymous in Greek culture (being out of breath, dying and losing one's soul are all conveyed by the single word *xepsy-hismenos*."[18] There is thus a common ground between the breath of the singer in lament and the last breath of the dying relation: "Many people believe that at the moment of death a person's soul . . . which is described as a breath of air . . . located in the area of the heart, leaves the body through the mouth."[19] I will show below that representations of cries are crucial elements of the music of Diamanda Galás.

Maniot laments are crucial elements in blood feuds.[20] On the surface, the call to revenge works to assuage grief by turning it outward. On a deeper level, it affirms loyalty to family over the state and thus radically reverses the classical Greek appropriation of women's role in lament centuries earlier.[21] The call to revenge also provides Maniot women with a voice that can address a wide variety of political issues.

Holst-Warhaft asserts that the texture of a woman's voice is crucial to lament: "We must at least be aware that the reactions of a contemporary audience to any lament, including those we find in classical tragedy, were as much conditioned by their musical structure, the timbre and pitch of the lead lamenter's individual voice, her sobs, moans, shrieks and sighs and by the polyphonic texture of the women's voices, as they were by the text."[22]

The importance of the texture and timbre of a woman's voice is reflected in the music of the Furies. The Furies sing music that binds; Holst-Warhaft describes it as follows: "To claim their victims, the Furies sing a magic 'binding song' while dancing in a ring. . . . Words are repeated, or nearly repeated, like incantations . . . together with the exclamations—the muttered spells of witches."[23] In addition to cries, mastery of vocal texture is also crucial to Galás's music, as I will show below.

Danforth suggests that music differentiates the lament of separation sung at weddings from the lament of separation sung at funerals, even when the texts are nearly identical; "When these songs are sung at weddings, the style is more forceful, vigorous, and joyful; the melody more elaborate, with trills and light melismatic phrases. At death rites the style is more somber and restrained, the melody flatter and less elaborate."[24] This quote suggests not only that the affect of a lament is more determined by the music than by the text but that it is the ornamentation of given musical materials that determines the affect of lament. If Danforth is right, then the outline of a melody can be used for a lament both at a wedding (lightly embellished with, e.g., neighbor notes, bent notes, appoggiaturas, trills, vibrato) and at a funeral (with a minimum of ornamentation). Such subtle differences would probably not be notated but would lie within the spontaneously executed "grain" of the singer's voice.[25]

Lamentation and Music: *Vena Cava*

Lamentation in the Greek tradition is a symbolic working out of the pain of loss at a wedding, exile, or death through ritualized acts, language, and music in public performances that incorporate individual suffering into a communal context. Lamentation frequently crosses and recrosses thresholds: between separation and incorporation, the world of the living and the world of the dead, pain and pleasure, expression and construction, mourning for the deceased and mourning for the self. And these thresholds are enunciated and crossed by a woman's speaking, singing, and crying voice.

I will explore below Diamanda Galás's *Vena Cava* from 1993 as lamentation: the work is dedicated to Galás's brother, Philip Dimitri Galás. There are no direct references to her brother in the text, but, according to the CD liner notes, some of the musical passages are taped excerpts from recordings that her brother made before his death—"There Is a Balm in Gilead" (vocals) and "When I Am Laid in Earth" (accordion).

The title of the work refers to a major vein that returns blood to the heart; this image thus condenses the images of the heart as source of emotion in popular and high culture, the heart as the center of the body's blood (infected with HIV), and the heart as the place of the soul's residence. Here is an overview of the work on a track-by-track basis with a few phrases from the text of each track and a few examples discussed in detail.

Track 1. "I wake up and I see the face of the devil and I ask him 'What time is it?'" (repeated over and over). A common feature of *Vena Cava* and much of Galás's work is repetition. As we saw in the first chapter, repetition can produce or erase a wide variety of meanings in a wide number of contexts. Repetition is crucial to lament since lament *is* a repetition, a working out of the significance of an already experienced trauma. On the surface, *Vena Cava* represents the hallucinations of a person suffering from AIDS-related dementia, and much of the work does represent the listening position of the mind of a deluded person. But, as I will show below, the listening positions produced by the music often shift, as in Maniot lament, and repetition of text and music cannot be assigned exclusively to any one listening position.

In the middle of the repetition of the line "What time is it?" the music enters quietly—synthesized, highly artificial notes, sustained and quiet. The array of taped music, noises, and electronically manipulated sounds gives the work an antiseptic quality. I find this the most disturbing of Galás's works, despite the manifest clarity of its artificial nature.

At 1:39, Galás shifts the timbre of her voice to a low question: "How do you feel today?" This suggests a visitor, relative, or doctor having come into the patient's room, and the rest of the track develops the antiphonal relation between these two "voices"—one high and whiny asking, "What time is it?" the other low and restrained asking, "How do you feel today?" At 3:16, the low, declamatory voice that had sounded like a visitor, relative, or doctor asks, "How much time do you want?" making him/her sound like the devil with whom the dying man/woman is bargaining for time.

At 3:36, the word *time* is electronically manipulated into the sound of a bird (it sounds like a crow to me) that echoes from channel to channel into the distance. In Greek lament, birds mediate between the worlds of the living and the dead: "Birds . . . are able to cross the boundary between the world of the living and the world of the dead.

What is more . . . birds are able to cross this boundary in a direction that nothing else can go except revenants: they can return from the world of the dead to the world of the living. They act as messengers who report to the living the condition of the dead in the underworld."[26]

What actually happens in the music, of course, is that the sounds of the birds get quieter; they do not get far away. For me, however, they sound as if they were receding into the distance for two reasons. First, I think that the ear distinguishes between close sounds and far sounds, not necessarily in terms of decibels, but more crucially in terms of noise. Most sounds have an aura of noise around them (one of the purest, least "noisy" sounds is a tuning fork held at the tip and struck with moderate force on a medium-hard surface such as one's skull). This aura of noise decays rapidly as its source moves away from the ear. Thus, sounds that have no audible aura of noise and are quiet *tend* to sound far away.[27] Second, there is an enormous sense of space in this work. While much of Galás's voice is close to the listening plane, voices, noises, sounds, and music echo into what sounds like infinite space.[28]

At 3:51, another voice enters and says, "We've been talkin' about you downstairs, and we don't think you're being realistic." This line gets repeated over and over and becomes transformed into gibberish— a reversal of the process discussed in chapter 1 in which children experience the meaningless sounds of the sonorous envelope divide and become organized in the acoustic-mirror stage and find relatively stable form in the mother tongue of the Symbolic Order.

At 4:48, a series of cries emerges in antiphonal response to the word *insane*. These cries sound like uncontrolled wails that echo into the distance and turn to nightmarish noises. At 5:24, Galás sings cries that recall the Maniot cry that breaks like a fissure from the hard surface of lament. These cries come from nowhere; they are frightening but quite controlled. Galás leaps from silence to the very top of her range and sings notes with an intense purity. (I will discuss these "structured cries" in the remarks on *Plague Mass* below.) Galás's highly controlled cries take over and give form to the less controlled cry of the man/woman dying of AIDS. This is a musical example of Galás identifying with the pain of someone mourning a loved one's immanent death.[29]

At 7:19, a noise emerges from the music's open spaces that sounds poised between a high sound emitted by an electronic device and a ringing in one's ears. This ambiguity opens the threshold between the man/woman dying of AIDS and the listener and his/her/our immediate environment. An iambic, quiet heartbeat emerges at 7:57. The grotesque atmosphere turns humorous from time to time in the work, as at 9:05, when Galás sings, "I'm fine Miss Thing; I just feel like singing 'The Battle Hymn of the Republic.'"

Track 2. "Porgi Amor" from Mozart's *The Marriage of Figaro.* This track shows how beautifully Galás can sing using conventional techniques. The aria is a representation of the dying man/woman's memory/imagination since the heavy echo continues throughout, and there are quiet, sustained electronic sounds throughout—like monitors in a hospital. At 3:10, the dying man/woman imagines having died, with a crowd of people looking down at him/her saying, "At last he is at peace." In the seconds that follow, Galás draws in her breath slowly and noisily and breathes out, barely comprehensibly, "free at last."

Track 3. "Amazing Grace." This track represents a radical revision of gospel music. First, there is an ironic sense of the placement of this music so early in *Vena Cava.* The text of "Amazing Grace" was written by a white slave merchant after surviving an intense storm at sea. The source of the music is unknown. It is clear from the first two tracks of the CD that the music represents the long and agonized death of a man/woman from AIDS. The song leads without transition to Galás's flat declamation of the following lines: "I dreamed I was lying in the green grass, and the wind was blowing softly, and blue was everywhere, and I saw heads popping out through the green grass, and it seemed as if they knew me." This surreal text condenses both the expressionistic idea of the return of the dead and green grass as an image of heaven in Greek poetry; the work adds a continuous texture of birds and insects sounding far away in the distance.

Track 4. Garbled sounds of medical staff discussing scheduling. Galás: "Yes, I like the TV." Television sounds in the background. At 2:00, the listener is placed in the position of the dying man/woman as we hear relatives whispering, "I just thought we'd have a small service; just the family, nothing big you know." The words disintegrate into the pure consonants of breath, tongues, and lips. From 10:16, Galás begins to produce a noise that sounds like a bow on a stringed instrument playing a note with too little speed and too much pressure; she gradually releases the pressure, and, at 10:24, the noise releases into a pure vowel that sounds into track 5.

Track 5. The line "Wait for me" turns into a heavy spondee "for me" like heavy breathing;[30] the line alternates with the line: "Take me down mother down to the cellar in a garbage bag." "Where's the old death bird"; the Christmas song "You'd Better Watch Out" bleeds in and out to applause on the television. "Silent Night" bleeds in and out. At 6:04: "Don't you know that you have destroyed me" (the voice of the dying person's mother, perhaps?).

Track 6. "Fishy fishy on the wall, who's the biggest fuck of all."

Track 7. "Stay awake little pony, stay awake. Don't let that maniac come in here." "Hush Little Baby." Galás sings this quite high in her range, quietly; this places her voice under enormous pressure. Her voice tightens throughout to the breaking point. "Silent Night"; television applause; "old dog bone"; "no surprises, no secrets, no needles, no puncture." A taped voice played so slowly it is incomprehensible.

Track 8. "I miss you; it's been so long; how are you? I'm fine; I've been out here so long, I remember us together, so green there; it's so black here." This sounds like a representation of the dead speaking through the lamenter. "Silent Night" close to the listening plane. "Silent Night" smears to silence—an acoustic equivalent of Francis Bacon's faces. The music ends with the listener located squarely in the position of the dying man/woman, who dies while remembering this Christmas song.

Vena Cava represents crossing the thresholds of listening positions, from the singer, to people in the hospital room (visitors, relatives, doctors), to the person him/herself, to the listener. There are frequent antiphonal structures that suggest conversation with the dying man/woman; there are frequent uncontrolled cries that are answered by Galás's structured cries. The work is dedicated to Galás's brother, but neither his name nor his relationship to the singer is present in the work, signifying the distance between the singer and the act of mourning; the work is clearly mediated with sophisticated electronic effects, and it freely borrows from classical and gospel music, commercial television, Christmas songs, and spirituals.

In other works, gospel and blues influences are more transparent. For example, her album *The Singer* (1992) contains powerful versions of "Put a Spell on You," "Swing Low, Sweet Chariot," and "Let My People Go" (written by Galás). Yet, even on this album, which flirts with presenting Galás as a sadomasochistic sex object (the CD has her photographed in a dark blue light wearing a leather jacket with straps tightly wrapped around her breasts), the words "we are all HIV+" are clearly visible on her fingers in the cover picture. *Plague Mass* (1990) is also a form of lamentation; it is a large-scale work devoted to people infected with HIV. Before listening to passages from *Plague Mass,* I would like to negotiate a transition to abjection—a psychoanalytic perspective on the culturally specific forms of lament whose musical representation we have been theorizing. In a nutshell, both lamentation and abjection negotiate *separation.*

Abjection and Music

Abjection has aesthetic, semiotic, theological, and psychoanalytic registers—all of which overlap. Aesthetically, sensations and representations of sensations that are extremely repulsive yet fascinating are abject —particularly representations of body *fluids* and *waste* such as blood, urine, semen, and feces, *decaying* flesh, sores on the skin, *decaying* food, and elements of all these that cross boundaries.[31] Semiotically, the abject runs constantly beneath the process of signification in which words represent (and are therefore cut off from) concepts of things; the abject is the semiotic residue that escapes (and is paradoxically produced by) signification. Theologically, rites of defilement are linked to rites of purification in many pagan religions, and dietary prohibitions are crucial particularly to Judaism. The image of the crucifixion in Christianity suggests the centrality of abjection as well. Psychoanalytically, the abject is that which is set aside by the psyche outside the economy of repression. The following discussion of Diamanda Galás's music will unpack these different registers of abjection through a reading of Julia Kristeva's *Powers of Horror.*[32]

Before focusing in some detail on *Plague Mass,* I would like to refer once more to the version of "Amazing Grace" performed in *Vena Cava.* A transcription of the song in E♭ major, as it might be sung in a more or less "neutral" fashion, is given in ex. 58. Example 59 suggests how Diamanda Galás sings the song.

Galás sustains many of what are half notes in the "neutral" version

Example 58. "Amazing Grace" in E♭ major.

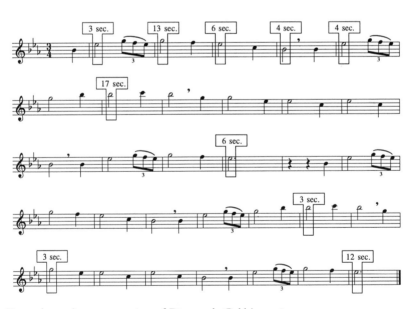

Example 59. A representation of Diamanda Galás's version
of "Amazing Grace" from *Vena Cava*.

for quite a long time. It sounds as if she were opening up the music and listening to what she heard inside each of these long and sustained notes. "Inside" the first G♮² in the second full measure, she hears a distant female choir, barely audible; this choir drifts around pitches that I cannot determine. After the song proper is over and Galás speaks the surrealist lines "I dreamed I was lying in the green grass," the female choir echoes *diminuendo* for thirteen seconds to silence. This echo signifies the abjection of a remainder, something that persists long after language emerges. Galás found these voices within a note of "Amazing Grace," and they remain as abjected bits of music after the song has ended.

Plague Mass (1990)

The work opens with a flat, declamatory question that is repeated: "Were you a witness?" The question and its sternly spoken repetition sound like a reproach, as if the rhetorical question were obviously answered no. The imperative of witnessing the death(s) in question suggests the function in lament of inscribing a death into the shifting contours of social space. What follows is a transcription from track 1:

> Were you a witness?
> Were you a witness?
> And on that holy day,
> And on that bloody day,
> Were you a witness?
> Were you a witness?
> And on that holy day,
> And on that bloody day,
> And on his dying bed,
> He asked me:
> "Tell all my friends, I was fighting, too."
> But to all cowards and voyeurs,
> There are no more tickets to the funeral;
> No. . . . No more tickets to the funeral.

Until the *no* followed by an ellipsis, the language is declaimed in a flat, severe tone echoing into the recesses of the cathedral of St. John

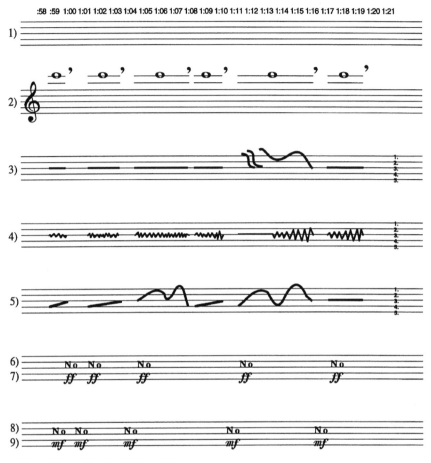

Example 60. Track 1, *Plague Mass*, 0:58–1:20.

the Divine in New York City in which the music was performed live. Right after the declamation of this *no,* Galás begins a series of cries that we have so far been linking to the cry that pierces the Maniot lament. There are many such passages in *Plague Mass* and other works by Galás in which cries alternate with declaimed monologue, antiphonal narration, and song. I would like to spend some time getting into Galás's cries, theorizing them as signifiers of abjection. According to Kristeva, the abject "beseeches a discharge, a convulsion, a crying out."[33] For a representation of this musical negation, see ex. 60.

First, a few remarks about the ideology and technique of the example. Peter Winkler discusses the ideological stain that transcription places on music in his excellent study of the voice of Aretha Franklin.[34] Winkler explores what transcription reveals in naming and describing the contours of a voice that resists conventional notation and how his own ideologically determined desires shape the results he sought. My own transcription is similarly charged with my own desire to mark Galás's voice, to understand it, to possess it. I have arranged the music into nine levels that represent different aspects of what I hear happening in the work.

Level 1 represents the left-to-right progress of phenomenal time as shown on the digital screen of the CD player. I decided for clarity's sake to notate seconds on each line; phenomenal time is thus notated as a span that connects points in time. There is, for example, one second that spans 0:58 to 0:59; what happens during that second is notated on various levels between the lines on which 0:58 and 0:59 are poised.

Level 2 represents the pitch that Galás sings in her cries; in *Vena Cava,* she sometimes cries, shrieks, moans, as any person might who is not a trained virtuoso; in *Plague Mass,* all her cries are highly studied and crafted soundings of notes at the top of a soprano's range. Since Galás bends notes extraordinarily, I could have notated much more pitch variation on level 2, with quarter tones edging the pitch up toward D♭ or down to B♮, for instance. I decided to notate C♮³ as the pitch structure of these cries since she begins and ends the series of cries squarely on C♮³ and because her bending occurs in waves, to be described below. I have done away with rhythmic notation entirely since I hear no fixed meter in this portion of the work. The pitch notation for each cry lasts as long as the C♮³ is notated. For example, the last cry in this series lasts for two seconds, from 1:17 to 1:19.

Level 3 represents what I call noise. In other chapters, I have discussed noise in aesthetic, cultural, and acoustic registers. Here, I am speaking acoustically, as if one could look at a graph of Galás's voice. Clearly defined lines would reflect "sounds"; thin, multiple, or thick lines would reflect "noise." I hear two kinds of noise in Galás's voice: noise as the result of too much pressure and too little air, on the one hand, and noise as the result of too little pressure and too much air, on the other.[35] A horizontal line on level 3 represents minimal noise; the pitch is sung "pure." Line 2 represents noise that is close to the "crushing" point; line 1 represents the noise of crushed pitches; anything above line 1 represents what can be described only as the vocal equivalent of static produced by little air speed and immense pressure on the vocal chords. Line 4 represents sound produced by much air speed and little pressure; line 5 represents sounds that are emptied of pitch content and sound like pure breath.

The breath marks that look like apostrophes refer, as in traditional vocal notation, to the singer taking a breath. There are three noise articulations that begin above line 1 in these cries. They sound like extreme versions of guttural articulations at the beginnings of notes in the vocal style of Elvis Presley or Buddy Holly.

Level 4 represents vibrato; a horizontal line on line 3 represents minimal vibrato; a wavy line from line 3, up to line 2, down to line 3, down to line 4, and back up to line 3 represents a wide vibrato such as would be acceptable in contemporary operatic performance practice. A wavy line from line 3, to line 1, to line 3, to line 5, and back to line 3 represents a very wide vibrato that reaches a semitone above and below the pitch.

Level 5 represents pitch variation. A horizontal line on line 3 represents no pitch variation; line 4 represents pitches approximately a quarter tone below the pitch notated on level 2; line 5 represents pitches a half step below the pitch notated on level 2; line 2 represents pitches approximately a quarter note above the pitch notated on level 2; and line 1 represents pitches a half step above the pitch notated on level 2.

Level 6 represents the sung text, level 7 the dynamic level of the sung text. Level 8 represents the spoken text, level 9 the dynamic level of the spoken text.

The antiphonal style of this series of negations and the way the sung *no* from 0:59 to 1:00 pierces the texture of declamation suggest Maniot lamentation. The alternation between *mezzo forte* spoken *no*s and excruciating *fortissimo* sung *no*s gives the music an element of control.

The sung *no*s are signifiers of abjection in two ways. First, their negation is so extreme it ruptures the denotative structure of the sentence in which the word *no* appears: "There are no more tickets to the funeral." The alternation between spoken *no*s and sung *no*s suggests a radical exclusion that repeats an escape from, but is trapped within, a boundary: "what is *abject,* radically excluded and draws me toward the place where meaning collapses." Or, "There are lives [abjection] not sustained by *desire,* as desire is always for objects. Such lives are based on *exclusion*. They are clearly distinguishable from those understood as neurotic or psychotic, articulated by *negation* and its modalities, *transgression, denial,* and *repudiation*."[36]

But the abject is not silent: "From its place of banishment, the abject does not cease challenging its master."[37] But who is the master of abjection in *Plague Mass*? On a simple level, the sung *nos* shown in ex. 60 challenge the society that has excluded people who are HIV+ from public view. Galás, like Antigone, is saying no, as well, to the patriarchal order.[38] In *Enjoy Your Symptom!* Žižek describes the Lacanian choice between the Name of the Father or the superego in the French phrase *père ou pire:*

> The original position of man *qua* being of language is decidedly that of *alienation* in the signifier (in the symbolic order): the first choice is necessarily that of the Father, which marks the subject with the indelible guilt pertaining to his very (symbolic) existence. . . . Yet Lacan's wager is that it is possible for the subject to get rid of the superego pressure by *repeating* the choice and thus exculpating himself of his constitutive guilt. The price of it is exorbitant: if the first choice [*père*] is "bad," its repetition is in its very formal structure "worse" since it is an act of *separation* from the symbolic community [*pire*]: Lacan's supreme example is here of course Antigone's suicidal "No!" to Creon.[39]

Example 60 suggests another aspect of abjection in the sounds of Galás's voice itself. First, she smears the pitch content of her cry around the C♮ up to D♭ in the seconds 1:07–1:08 and 1:15–1:16 and down to B♮ at the beginning of the second 1:04–1:05. This smearing of boundaries suggests a paradoxical aspect of abjection; it can signify *drawing* boundaries with the side-by-sideness of psychic apparatus and the excluded abject discussed above, and it can signify *erasing* boundaries, such as in the representations of horrid oral/anal/genital substitutions that permeate the film *The Cook, the Thief, His Wife, and Her Lover.* This drawing/erasing of boundaries suggests a double, semiotic register of abjection. Abjection is produced by all stages of developing subjectivity from the separation of our bodies from those of our mothers, from the separation of our voices from those of our mothers, from the separation of our mothers' voices from those of our fathers, and from the separation of words from things. Such separations produce abject residues at each stage and belong to the primary register of semiotic abjection. These primary abjections are produced when *boundaries are drawn*. Secondary abjection fantasizes a return back across these thresholds. These secondary abjections are produced when *boundaries are erased*. Kristeva associates this regressive register of abjection with the consequences of renouncing the father (the *ou pire* discussed above): "It is worth noting what repercussions such a foreclosure of the Name of the Father have on language. That of the borderline patient is often abstract, made up of stereotypes that are bound to seem cultured; he aims at precision, indulges in self-examination, in meticulous comprehension, which easily brings to mind obsessional discourse. But there is more to it than that. That shell of ultra-protected signifier keeps breaking up to the point of desemantization, to the point of reverberating only as notes, music, 'pure signifier' to be reparcelled out and resemanticized anew."[40]

Galás often tears meaning from sound in her work, as in the passage represented in ex. 60. And, along the regressive trajectory back across the threshold that had separated words from things, we come to the noise that lies at the heart of the acoustic mirror, as discussed earlier.[41] Galás crushes the pitch $C\natural^3$ as discussed above in the seconds 1:04–1:05 and 1:11–1:12, and she articulates crossing the threshold between pitch and noise through too much pressure/too little air from 1:12 to 1:14. The regressive trajectory suggests a fantasy of the body of the mother—a crucial site of abjection. We have seen throughout this book how the gender specificity of the sonorous envelope and acoustic mirror produces a highly charged ambivalence associated with the voice of the mother: "The abject confronts us . . . and this time within our personal archaeology, with our earliest attempts to release the hold of the *maternal* entity even before existing outside of her, thanks to the autonomy of language. It is a violent, clumsy breaking away, with the constant risk of falling back under the sway of a power as securing as it is stifling."[42]

Cries that erupt in unmetered time signify abjection in yet another way. Kristeva distinguishes the economy of the unconscious with its negations that propel a variety of psychic returns, on the one hand, and the economy of the abject, on the other, in which time is at once infinite and explosive:

Once upon blotted-out time, the abject must have been a magnetized pole of covetousness. But the ashes of oblivion now serve as a screen and reflect aversion, repugnance. The clean and proper (in the sense of incorporated and incorporable) becomes filthy, the sought-after turns into the banished, fascination into shame. Then, forgotten time crops up suddenly and condenses into a flash of lightning an operation that, if it were thought out, would involve bringing together the two opposite terms but, on account of that flash, is discharged like thunder. The time of abjection is double: a time of oblivion and thunder, of veiled infinity and the moment when revelation bursts forth.[43]

Example 61 is from track 2 of the work; it reworks the lines with which the piece opens and turns the accusatory question "Were you a witness?" into a horrid hiss. The example shows the register of noise that Galás uses to drain spoken words of vowels; the example shows that, at 2:13, Galás splits the word *witness* into its two syllables and drains the syllable-*ness* of the short *e* until only a sinister hiss remains. The example shows with two *x*'s a unique sound at 2:19. Right at the point at which the short *e* is almost entirely drained from the syllable -*ness*, Galás opens her mouth widely, twice, in demonic acoustic smiles that transform the short *e* into *ah* right before the vowel gets extinguished altogether. While ex. 60 had shown Galás crossing the threshold from pitch specificity to crushed noise, ex. 61 shows Galás crossing the threshold between language and pure sound by subtracting vowels from consonants. Although I concentrate on Kristeva for the reasons cited above, the way that Galás turns beautifully sung notes to noise is like the acoustic equivalent of Georges Bataille's flowers, in which lovely petals surround an obscene, hairy center: "The interior of a rose does not at all correspond to its exterior beauty; if one tears off all

Example 61. "Were You a Witness?" from *Plague Mass,* track 2, 2:07–2:21.

2:07	2:08	2:09	2:10	2:11	2:12	2:13	2:14	2:15	2:16	2:17	2:18	2:19	2:20	2:21	2:22	2:23	2:24

And on that	were			xx				
Holy Day,	you							
and on that	a							
Bloody day,	witn————————————— ss		ē vowel subtracted from syllable "ness"				xx: as the ē vanishes, Galás' mouth opens to ā whispered sounds before the "ss"	

of the corolla's petals, all that remains is a rather sordid tuft."[44] For Bataille, the flower is abject because of a *lack* of relation between the beauty of the petals and the obscenity of its center. Notes at the top of a soprano's range are like flowers that Galás mutilates petal by petal to reveal the pure noise that resides within the human voice.[45]

Track 4 contains passages from the Old Testament and texts composed by Galás; the liner notes are misleading since they show all the passages from Leviticus followed by those composed by Galás; the music is composed of passages from Leviticus interrupted by and juxtaposed to texts as shown below:

[Leviticus 15:]

When any man hath an issue out of his flesh
because of his issue he is unclean;
Every bed whereon he lieth is unclean;
and everything whereon he sitteth unclean;
and whosoever touches his bed shall be unclean;
and he that sitteth whereon he sat shall be unclean;
and he that touches the flesh of the unclean becomes unclean;
and he that be spat on by him unclean becomes unclean.

[Excerpt from Psalm 22:]

Strong bulls of Baashan, do beset me round.
They gape upon me with their mouths
as a ravening and a roaring lion.
But thou, O Lord shall laugh at them,
Thou shalt bring them down,
into the pit of destruction
greedy and deceitful men shall be exposed as vermin
And their days as iniquity.

[Return to Leviticus 15:]

And who soever toucheth anything under him shall be unclean;
And he that beareth any of those things shall be unclean;
And what saddle he rideth upon is unclean;
and the vessel of earth that he touches unclean;

[Excerpt from Psalms 58 and 59 and text by Diamanda Galás:]

Deliver me from mine enemies,
Defend me from them that rise up against me;
Deliver me from the workers of iniquity
and save me from bloody men.
For lo, they lie in wait for my soul;
The wicked are gathered against me,
not for my transgressions, not for my sin, O Lord.
They run and prepare themselves without my help, without my fault,
Awake to help me and behold:
Swords are in their lips, for who, say they, doth hear.
But thou, O Lord, shall laugh at them.
The God of my mercy shall let me see my desire upon my enemies.
And at evening, let them make a noise like a dog,
and go around about the city.
Let them look up and down for meat,
and grudge if they be not satisfied.
Break out the great teeth of the young lions,
Break out the great teeth of the young lions,
and when they laugh at the trial of the innocent,
Let them be cut as in pieces!

[Return to Leviticus 15:]

And if any man's seed of copulation go out from him, he is unclean;
Every garment, every skin whereon is the seed, unclean;
And the woman with whom this man would lie will be unclean;
And whoever touches her will be unclean.
This is the law of the plague,
to teach when it is clean and unclean.

[Text by Diamanda Galás:]

The Devil is an impotent man.
He says it nice and plays himself off as the friend.
He tries to make you uncertain
so your hands shake
and then he tells you, you're insane
when you call him by his rightful name:
Impotent homophobe and coward!

So you will miss when you aim at this evil man
who cannot get it up
except
in the TV public operating room
of another man's misfortune!

[Return to Leviticus 15:]

And the priest shall look upon the plague
for a rising, and for a scab, and for a bright spot.
And the priest shall shut up he that hath the plague;
He shall carry them forth to a place unclean;
He shall separate them in their uncleanness;
This is the law of the plague,
to teach when it is clean and when it is unclean.

In this portion of *Plague Mass,* Galás directly confronts the quint-essential text of exclusion in the Old Testament. The added text by Galás makes clear her political commitment to bringing the suffering of people infected with HIV before the public eye. The devil is un-cloaked as an "impotent homophobe" whose cowardice is central to the sensationalist media. But where is purification in the text? Kristeva suggests that the economy of abjection involves two elements that occur not diachronically, one after the other, but synchronically, at the same time: immersion and purification. I will show how Galás's music represents these two registers below.

Galás's setting of the text cited above superimposed three layers of sound: (1) a continuous percussion line, (2) Galás's declamatory de-livery of text with typical Galás cries (to neutral vowel sounds), and (3) male voices. The piece opens with percussion; at 0:00, there is a *for-tissimo* bass drum attack with a secondary hissing sound of very short duration. The bass drum sound resounds into voluminous space and is repeated every seven seconds until 0:28, when other drums enter, the dynamic is lowered to *mezzo forte,* and the music is metered in a mod-erate $\frac{4}{4}$, subdivided into eighth notes. The first twenty-eight seconds thus present four large beats lasting seven seconds that then get di-vided, separated, into a moderate $\frac{4}{4}$ at 0:28. At 0:36, the initial second-ary hissing sound emerges from its hiding place into the foreground;

it articulates the entry of the male voices and is an example of musical sneaking.[46] The male voices sing *piano* and add pitch structure to the piece; they sing vowels—long *ee*'s, short *a*'s, and long double *oo*'s—to B♭. They smear the note down almost a half step to A♮$_1$ on the short *a* vowel; thus, the articulation sounds almost like a single lower neighbor decoration of B♭$_1$.[47] At 0:46, Galás begins to declaim text in a tight, *forte,* sneering tone. These three layers of music continue to 1:49, concluding with the line "And he that be spat on shall be unclean." The sound is ritualistic, as if Galás were staging the pronouncement of the law of the plague herself. A series of cries erupts from 1:50 to 2:05; these function as cathartic responses to the horror of the law of the plague in which the Old Testament text is seen as a double for contemporary society's exclusion from public view of AIDS patients. Not only are these cries emotionally cathartic, but they also represent the shifting subject positions within the purification process itself. Galás's declamation from 0:00 to 1:49 represents the voice of the law that separates; her voice from 1:49 to 2:05 represents the voice of an artist identifying with those who are now dying of AIDS. The structure of these cries is similar to the cry shown in ex. 60, with one difference; the pitch structure is not one note that is crushed into noise but the interval of a tritone— the "devil in music" in Western sacred music. Galás smears and crushes the downward tritone from C♮^{2} to F♯^{1} from 1:50 to 1:56 and from 1:57 to 2:04, ending in an unpitched, pinched-off, acoustic grimace.

From 2:06 to 2:51, Galás declaims the lines from "Strong bulls of Baashan do beset me round" to "and their days to iniquity." The male voices cease, and the metered percussion becomes fragmented to what sounds like improvised *mezzo forte* attacks on the bass drum. Galás shifts the position of her voice from the voice of the law that separates to the voice of someone in need of divine intervention. At 2:52, a series of scorching cries begins, with cries beginning on high C♮, D♮, and even E♮. These cries alternate with a series of (for me) horrifying and disgusting sounds that remind me of the "binding song" described above. This binding song involves the *mezzo forte* articulation of three sounds: (1) *sh* + a short *u*, (2) *g* + a short *u*, and (3) *d* + a short *u*. Galás speaks these sounds as quickly as possible in the pitch area between B♮ and B♭ an octave above middle C♮. Together with the initial male voices that also smear this pitch class, B♭ signifies in this section the abjection of the voice stripped of its signifying function. Throughout this portion of the work, a new element is added: a heavy breathing, sneaking into the texture from silence, articulating quarter notes on beats 1 and 3 of $\frac{4}{4}$ that (re)emerges around 3:00.

After the line "Let them be cut as in pieces," a series of cries and "binding music" is accompanied by the male voices, which have begun to move up the chromatic scale from their initial B♭; here, they articulate the clear motion C♯-D♮-C♮. This continuous sound is accompanied by Galás's declamation of the lines "And if any man's seed of copulation go out from him, he is unclean" to "This is the Law of the Plague, to teach when it is clean and unclean." During this passage, the heavy breathing that had occurred on beats 1 and 3 becomes quieter but quicker—occurring on each *upbeat*. From 8:16 to 8:28, Galás sustains the long *e* vowel of the second syllable of *unclean* for twelve seconds while her voice is superimposed with a tape of herself singing the same word; her taped voice tears away from this electronically produced unison—a horrid representation of the acoustic mirror. There is another way of understanding this "tearing away." The acoustic-mirror phase occurs along the way to socialization that will lead to language acquisition and the law (Žižek's *père*); tearing yourself away from the acoustic mirror places you at the threshold of the Real (Žižek's *pire*). This horrifying moment of threshold crossing is articulated in the music through the most intense cries in the music thus far, which are interrupted by repeated fragments of the taped voice "unclean" tearing away from Galás's more phenomenally "real" voice singing the same "unclean" from 8:30 to 8:50.

The track ends with Galás singing the final "unclean" as a descending perfect fifth from C♯ to F♯. This perfect fifth is then blurred by a low C♮$_2$ played by the synthesizer; this note decays to silence and reminds us of the tritone (F♯-C♮) that Galás had smeared earlier in the piece. Galás's music represents an immersion in abjection in the setting of the notated passages from Leviticus and the Psalms; her music releases a cathartic identification in the settings of her own texts and in the structured cries that re-mark classic climactic notes at the top of a soprano's range.

Track 11 is declaimed in Italian: "Sono l'Antichristo." There are *no* Galás cries in this track, just declaimed text, a very hard and bright percussion section that articulates the slow $\frac{4}{4}$ rhythm with rapid groups of notes played on the synthesizer that sound like insect calls speeded up as decorative, rhythmic appoggiaturas. There is a quiet synthesized accompaniment that sounds poised between male voices and low strings. The text is given below. Galás declaims the Italian; the English translation of each line is provided to the right:

Sono la prova	I am the token
Sono la salva	I am the salvation
Sono la carne macellata	I am the butcher's meat
Sono la sanzione	I am the sanction
Sono il sacrificio	I am the sacrifice
Sono il Ragno Nero	I am the black spider
Sono il scherno	I am the scourge
Sono la Santa Sede	I am the Holy Fool
Sono le feci dal Signore	I am the shit of God
Sono lo signo	I am the sign
Sono la pestilenza	I am the plague
Sono l'Antichristo	I am the Antichrist

In "Sono l'Antichristo," the understood "I" speaks in each stanza, not the abjection of separation and exclusion, but the abjection that erases boundaries among holy, profane, and signifying categories. On the surface, the rhetoric seems ontological; it is, in fact, topological—abjection as that place that disturbs stable identity: "It is thus not lack of cleanliness or health that causes abjection but what disturbs identity, system, order." But, more important, abjection is linked to the body of Christ. This text represents an abject version of the Eucharist; Kristeva describes the Eucharist as follows: "The *division* within Christian consciousness finds in that fantasy, of which the Eucharist is the catharsis, its material anchorage and logical node. Body and spirit, nature and speech, divine nourishment, the body of Christ, assuming the guise of a natural food (bread), signifies me both as divided (flesh and spirit) and infinitely lapsing."[48] "Sono l'Antichristo" lacks cathartic release (thus the absence of structured cries) as equations erase boundaries among disease, signification, shit, and God. Galás's voice splits off from itself, and it often becomes difficult to distinguish the phenomenal voice we first identify as "hers" at the outset of the track from the taped voice that veers away, returns, and veers away again.[49] This veering away and returning to one's own voice is an extended acoustic mirror fantasy in which the ambivalence of the acoustic mirror is a signifier of abjection. The bass line that accompanies Galás's voice drifts modally away from and eventually returns to a low A♮.

Example 62 shows the pitch structure and approximate duration of notes of the first minute and twenty seconds of the piece. This bass line also suggests the slow, stepwise motion of Gregorian chant—a working out of a modal scale on A with secondary material on the D♮ a perfect fourth higher. The material based on D has another function, however; it anticipates the "Dies Irae" theme prominent in the last movement of Berlioz's *Symphonie fantastique* that will become explicit in track 12. The bass accompaniment thus musically foreshadows a call to final judgment as *Plague Mass* draws to a close. As the piece ends, the bass articulates an oblique wedge, with the low A♮ sustained over a chromatic ascent connecting the low A♮ to the D♮ above it, followed by a modal ascent to G♮ and a falling fifth from E♮ down to A♮. The chromatic ascent signifies the musical language of nineteenth-century harmony and brings the appearance of the "Dies Irae" of track 12 closer.[50]

The work ends with a bluesy version of "Let My People Go." With this familiar song, Galás reaches out to her audience; after an hour-long representation of abjection, this song sutures a sustained separation that Galás has drawn between herself and the audience. The first half of the concert that I saw consisted of excerpts from *Plague Mass;* this is the only concert I have ever seen in which there was intentional distance created between performer and audience—a highly ambivalent interpellation.[51] This distance is created by the painful noise level of the music, the images of explicit abjection (Galás's body soaked in blood), and implicit abjection (the complex series of identification with and purification from the suffering of people infected with HIV). With "Let My People Go," the floodgates of identification between audience and performer open. The musical materials are basically the same as those (mis)used by Oi musicians from the blues. While Oi produces a deadly but ingenious music that affirms musically what it denies textually, Diamanda Galás uses the blues so that her audience can identify with her through the register of racial injustice, onto which members of the audience can transpose their fear of identification with people

Example 62. Track 11, *Plague Mass*, "Sono l'Antichristo,"
bass line of the opening.

Example 63. "Let My People Go," from *Plague Mass,* the opening melody.

infected with HIV. Example 63 shows the basic melody of the song that enters after open B♮ octaves in the lowest register of the piano.[52] Note two very familiar elements in the melody: (1) the minor third B♮-D♮ within which the melody moves and (2) the lowered seventh scale degree. Galás sings the melody in a flexible rhythm that the example only approximates, with long pauses for breath at the spots marked on the example. In this version of the song, there are no cries that would have signified cathartic release or a shift in subject position.

A crucial repetition of lines from the beginning of *Plague Mass* provides the repetition that is crucial to abjection—the emergence from identification to a redrawing of the boundaries of the ego. The lines are as follows:

> And on that Holy Day
> And on that Bloody Day
> And on his dying bed,
> he told me, "There are no more tickets to the funeral
> There are no more tickets to the funeral
> There are no more tickets to the funeral
> The funeral is crowded."

The differences between these lines and those at the outset of *Plague Mass* are both obvious and minute; they are crucial, however, for a sense that one has arrived at a place almost identical to, but different from, the place from which one had begun. I find Diamanda Galás's representations of abjection productively open-ended, however; each cry could emerge again and again from a declamatory texture; Galás could crush over and over again the pitch content of each cry; cries can release a cathartic affect as the representation of the voice that separates turns to the voice of that which has been separated from the law, over and over again. This continuous attraction to and repulsion from a signification is typical of abjection: "Unflaggingly, like an inescapable boomerang, a vortex of summons and repulsion places the one haunted by it [the abject] literally beside himself."[53]

Lamentation and Abjection

Lamentation and abjection share structures of separation, repetition, and representation, as has been suggested above. And a series of represented reversals (affective, logical, rhetorical) also link lamentation and abjection. In lamentation—the pleasure of lament and the pain of the occasion, the pleasure of incorporation and the pain of separation, the rites of mourning and a call to revenge, a tight structure and one broken by spontaneous cries. In abjection—the divisions that separate us from and yet pull us back to the body, the voice of the mother, the repulsive abjected substance and the purity such abjection produces, defilement and purification, the abject and its close relation to the sublime. But do these parallels occupy the same logical space? I think not. Lament oscillates between the poles mentioned above, but it does so with clear one-to-one correspondences to a time, a place, an occasion, and a social context. The abject is more paradoxical; it both evades and constitutes psychic structures.

The Abject and the Sublime

In the chapter on Schubert and the gaze, I introduced the structure of Lacanian psychic apparatus—the cut circle that cannot close, the circulation blocked by the *objet a*.[54] The *objet a* is paradoxical. On the one hand: "The *objet a* is not a positive entity existing in space, it is ultimately nothing but a certain *curvature of the space itself* which causes us to make a bend precisely when we want to get directly at the object."[55]

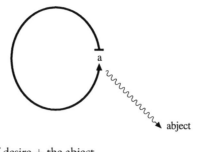

Example 64. The structure of desire + the abject.

On the other hand, the *objet a* is often described as a thing with just a little bit of otherness, and Žižek asserts in *Looking Awry* that images in literature and film can represent the *objet a*.[56] There are connections among the *objet a,* the voice of Diamanda Galás, the abject, and the sublime.

The abject is crucially connected to the Symbolic Order. According to Kristeva: "Abjection, just like *prohibition of incest* is a universal phenomenon; one encounters it as soon as the symbolic and/or social dimension of man is constituted, and this throughout the course of civilization."[57] This connection between the abject and the symbolic may sound counterintuitive. Could one not just as well assert that the abject is associated with the Imaginary Order, with the body of the mother, as Kristeva so often emphasizes? The abject *does* represent separation that occurs in prelinguistic stages of development. But these separations are retrospectively named from a position within the Symbolic Order. Anyone who has raised a child knows that very young children are not disgusted by fecal matter. Once *language* sets in, children "feel" disgusted by body fluid, fecal matter, slime, etc. Within a structure of desire made possible by language acquisition, I would like to argue that the abject can be represented by Lacan's cut circle, as a substance that drains off in a downward spiral from the *objet a*. See ex. 64.

Galás's voice separates noise from sound; it splits notes open; it drains vowels from words; it is loud, threatening, and heavy. Her voice draws and obliterates the boundary between familiar sounds, melodies, techniques, and the abject substance that is their support. This is the structure of Galás's voice as a representation of abjection. How is the sublime related to the abject?

In *The Critique of Judgement,* Kant opposes beauty to the sublime: "The beautiful in nature is a question of the form of the object, and this consists in limitation, whereas the sublime is to be found in an object even devoid of form, so far as it immediately involves, or else by its presence provokes, a representation of *limitlessness.*"[58] Kant divides the sublime into the mathematical and the dynamic sublime. The mathematical sublime is a representation that suggests infinite space or time —a series infinitely divisible or expansive.[59] The dynamic sublime is a representation of *might* or power that is beyond comprehension. For Kant, the essence of the sublime is not within the object but within the viewing subject whose horizon of perception seems to be expanded by the mathematically or dynamically limitless representation: "True sublimity must be sought only in the mind of the judging Subject, and not in the Object of nature that occasions this attitude by the estimate formed of it."[60] Galás's voice is mathematically sublime in its capacity to signify for a listener a seemingly infinite division of sound from noise. It is dynamically sublime in its capacity to signify for a listener immense power and range.

Žižek understands the sublime in terms of a paradox that closely resembles the paradox of the *objet a:* "The paradox of the Sublime is as follows: in principle, the gap separating phenomenal, empirical objects of experience from the Thing-in-itself is unsurmountable—that is, no empirical object, no representation . . . of it can adequately present . . . the Thing . . . ; but the Sublime is an object in which we can experience this very impossibility, this permanent failure of the representation to reach after the Thing. Thus, by means of the very failure of representa-

Example 65. The structure of desire + the abject + the sublime.

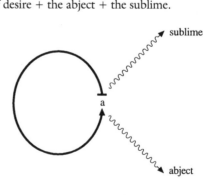

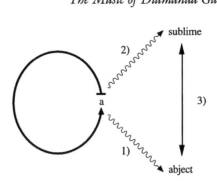

Example 66. The structure of desire + the abject + the sublime + a path connecting the abject to the sublime.

tion, we can have a presentiment of the true dimension of the Thing."[61] The abject and the sublime are representations that veer away from the *objet a*. See ex. 65.

The abject is a representation of the thingness of the limit on a downward spiral; the sublime is a representation of the (impossible beyond) the limit of the thing on an upward spiral. But I think that the abject and the sublime are more intimately bound up with one another. My own sense of Galás's music requires such a possibility. I find her music at once abject and sublime. Example 66 represents such a connection between the abject and the sublime.

The relation between the abject and the sublime represented by line 3 is a paradox. On the one hand, the abject and the sublime can turn into one another. Disgust at Galás's voice can turn into an acoustic Kantian sublime, either mathematical or dynamic. Yet, on the other hand, the abject and the sublime are both *simultaneously* produced at the impossible impasse of the *objet a*.[62] It is precisely this paradox that causes Galás's voice to be both abject and sublime at the threshold of the Real.

NOTES

Introduction

1 Lawrence Kramer, *Music as Cultural Practice* (Berkeley: University of California Press, 1990). See, especially, the chapter "Music as Expressive Doubling."

2 See Susan McClary, *Feminine Endings* (Minneapolis: University of Minnesota Press, 1991); and Julia Kristeva, *Powers of Horror,* trans. Leon S. Roudiez (New York: Columbia University Press, 1982); and Carolyn Abbate, *Unsung Voices* (Princeton: Princeton University Press, 1991).

3 V. Kofi Agawu, *Playing with Signs* (Princeton: Princeton University Press, 1991).

4 The distinction between musical things and spaces is similar to a distinction in semiotics between a "speaking subject" and a "subject of the speech." See Émile Benveniste, *Problems of General Linguistics,* trans. Mary Elizabeth Meek (Coral Gables, Fla.: University of Miami Press, 1971). See also Kaja Silverman, *The Subject of Semiotics* (New York: Oxford University Press, 1982), 43–48, and 195–98. For a discussion of the relation between signifiers and ideology, see Louis Althusser, "Ideology and Ideological State Apparatuses (Notes toward an Investigation)," in *Lenin and Philosophy,* trans. Ben Brewster (New York: Monthly Review Press, 1971), reprinted in *Mapping Ideologies,* ed. Slavoj Žižek (New York: Verso, 1994). See also Slavoj Žižek, *Metastases of Enjoyment* (London: Verso, 1994), 57–62.

1 Music as Sonorous Envelope and Acoustic Mirror

1 For a discussion of oceanic fantasies and subjectivity, see Sigmund Freud, *Civilization and Its Discontents,* trans. and ed. James Strachey (New York: Norton, 1961).

2 See, in particular, Kaja Silverman, *The Acoustic Mirror* (Bloomington: Indiana University Press, 1988); Michel Chion, *La voix au cinéma* (Paris: Cahiers du cinéma, 1982); and, for an introduction to sound and cinema, "Cinema/Sound," *Yale French Studies,* no. 60 (1980). See also Slavoj Žižek, *Looking Awry* (Cambridge, Mass.: MIT Press, 1991), 40.

3 "Si la voix maternelle contribue à constituer pour l'enfant le milieu agréable qui l'entoure, le sustente et le choie, elle peut, inversement, en cas de refus massif ne devenir que pénétration agressive et ténébrante contre laquelle il n'a guère de protection à déployer. On peut avancer qu'elle est le premier modèle d'un plaisir auditif et que la musique trouve ses racines et sa nostalgie dans une atmosphère originelle—à nommer comme matrice sonore, maison bruissante" (quoted and translated in Silverman, *The Acoustic Mirror,* 84–85). Silverman omits that part of the French that opens the possibility for the sonorous envelope to be experienced negatively—as a structure of entrapment. Michel Chion's theory of the voice in cinema is based on this negative aspect of the mother's voice, as Silverman points out in other passages in *The Acoustic Mirror.* See *La voix au cinéma,* 30, 44, 48–49. Esther Bick shows clearly how a child's identification with the touch, smell, and voice of the mother can lead to pathological development in cases of neglect; see "The Experience of the Skin in Early Object Relations," *International Journal of Psycho-Analysis* 49 (1968): 484–85. See also Guy Rosolato, "La voix," in *Essais sur le symbolique* (Paris: Gallimard, 1969), 292; Didier Anzieu, "L'envelope sonore du soi," *Revue française de psychanalyse* 37, no. 1 (1974): 161–62; and Denis Vasse, *L'ombilic et la voix* (Paris: du Seuil, 1974), 1–23. See also Claude Bailblé, "Programmation de l'écoute (2)," *Cahiers du cinéma* 293 (1978): 5–12.

4 For an introduction to semitonal voice leading, see Robert Bailey, "Analytical Study," in *Prelude and Transfiguration from Tristan and Isolde* (New York: Norton, 1985).

5 Imagine the left-hand part of the beginning of the first movement of Beethoven's *Moonlight* Sonata; slow down the harmonic rhythm even more, delete the melody, make the harmonic progression more static, and you would have the basis of a new minimal composition in the style of Philip Glass.

6 The music of Philip Glass seems to me to represent the former kind of sonorous envelope with the greatest consistency—music as fantasy thing that recalls an experience that cannot be remembered transparently.

7 At the end of the *Lyric Suite* of 1926, Berg again quotes the opening of the "Prelude to *Tristan and Isolde,*" this time very directly, having the initial A♮-F♮ interval come out of the twelve-tone permutations of the last movement. For a thorough treatment of Berg's music, see Douglass Jarman, *The Music of Alban Berg* (Berkeley and Los Angeles: University of California Press, 1979).

8 Writers differ on when the sonorous envelope begins and ends. It is more important to realize that the stages outlined here and elsewhere in the book *overlap.* They are phenomenally experienced in linear time, yet each experience refigures the structure and/or significance of the previous stage. Residues of each stage are left over and dealt with in a wide variety of ways to be discussed throughout the book.

9 For an introduction to the mirror stage, see Jacques Lacan, "The Mirror Stage," in *Écrits* (New York: Norton, 1977), 1–7. A list of terms is provided at the outset of the *Écrits;* see also the glossary of terms at the end of Jacques Lacan, *Four Fundamental Principles of Psychoanalysis,* ed. Jacques-Allain Miller, trans. Alan Sheridan

(New York: Norton, 1978). See also the chapter on psychoanalysis in Kaja Silverman, *The Subject of Semiotics* (New York: Oxford University Press, 1983).

10 For an introduction to the Imaginary Order, see the psychoanalytic chapter mentioned in the preceding note from Silverman's *Subject of Semiotics*. See also Fredric Jameson, "The Imaginary and Symbolic in Lacan," in *Ideologies of Theory* (Minneapolis: University of Minnesota Press, 1988), vol. 1.

11 The difference between the binaries of the Imaginary Order and the signification of the Symbolic Order is crucial. Because the entire narrative of developing subjectivity is a symbolic and highly mediated retrospective construction, the Imaginary Order's binaries are much more harshly mutually exclusive than language can grasp; language takes the place of the Imaginary binaries by complicating its categories. For example, within language, the signifier stands for the missing thing (thus Žižek's claim that in the beginning was metaphor: the signifier stands for symbolic presence in absence); while the thing can never be completely *present,* on the one hand, it can also never be totally *absent* in signification. The Symbolic Order provides the subject with a compromise to the Imaginary Order's binaries, as if to say, "You'll never have anything completely, but you'll always have something incompletely." Late in his career, Lacan developed his third category, the Real, to be described in greater detail in subsequent chapters. For an introduction to the Imaginary/Symbolic/Real triangular structure, see Žižek, *Looking Awry,* 130–40.

12 For example, some pieces by Adams quote more directly than the example above from *Nixon in China.* Measures 223–29 of Adams's *Fearful Symmetries* (1988) quote a passage from the Berlioz *Symphonie fantastique* (mm. 463–84) quite directly. In Berlioz, a progression of chords in first inversion ascends through a C-C octave with a quickening harmonic rhythm that leads to a powerful dominant. In Adams, a progression of chords in first inversion ascends through a G-G octave with quickening harmonic rhythm that leads to a tone cluster in which B♭, A♭, and G♭ are superimposed on a B-F tritone in the bass. For musical illustrations of these passages, see David Schwarz, "Listening Subjects: Music, Psychoanalysis, and the Music of John Adams and Steve Reich," in *Keeping Score: Music, Disciplinarity, Culture,* ed. David Schwarz, Anahid Kassabian, Lawrence Siegel (Charlottesville: University Press of Virginia, in press).

13 My thanks to Dave Headlam for pointing this piece out to me and for suggesting the possibilities for applying psychoanalytic concepts to its structures and techniques.

14 See the end of the next chapter, in which I discuss the wall of noise fading *in* to the music at the end of "I Want You (She's So Heavy)" by the Beatles.

15 For a more extended discussion of the spatial implications of listening, see the "Intruder" chapter.

16 For an introduction to the distinction between *look* and *gaze,* see Kaja Silverman, introduction to *Male Subjectivity at the Margins* (London: Routledge, 1992), and my chapter 3. See also the "Intruder" chapter, in which I discuss in some detail the differences between the *listening look* and the *listening gaze.* For discussion of the

gaze in psychoanalytic criticism, see Slavoj Žižek, *Enjoy Your Symptom* (New York: Routledge, 1992), 113–14, 126–27; *Looking Awry,* 72, 91–93, 114–16; *Metastases of Enjoyment* (London: Verso, 1994), 73–74; *The Sublime Object of Ideology* (London: Verso, 1989), 105–7; and *Tarrying with the Negative* (Durham, N.C.: Duke University Press, 1993), 63–65.

17 In the chapter on Schubert and the gaze, I discuss both the visual gaze and its musical counterpart in "Ihr Bild" by Franz Schubert.

18 For another example of a similar moment of the representation of regressive threshold crossing in Steve Reich's music, see "Come Out," in which the phrase *come out* from the line "I had to like open the bruise up and let some of the bruise blood come out to show them" becomes dislodged from the declarative sentence. As in "It's Gonna Rain," *come out* turns into an imperative phrase aimed at the listener.

19 The representation of repetition, however, has no universal function; it is completely context dependent. Here are just a few ways in which it can function. Repetition can *emphasize* meaning. In *The Waste Land,* the repetition of the line "HURRY UP PLEASE ITS TIME" is used to represent the urging of a bartender in a British pub that his customers should leave. Repetition can also *strip meaning* away from a text. Children's fascination with repeating words over and over is supported by a fantasy of stripping language of its conventionality to reveal the "pure sounds" out of which it sprang. Repetition can also reinforce textual boundaries, such as in the movie *Apocalypse Now,* in which the song "The End" by the Doors opens and closes the film. Binary repetition can also create *a shift to another level of meaning.* For example, in John Cage's piece for piano "A Room," the first version can be heard naively as an object; the second version presents the same pitches altered at the piano. In the second version, we hear hearing. In *repetition compulsion,* a subject attempts through symbolic repetition to protect him/herself from trauma. *Continual repetition* is basic to current evolutionary theory, which holds that accidents arising from multiple repeated divisions of cells is crucial to life as we know it. Continual repetition is represented in the film *Before the Rain,* in which the dynamic of ethnic violence takes the form of a spiral—the dynamic seems to repeat itself endlessly, but subtle shifts in its structure occur because of accidental variants. My thanks to Dennis Foster for this last idea.

20 Framing is also essential in film for creating distance between the viewer and the main action. Think of *Blue Velvet,* in which the descent into and emergence out of the ear encloses Jeffrey's fantasy. The girl's voice-overs at the beginning and end of *Cape Fear* also point to the large-scale significance of the film as a symbolic working out of the young girl's ambivalence toward her father.

21 At the end of the next chapter, I will introduce the Lacanian Real into the discussion; the noise evoked in this piece by Reich can be considered a musical representation of the Real—the "stuff" that paradoxically emerges from and is constitutive of the Symbolic Order. For an introductory illustration of the Real, see the discussion of photograph #314E by Cindy Sherman in the next chapter.

22 Guy Rosolato characterizes the relation between language and noise as follows:

"[Noise] exists as a unique illustration of the voice before the Word in which man strips himself of words" ("[L'éclat] existe comme une singulière illustration de cette Voix d'avant la Parole, où l'homme se dépouille des mots"; "La voix," 292). It should be pointed out that the French word *éclat* covers a semantic field far larger than any single English word; its meanings include "noise," "cry," and "burst of sound." *Parole* with a capital *P* suggests both the spoken word and the word of God. In the passage at hand, Rosolato subtly compares *Parole* and the prelinguistic voice of the child (*Voix* with a capital *V*). The word *mots* (written words) refers to the language of the Symbolic Order. My thanks to Philip Solomon of the Department of Foreign Languages at Southern Methodist University for assistance with this translation.

23 In this movie, the hissing sound of a candle going out into molten wax at the beginning of the movie "bleeds" into the sound of steam from a train during the war.

24 In *Beyond the Pleasure Principle*, Freud discusses repetition compulsion as an expression of anxiety that he distinguishes from fear and fright: "'Anxiety' describes a particular state of expecting the danger or preparing for it, even though it may be an unknown one. 'Fear' requires a definite object of which to be afraid. 'Fright,' however, is the name we give to the state a person gets into when he has run into danger without being prepared for it; it emphasizes the factor of surprise." For Freud, anxiety and repetition compulsion are intimately bound up with one another. See Sigmund Freud, *Beyond the Pleasure Principle*, trans. and ed. James Strachey (New York: Norton, 1961), 11.

25 "Nous voudrions mettre en évidence l'existence, plus précoce encore, d'un miroir sonore, ou d'une peau auditivo-phonique, et sa fonction dans l'acquisition par l'appareil psychique de la capacité de signifier, puis de symboliser" (Anzieu, "L'enveloppe sonore," 162). Esther Bick takes the metaphor sound as skin quite literally in her work: "The need for a containing object would seem, in the infantile unintegrated state, to produce a frantic search for an object—a light, a voice, a smell, or other sensual object. . . . Material will show how this containing object is experienced concretely as a skin" ("The Experience of the Skin," 484). See also Didier Anzieu, *Le moi-peau* (Paris: Bordas, 1985), trans. Chris Turner as *The Skin Ego* (New Haven, Conn.: Yale University Press, 1989).

26 Silverman, *The Acoustic Mirror*, 80.

27 See Anzieu, "L'enveloppe sonore du soi," 167–68. Anzieu points out that psychoanalysts disagree on one aspect of the acoustic mirror—whether the child first makes as many different sounds as possible, followed by a narrowing down to match those of the mother, or whether the child seeks to imitate the sounds of the mother from the outset of the acoustic mirror and imitation takes time to perfect (ibid., 168).

28 See also Guy Rosolato: "[The mother's voice] carries, in effect, the first *introjections* preparatory to identification" ("[La voix maternelle] porte, en effet, les premières *introjections* préparatoires aux identifications"; "Entre corps et langage," *Revue française de psychanalyse* 37 [1974]: 80).

29 See Ovid, *The Metamorphoses,* trans. Rolf Humphries (Bloomington: Indiana University Press, 1955), 68–69. Echo is female; and, as she pines away in the forest, only her voice remains—an ancient representation of the acoustic mirror: "She frets and pines, becomes all gaunt and haggard, / her body dries and shrivels till voice only / And bones remain, and then she is voice only / For the bones are turned to stone. She hides in the woods / And no one sees her now along the mountains, / But all may hear her, for her voice is living" (p. 69).

30 For more musically detailed examples of the acoustic mirror in contemporary music, see David Schwarz, "Listening Subjects: Semiotics, Psychoanalysis, and the Music of Steve Reich," *Perspectives of New Music* 31, no. 2 (Summer 1993): 24–56.

31 For another example of a representation of an acoustic mirror in Steve Reich's music, see *Piano Phase* (1967).

2 The Beatles' "I Want You (She's So Heavy)"

1 Applying analytic tools designed for classical music to popular music can produce critical and ideological problems. In general, I think that temporality functions differently in classical and popular musics; thus, I avoid Schenkerian voice-leading accounts of unfolding pitch structures in popular music. The predominantly European approach to popular music studies focuses on the function of popular music in a social context; such an approach avoids formal, analytic, and musical-theoretical approaches as inappropriately "aesthetic." European popular music studies attitudes are slowly changing, however, moving in the direction of grounding claims about music in details of the music itself. For an alternate view, see Walter Everett, *Music of the Beatles: An Analytical History* (Oxford: Oxford University Press, in press).

2 The turn from forty-five-rpm singles to albums played at thirty-three rpm is an important one in the history of rock. Longer songs and albums composed as wholes broadened listeners' horizons significantly over the two-minute, thirty-second time span—the typical duration of classic rock-and-roll songs of the mid-1950s.

3 I use the phrase *wall of noise* as an indirect tribute to Phil Specter's "wall of sound" productions of the 1960s. Specter's productions of Ike and Tina Turner, the Ronettes, the Beatles, and the Stones were all heavily produced with massive overdubbing. See Katherine Charlton, *Rock Music Styles* (Madison, Wisc.: Wm. C. Brown, 1994).

4 See Mark Lewisohn, *The Beatles Recording Sessions* (New York: Harmony, 1988), 173.

5 See ibid., 168–92. Lewisohn is not precise on the question of which master tape was used for each of these sections of the 20 August final version of "I Want You (She's So Heavy)."

6 These examples are derived from material published in *Beatles* (Milwaukee: Hal Leonard, 1989). These excerpts are used with the permission of the publisher.

7 Below, I will discuss how this song and others like it from the blues tradition use

the jazz technique of scatting. The use of a common jazz *harmony* in the introduction subtly evokes the sound of jazz before the explicit appearance of a crucial jazz *technique* later in the song.

8 Perhaps I am imposing a classical expectation on this dominant chord. Subdominant harmonies often follow dominant harmonies in popular music, as in the "typical" twelve-bar blues formula I-IV-I-V-IV-I-(+ wraparound).

9 Such language might suggest the classical technique of prefiguring larger structural elements *in nuce* at the beginning of a composition. Schoenberg's notion of a piece of music's *Grundgestalt* or Schenker's motivic parallelism are examples of such techniques. I mean the emergence of the chords at hand to be specific, cross-referential "solutions" to the "problem" of the augmented triad in m. 3 of this song.

10 Susan McClary has convincingly pointed out that madness and chromaticism have long been connected in Western art music. See her *Feminine Endings: Music, Gender, and Sexuality* (Minnesota: University of Minnesota Press, 1991), chap. 2.

11 Referring to "I Want You (She's So Heavy)," George Harrison said: "It has John playing lead guitar and singing the same as he plays" (*Rolling Stone*, no. 44 [18 October 1969], 8). My thanks to Walt Everett for this citation.

12 One of the earliest examples I have heard of scatting is the first version of Robert Johnson's "Come on in My Kitchen." Other examples include "Lord, I Just Can't Keep from Cryin' " by Blind Willie Johnson, "Within You/Without You" from *Sgt Pepper's Lonely Heart's Club Band,* Janis Joplin's "Move Over" from *Pearl,* and "Six Strings Down" by Jimi Vaughan.

13 I do not mean to make an argument for a universal truth here. On the one hand, I do believe that representations of the sonorous envelope and acoustic mirror make music and listening possible for a number of subject positions; on the other hand, styles, social contexts, and historical moments have a specificity that must be coordinated to psychoanalysis. In the song at hand, I think that a number of factors come together to suggest a connection among Lennon's simultaneous scatting of his guitar solo, his vocal solo, the acoustic mirror, and ambivalence toward a female object of desire. For a discussion of why acoustic-mirror fantasies are so often ambivalent, see the previous chapter.

14 For examples of subtle acoustic-mirror effects in 1950s rock that do not involve explicit scatting, see Buddy Holly's "Words of Love," in which the voice is double-tracked, and several early recordings of Elvis Presley, in which heavy echoing is used in the recording process. In an unpublished paper Peter Winkler discussed Elvis Presley's slurred diction in "It's Alright" as an indication of a regressive fantasy involving his mother: "Blackface Minstrelsy Past and Present: The Case of Elvis Presley" (paper presented at the seventh national meeting of the International Association for the Study of Popular Music/USA, Denton, Texas, October 1992).

15 This acoustic stain is like the tain in the mirror described by Žižek. The tain is the appearance of the black substance behind the surface of the mirror that shows through a scratch. Žižek argues (after Rodolphe Gasche) that the tain is both a signifier of the limit of philosophy and a support of subjectivity. See Slavoj Žižek, *For*

       They Know Not What They Do (London: Verso, 1991), 89–91. "I Want You (She's So Heavy)" pushes against such a limit with relentless force by the end of the song.

16   To the nonmusician, it may sound odd to call an instrumental melody a voice. In fact, it is a commonplace in music pedagogy and critical discourse.

17   See Didier Anzieu, *The Skin Ego,* trans. Chris Turner (New Haven, Conn.: Yale University Press, 1989), 164.

18   Nevertheless, vestiges of this contagious echo of acoustic mirroring do abide into adulthood. One can feel "automatically" sad, e.g., listening to the cries of a complete stranger. The contagious cry of developing subjectivity must, in part, make such identification possible.

19   Vocal style in the blues and rock and roll has blurred the binary opposition between speech and music since it began with the slave hollers of the American South. Robert Johnson often sings some of his lines in his Mississippi Delta blues of the 1930s like a synthesis of crying, calling, and singing; shouts and screams are common in rock and roll of the 1950s and 1960s. In "Baby," Janis Joplin splits her voice into multiphonics, and, for a full spectrum of sounds that divide the sound/music continuum, see the chapter on Diamanda Galás.

20   *Beatles in Their Own Words,* ed. Barry Miles (New York: Omnibus, 1978). My thanks to Walt Everett for showing me this quotation.

21   I do not mean to suggest that subjects become engendered after the acoustic-mirror stage; the research that I have read does not assert differences between the cries of male and female children during the acoustic-mirror stage.

22   "C'est un cri de puissance, pour exercer un pouvoir, marquer un territoire, un cri structurant, *attendu.* S'il y a dans ce cri quelque chose de bestial, c'est comme dans l'identification du mâle à l'animal totémique. L'exemple le plus célèbre en est le cri du Tarzan hollywoodien, fabriqué dans les années 30 à partir de cris multiples d'animaux: cri phallique par lequel le mâle parade et fait sonner sa puissance virile" (Michel Chion, *La voix aux cinéma* [Paris: Cahiers du cinéma, 1952], 69). My thanks to Philip Solomon of the Foreign Language Department of Southern Methodist University for his assistance in French-to-English translations.

23   "Le cri de la femme, lui, c'est plutôt le cri d'un être humain sujet du langage face à la mort. . . . Le cri de l'homme délimite un territoire, le cri de la femme renvoie à l'illimité" (ibid.).

24   For me, this scene on the steps of the opera house has an operatic quality—an inversion, perhaps, of the opera the audience had been seeing inside. Michael's scream is thus intimately related to music; just as his son has sung in melismatic tones on the stage inside, Michael himself screams several agonizing seconds of silence before the sound emerges on the inverted stage of the steps outside. Žižek describes two kinds of screams, the scream of release (like Sonny's) and the scream that gets stuck in the throat (like Michael's). See *Enjoy Your Symptom!* (London: Routledge, 1992), 117.

25   For a clear example of a scream associated with an appearance of the Real, see the film *Reflecting Skin.* The film is about the coming of age of a young boy in a world

he is unable to understand. He witnesses the social and personal dysfunction of the adults around him, and the movie ends with him screaming at a world that at once demands and yet resists his understanding. For more thorough interrogations of screams, see also the chapter on Diamanda Galás.

26 I think that the *beginnings* of rock songs are often more important than their endings, aside from the issue that temporality in popular music is different than in classical music. In classical, tonal music, as Schenker has shown us, all elements of pitch structure unfold basic materials that aim toward and prefigure in complex ways the final cadence. Temporality in popular music is very different, however. Gospel songs assemble layer after layer at the beginning; blues songs often lock into place after a brief introduction; rock songs often "snap" into place ("Gimme Shelter" by the Rolling Stones, "A Hard Day's Night" by the Beatles, and "Heilige Lieder" by Die böhse Onkelz; for a discussion of this song and the phenomenon of "snapping into place," see the Oi chapter).

27 This lack of movement is not a necessary characteristic of the augmented triad; augmented triads do not occur with enough regularity in popular music for them to have any predictable function. Within this song, the augmented triad's symmetrical division of the octave represents being trapped within a fantasy of the acoustic mirror.

28 For a more detailed discussion of how music can impinge on the listener's space, see the "Intruder" chapter.

29 For a discussion of the listening gaze as a representation in music, see chapter 1; see also the end of the "Intruder" chapter and the chapter on Schubert and the gaze.

30 In his early work, Lacan distinguished between the Imaginary Order and the Symbolic Order. In his later work, he added a third term to this binary—the Real. For discussion of the Real, see Žižek, *Enjoy Your Symptom!* 20–22, 113–16, 123, 126, 140; *For They Know Not What They Do,* 154, 101–2, 112, 201; *Looking Awry* (Cambridge, Mass.: MIT Press, 1991), 14–15, 31–32, 104–6, 120, 128–30, 134–36; *Metastases of Enjoyment* (London: Verso, 1994), 30, 199–200; *The Sublime Object of Ideology* (London: Verso, 1989), 2–3, 78–79, 132–33, 169–73, 182–85; and *Tarrying with the Negative* (Durham, N.C.: Duke University Press, 1993), 35–36, 43–44, 103–4, 118–19, 178–79.

31 My thanks to Cindy Sherman and Metro Pictures for permission to use a slide of #314E in this book.

32 Other systems of thought account for a similar category in different ways. *God* covers a semantic field that in many contexts would include the Real; the Kantian notion of noumenon suggests the Real—the thing-in-itself beyond the limits of phenomenal experience. For a discussion of the relation between Kant's noumenon and the Real, see Žižek, *For They Know Not What They Do,* 217–20.

33 These photographs are a rich, glossy red in their original forms, clearly suggesting flesh beneath facial skin.

34 For a discussion of the mirror stage, see Jacques Lacan, *Écrits,* trans. Alan Sheridan (New York: Norton, 1977), chap. 1. From around six months of age, the child still

limited by motor incapacity sees itself in the mirror and holds in intense delight the fullness of its whole reflection. As the child gains motor capacity, it "realizes" that the image in the mirror is "flat"—not whole at all. This shift in the mirror stage (from motor incapacity and grasping the whole image as one's own to motor capacity and a sense of the image's flatness) marks a shift toward language acquisition. The presence that stands for the absence in the mirror is, of course, language. For a discussion of the structure of language as mirror-image substitute, see Sigmund Freud, *Beyond the Pleasure Principle,* trans. and ed. James Strachey (New York: Norton, 1961), 13–17. Diamanda Galás also incorporates mirror misrecognition into her work. Referring to her work in the 1970s she says: "I would perform dressed in black with my back to the audience; I would wait until something else that was not me anymore would emerge" ("Interview with Diamanda Galás," by Andrea Juno, in *Angry Women* [San Francisco: Re/Search Publications, 1991], 9). "No One Home but Me" was produced by the BBC and broadcast in 1994.

35   In *Looking Awry,* Žižek offers another example of the Real from a film entitled *The Unpleasant Profession of Jonathan Hoag.* In the crucial scene, a couple is warned not to open the car window while driving home from a picnic: "[The wife] complied [with the husband's command to open the window], then gave a sharp intake of breath and swallowed a scream. He did not scream, but he wanted to. Outside the open window was no sunlight, no cops, no kids—nothing. Nothing but a grey and formless mist, pulsing slowly as if with inchoate life. They could see nothing of the city through it, not because it was too dense but because it was—empty. . . . It merged with the frame of the window and began to drift inside. 'Roll up the window!' She tried to obey, but her hands were nerveless; he reached across her and cranked it up himself, jamming it hard into its seat. The sunny scene was restored. . . . This 'grey and formless mist, pulsing slowly as if with inchoate life,' what is it if not the Lacanian real, the pulsing of the pre-symbolic substance in its abhorrent vitality?" (pp. 14–15). It is precisely the proximity between the gray substance and the suburban images that marks the space of the Real.

36   At the outset of this chapter, I implied a similarity between the "walls of noise" in "A Day in a Life" and "I Want You (She's So Heavy)." In fact, the "walls of noise" sound quite different in these songs. In "A Day in a Life," the wall of noise sounds like a mass of recorded fragments of conversations, musical passages, ambient street noises, etc. It is more an intensely complex sound collage than the white noise in "I Want You (She's So Heavy)."

37   For me, the music represents the impotent gaze of the listener in the finale of this song. We hear everything but are mute—like musical analogues of the character in Hitchcock's *Rear Window* who observes all but cannot move. See Žižek, *Metastases of Enjoyment,* 73–75.

38   Žižek, *Looking Awry,* 104–6.

39   This pun is intentional. By *symbolic,* I mean both a rupture of a one-to-one correspondence between image or sound and meaning and a rupture of the symbolic order out of which the Real emerges.

40 "I Want You (She's So Heavy)" was the last song on side 1 of *Abbey Road* as an LP. For me, the slash at the conclusion of the song is reminiscent of the sound of automatic turntables that occasionally pulled the tonearm off the record before the music had concluded. This idea would synthesize the slash as something in the ear, a product of creative decision making, and a function of a mechanical structure both external to, yet crucial for, representation. For a cover of "I Want You (She's So Heavy)," see *Picture of a Thousand Faces* by the Eric Gales Band (Elektra Records, 1993). The Gales band transposes the song to A-flat minor and opens with a transposed augmented triad (Ab-C-E) that corresponds to the augmented triad at the end of the introduction of the Beatles' version. The Gales version adds a lovely and barely perceptible acoustic mirror—the lead voice is slightly out of phase with himself. My thanks to Miguel Panetta for pointing out this version to me.

41 Lewisohn, *The Beatles Recording Sessions,* 191.

3   Schubert's *Winterreise*

1 For an introduction to Schenkerian analysis, see Allen Forte and Steven E. Gilbert, *An Introduction to Schenkerian Analysis* (New York: Norton, 1982); and Allen Forte, "Schenker's Conception of Musical Structure," *Journal of Music Theory* 3, no. 1 (April 1959): 1–30.

2 See Gregory Proctor, "Technical Bases of Nineteenth-Century Chromatic Tonality" (Ph.D. diss., Princeton University, 1978); Patrick McCreless, "Schenker and Chromatic Tonicization: A Reappraisal," in *Schenkerian Studies,* ed. Hedi Siegel (Cambridge: Cambridge University Press, 1990); and Matthew Brown, "The Diatonic and Chromatic in Schenker's Theory of Harmonic Relations," *Journal of Music Theory* 30, no. 1 (Spring 1986): 1–34.

3 My thanks to Jenny Kallick of the Music Department, Amherst College, for help in clarifying this large-scale claim about nineteenth-century music.

4 See the first chapter of Slavoj Žižek, *Enjoy Your Symptom!* (New York: Routledge, 1992).

5 For a discussion of *Winterreise* that compares the text and details of voice leading in the music, see Walter Everett, "A Schenkerian View of Text-Painting in Schubert's Song Cycle *Winterreise*" (Ph.D. diss., University of Michigan, 1988). My work owes much to Everett, especially his notion that two half-step motions (Bb-C♮ and E♮-F♮) are crucial elements that connect the songs to one another.

6 This sense of the narrator always having been *fremd* suggests to me a profoundly repetitive psychic structure behind the text and music of *Winterreise.* As a representation that negotiates an already-given loss, the work is a lamentation. For a theory of lamentation, see the chapter on Diamanda Galás. Susan Youens also speaks of *Winterreise* as a lament, although she theorizes neither what lamentation is nor how it can be represented in music. See her *Retracing a Winter's Journey: Schubert's Winterreise* (Ithaca, N.Y.: Cornell University Press, 1991).

7 Charles Rosen also points out a crucial feature of the cycle of poems: "All the events

take place before the cycle begins, and we are not even sure what they were" (his *The Romantic Generation* [Cambridge, Mass.: Harvard University Press, 1995]).

8   Youens (*Retracing a Winter's Journey*) does point out, however, that groups of songs are connected by keys that tend to suggest a state of mind—an expression of *Affektenlehre*. There is, for example, the motive of steady eighth notes to denote wandering (p. 74), irregular accents to denote stumbling (p. 75), the key A major to connote "dance songs about illusions of light and love" (p. 75), a cyclic unity to the first part of the cycle ("Gute Nacht" is in D minor; "Einsamkeit" was in D minor, before Schubert transposed the song down to B minor) (p. 97), and a connection between C minor and a sinister presence of death (pp. 100–101).

9   The English translations of the poems are taken from *Schubert: The Complete Song Texts,* trans. Richard Wigmore (New York: Schirmer Books, 1988). The translation of "Gute Nacht" is on pp. 364–65. Subsequent documentation of English translations is given in the text.

10 Žižek cautions us against the notion that the arbitrariness of the relation between signifier and signified lies within this binary alone. Žižek asserts that the arbitrariness of signification lies in the fact that there is no position from which it would be possible to utter the definitive idea that signification is arbitrary. See Slavoj Žižek, *For They Know Not What They Do* (London: Verso, 1991), 200.

11 The arrival of the letter at its first destination is a metaphor for living in social space and functioning according to the arbitrary rules of the Symbolic Order. We collectively "agree" to accept the arbitrary structure of the sign; we thus can (and must) remember to forget the arbitrary basis of the structure that holds together social space. The arrival of the letter at its second destination is a metaphor for a slippage in this collective, unspoken, "agreement." For whatever reason, the arbitrariness at the heart of social space appears as an awful thing, a void that contains nothing. The machinery of signification "goes on" without its ability to structure subjects in a community. Thus, the subject seems to forget to forget; he/she sees "all" and "nothing," cut off from his/her own subjectivity and social space.

12 For a general exposition of this reading, see Youens, *Retracing a Winter's Journey,* 102–3. For detailed readings of the implications of this binary in individual songs, see her discussions of "Gute Nacht" (p. 129), "Der Lindenbaum" (p. 163), "Rückblick" (p. 193), "Irrlicht" (p. 200), "Frühlingstraum" (p. 211), "Im Dorfe" (p. 255), and "Täuschung" (p. 270).

13 For an extraordinary account of "Auf dem Flusse," see David Lewin, "Auf dem Flusse: Image and Background in a Schubert Song," in *Schubert: Critical and Analytical Studies,* ed. Walter Frisch (Lincoln: University of Nebraska Press, 1986). Lewin argues that the conflict between the E minor with which the song begins and E major in the middle portion of the song (a diachronic argument) is also present in the layers of music itself across the entire song (a synchronic argument); the vocal line and the left hand of the piano project E major with the crucial pitch G♯, while the right hand of the piano projects E minor with the crucial pitch G♮. For Lewin, this layering of mode in the music represents the narrator's questioning of his experience and the metaphoric structure of his understanding of his experi-

ence. For Lewin, the narrator's insecurity of whether his heart is like the frozen surface of the river beneath which water/passion/blood still flows is embodied in this (synchronic) enclosure of E minor by the E *major* of the outer voices.

14 Part 1 of *Winterreise* contains ten songs in minor keys and two in major keys. Part 1 sounds, therefore, like a musical representation in touch with the narrator's immediate experience. Part 2, on the other hand, contains six songs in major, six in minor. Part 2 sounds, therefore, like a musical representation out of touch with the narrator's experience as he retreats more and more into fantasy, dream, and hallucination. For an explanation of the part 1/part 2 binary in *Winterreise,* see n. 15 below.

15 For an extended interpretation of *Winterreise* based on this part 1/part 2 opposition, see Richard Kramer, *Distant Cycles* (Chicago: University of Chicago Press, 1994). Kramer discusses the first half of the cycle as "Winterreise I" and the second half as "Winterreise II." For me, Schubert's "second" *Winterreise* is a musical "rewriting" of his "first" *Winterreise.* Of course, the "whole" cycle of twenty-four songs begins with "Gute Nacht" and ends with "Der Leiermann," but I agree with Kramer that there is something provisionally self-contained about part 1: "Gute Nacht" is in D minor, the original key of "Einsamkeit," which concludes the "first" *Winterreise,* and "Einsamkeit" represents a traumatic memory of the "sigh" first heard in "Gute Nacht." Schubert's "second" *Winterreise* deepens the exploration of the relation between conventionality and traumatic loss to be explored below. For an account of the order of the publication of Müller's poems, see n. 24 below.

16 *Winterreise* is part of a tradition of setting poetry cycles to music that was not uncommon in the late eighteenth, early nineteenth century in German states. German poetry cycles began with poems based on the Petrarchan models of sonnets arranged in cyclic structures that evoked natural cycles. Poetry cycles were written by Novalis, A. W. Schlegel, Ludwig Tieck, Goethe, and others. Uhland was the first German poet to abandon traditional forms and to use German folk forms for his cycles. In *Wanderlieder* of 1813, Uhland established the paradigm for cycles that depict the literal and metaphysical wanderings of the Romantic hero: (1) departure from the sweetheart, (2) recounting his experiences with her in her absence, (3) walking in the woods, (4) wandering at night, (5) arrival at a village after a winter trip, (6) encountering a friendly landlord, (7) leaving the village, and (8) returning home to the beloved. Wilhelm Müller followed Uhland's lead in a turn from classical sources. His *Wanderlieder eines rheinischen Handwerksburchen* of 1820 was based on Uhland's model of *Wanderlieder,* with a crucial departure; Müller ends the cycle inconclusively. His *Die schöne Müllerin* was written in 1816–20. Müller published *Winterreise* in various editions in 1823.

17 Charles Rosen points out that the beginning of the vocal line of "Gute Nacht" is especially poignant: "The opening of the vocal line is at once painful and casual: the first note is an awkwardly difficult high F, but it is there unaccented, almost in passing." See his *Romantic Generation,* 124.

18 The emphasis of the past tense is mine. Notice the emphasis in the poem on the *gaze* as the narrator's eye opens.

19 Chords are said to be spaced naturalistically with large intervals at the bottom,

smaller intervals at the top. This is roughly the structure of the overtone series. Schubert's spacing of thirds at the bottom of this chord produces a thicker, muddier sound than if, e.g., he had spaced the chord with an A♮ octave in the left hand and had left the right hand as is. Such spacing is considered modern, antinaturalistic. See, e.g., the spacing of the E-minor referential chord in the first movement of Stravinsky's *Symphony of Psalms.*

20   Schubert's original key for "Einsamkeit" was D minor; perhaps he wanted the large-scale cross-reference between the D minor of "Gute Nacht" and the A minor of "Die Wetterfahne" to be answered by the A major of "Der Frühlingstraum" and D minor of "Einsamkeit."

21   The reader should remember that in Schubert's original key, this sigh would have been an A♭ moving to a G♮. In m. 37, however, Schubert's original key would have resulted in G♭-F♮, a reappearance of the large-scale F♯-F♮ sigh that spans "Gute Nacht" with F♯ enharmonically respelled as G♭.

22   Richard Kramer hears this passage as well as profoundly disruptive, although his means of describing the disruption are different from mine: "[In m. 24,] the *tremolando* aggravates the breach, healed in the chromatic return to A in the bass at m. 28. The motion between A and B♭, readdressed, now yields the desperate phrase at 'Als noch die Stürme tobten.' Everything is at loose ends" (*Distant Cycles,* 167).

23   Augmented-sixth chords have the effect of slamming home the significance of being flooded by traumatic shock in "Der Frühlingstraum," as well. See mm. 16, 18, 20, and 22 as the music moves through first-inversion tonicizations of E minor, D minor, G minor, and A minor.

24   Müller published *Die Winterreise in 12 Liedern* in 1823 in *Urania.* This is the first edition that Schubert found early in 1827, and it represents the first part of the cycle as we know it. Müller published an additional ten poems in the 13 and 14 March editions of *Deutsche Blätter für Poesie, Literatur Kunst und Theater:* "Der greise Kopf," "Letzte Hoffnung," "Die Krähe," "Im Dorfe," "Der stürmische Morgen," "Die Nebensonnen," "Der Wegweiser," "Das Wirtshaus," "Muth," and "Der Leiermann." In 1824, Müller added "Die Post" and "Täuschung" to the cycle and published it as *Lieder des Lebens und der Liebe: Winterreise* in *Gedichte aus den hinterlassenen Papieren eines reisenden Waldhornisten.* While Müller changed the order of the poems for this final version of the cycle, Schubert maintained the ordering of the poems as he had found them early in 1827; when he encountered the rest of the cycle, he set part 2 to Müller's new ordering in the order in which they occur, with one exception. Schubert switched the order of "Muth" and "Die Nebensonnen" so that "Die Nebensonnen" would be the penultimate song in the cycle. Wilhelm Müller, *Gedichte,* ed. James Taft Hatfield (Berlin: Behr's Verlag, 1906).

25   The post horn refers both to the title of Müller's final title of his poetry cycle (see n. 24 above) and to the conventional sound in German social space of actual post horns. The post horn consisted of one very small coil until the early seventeenth century. In the late eighteenth century, post horns had three coils and could play pitches to the sixth or eighth partial of the overtone series. By 1820, post horns had crooks and tuning slides. Most German post horns were in F, but other keys were

possible. See "Post Horn," in *The New Grove Dictionary of Musical Instruments,* ed. Stanley Sadie (London: Macmillan, 1984), 3:142–43.

26 There is an extraordinary representation of trauma in "Der Wegweiser." The meter, mode, and texture recall "Gute Nacht." Toward the end of the song, Schubert writes passages saturated with the reiteration of G♮. The song seems to be about the wandering of the narrator that was prefigured in "Gute Nacht." A closer look at the text, however, suggests that the narrator is frozen in terror, straining desperately to move: "Einen Weiser seh ich stehen unverrückt vor meinem Blick" ("immovable before my eyes" [Wigmore, trans. 380]). The reiterated G♮s signify at once the narrator's horror and a confusion within the gaze. The line "unverrückt vor meinem Blick" suggests that volition has been externalized from the narrator onto the sign that points the way. It is as if the sign will not look away from the narrator and let him pass. The German contains a delightful pun on the word *unverrückt;* the verb *verrücken* means "to move aside, to slip"; the negation of this verb through the *un-* prefix signifies the state of the narrator's paralysis transposed outward onto the sign. The adjective *verrückt* means "crazy" or "insane" in everyday German.

27 Susan Youens discusses the various possibilities for encoding what Müller means by "three suns" (*Retracing a Winter's Journey,* 291–92).

28 The arrival of a letter at its second destination is related to making the Real appear. For an introduction to the Real, see the chapter on the Beatles and a discussion of photograph #314E by Cindy Sherman.

29 In *Distant Cycles,* Richard Kramer discusses "Der Leiermann" in terms of the significance of the original key, B minor, and various details that recall songs earlier in the cycle, especially "Auf dem Flusse." Kramer shares my sense that "Der Leiermann" represents a unique register of signification: "Der Leiermann, about neither past nor future, drones its mantic questions in a timeless present" (182).

30 The hurdy-gurdy is an instrument with a rich past in European culture. It was used in sacred as well as secular contexts throughout the Middle Ages. It had both melodic and drone strings, a crank that vibrated the strings as a kind of "bow," and a keyboard. There are twelfth-century representations of two people playing a large hurdy-gurdy—a curious historical corollary to my psychoanalytic interpretation of the psychic "split" that the song at hand represents. While the twelfth-century instrument was rather large, the smaller thirteenth-century hurdy-gurdy became an instrument commonly associated with wandering musicians. Although incorporated into a wide variety of "high" and "low" musical functions, the hurdy-gurdy became associated with beggars and social outcasts, particularly in the seventeenth century. Variants of the hurdy-gurdy persisted through the eighteenth and nineteenth centuries, including "distant" variants in the twentieth century. See "Hurdy-Gurdy," in *The New Grove Dictionary of Musical Instruments,* 2:260–64.

31 Charles Rosen hears something similar in the phrase structure of "Der Leiermann": "Melody and accompaniment turn in steady, unexpressive circles, like the arm of the musician. All the phrases revolve: they mimic the gestures of the organ-grinder" (*The Romantic Generation,* 194).

32 The hypnotic effect of the music that sets these stanzas is intensified by the fact

that what I characterize as units a, b, c, d, e, and f are all very similar to one another. I call them by different letters just so I can hear the precision of the large-scale repetition that Schubert has composed. A high degree of similarity causes small differences to stand out; for me, the added voice exchanges in mm. 23 and 45 are poignant. Voice exchanges tend to sound reassuring in tonal music; a musical space is transparently opened, marked, and mastered. For Schubert to decorate the bleak motives of this song with voice exchanges is an example of his keen sense of musical irony.

33   I am not speaking of harmony in a completely functional sense; the B♮-F♯ drone neutralizes all harmonies above it. The whole piece is one enormous prolongation of B minor on a deep structural level.

34   The second part of the cycle stresses the instrumentality of music. One of the few changes in the order of poems that Schubert made in his settings of part 2 was to move "Die Post" from an early position in Müller's revised publication to open part 2. "Die Post" locates musical representation in an actual instrument; the post horn signifies the instrumentality of social space. The cycle ends with a representation of another musical instrument—the hurdy-gurdy, the instrument of the social outcast. For a discussion of these instruments, see nn. 25 and 30 above.

4   Schubert's "Der Doppelgänger" and "Ihr Bild"

1   Richard Kramer uses a single Schenkerian voice-leading sketch to suggest that motivic details connect the Heine settings in *Schwanengesang*. I have also suggested harmonic and textual unity in the Heine settings of *Schwanengesang* using extensions of Schenkerian voice-leading techniques. See Richard Kramer, "Schubert's Heine," *19th-Century Music* 8, no. 3 (1985): 213–25. While Kramer focuses on a single semitone, I propose that a single, chromatic, ascending line (F♯, G♮, A♭) connects crucial pitches of the songs arranged in the order in which Heine wrote the texts. I also discuss a large-scale harmonic structure that gives the cycle coherence in terms of the order of the songs *as published*. See David Schwarz, "The Ascent and Arpeggiation in 'Die Stadt,' 'Der Atlas,' and 'Der Doppelgänger' of Franz Schubert," *Indiana Theory Review* 7, no. 1 (Spring 1986): 38–50.

2   Lawrence Kramer has influenced my sense of representing doubles in music; see, in particular, his "Music as Expressive Doubling," in *Music as Cultural Practice* (Berkeley and Los Angeles: University of California Press, 1990), chap. 1. See also his "The Schubert Lied: Romantic Form and Romantic Consciousness," in *Schubert: Critical and Analytical Studies,* ed. Walter Frisch (Lincoln: University of Nebraska Press, 1986), 223.

3   "Der Doppelgänger" and "Ihr Bild" are from Heine's cycle of poems *Die Heimkehr* (1823–24). The cycle consists of eighty-eight lyrics and a concluding poem, "Götterdämmerung"; "Der Doppelgänger" is poem 20, "Ihr Bild" poem 23.

4   This binary structure is like the two destinations of notes discussed in the preceding chapter. In "Why Notes Always Reach Their Destination (at least once) in

Schubert's *Winterreise*," I discuss the first arrival of notes at their destination when self-conscious, conventional representation is in place; notes arrive at their second destination when conventional structures show signs of strain. Much of this chapter on the gaze can be understood as a composing-out of notes reaching their second destination to reflect back on the subject the emptiness of his fantasy support.

5 One might ask, Why "male"? Žižek has shown that the gaze articulates subject positions that situate representations of men and women in social space. The song at hand suggests a male narrator gazing at the image of his female beloved through the pronoun *ihr*, which clearly translates "her picture." The poem also belongs to a revision of the tradition of courtly love in German Romantic poetry in which male subjectivity is seen to be contingently structured around desire for an object that is a projection of the self.

6 Heinrich Heine, *Buch der Lieder* (Berlin: Fischer, n.d., 121–22. Some of the spelling in this edition seems archaic to the contemporary reader; thus, e.g., I refer to *Doppelgänger*, not *Doppeltgänger*, and *Tränen*, not *Thränen*.

7 *The Complete Poems of Heinrich Heine: A Modern English Version*, trans. Hal Draper (Boston: Suhrkamp/Insel, 1982), 85. My psychoanalytic and musical interpretation of these songs depends on the language of the German original; these English translations should be used as general guides only.

8 I will use the word *look* to suggest a literal, denotative glance; I will use the word *gaze* to suggest a look that has been taken beyond mirror identification and has been inscribed in language, social space, and the law.

9 D♯ minor is often considered the musical *chromatic* double of the *diatonic* mediant D major. This notion of a chromatic double that emerges out of a diatonic double is strengthened in the music; the chromatic ascent in mm. 43–46 moves through the diatonic D major to D♯ minor with the pitch F♯1 connecting both sonorities on the word *äfft*, "mock, imitate, ape."

10 See Sigmund Freud, "The Uncanny," trans. Joan Riviere, in *On Creativity and the Unconscious* (New York: Harper & Row, 1958), 141, 143.

11 See Kramer, "The Schubert Lied," 223.

12 Ibid., 219.

13 See Sigmund Freud, *Beyond the Pleasure Principle*, trans. and ed. James Strachey (New York: Norton, 1961), 10–17.

14 See ibid., pts. 6–7.

15 For an introduction to the *objet a*, see Slavoj Žižek, *Enjoy Your Symptom* (London: Routledge, 1992), 48–49, 76, 96, 126; *For They Know Not What They Do* (London: Verso, 1991), 148, 231, 234–35, 257; *Looking Awry* (Cambridge, Mass.: MIT Press, 1991), 6, 38, 77, 94–95, 133–35; *The Sublime Object of Ideology* (London: Verso, 1989), 53, 65, 184–85, 95, 163; and *Tarrying with the Negative* (Durham, N.C.: Duke University Press, 1993), 36, 66. Lacan's cut circle is sometimes used to represent desire or drive in the psychoanalytic literature. The Beatles' "I Want You (She's So Heavy)" represents *drive* as the music repeats its introductory phrase fourteen times. In the chapter on Diamanda Galás, I argue that her voice represents *desire*

as it splits the *objet a* into the sublime and the abject. See n. 17 below for a distinction between drive and desire in "Der Doppelgänger" and "Ihr Bild," respectively.

16   Žižek, *Enjoy Your Symptom,* 48.

17   I hear a musical representation of *drive* in "Der Doppelgänger" and a musical representation of *desire* in "Ihr Bild." Drive describes a pleasure in displeasure around the cut Lacanian circle; desire describes a circulation around the cut Lacanian circle that strives for but always slips past the object. A representation of repetition at a limit in which motion itself seems to become the thing suggests drive; a representation of repetition that veers away from the limit and becomes at once empty and transformed suggests desire. See Slavoj Žižek, "In His Bold Gaze My Ruin Is Writ Large," in *Everything You Always Wanted to Know about Lacan but Were Afraid to Ask Hitchcock,* ed. Slavoj Žižek (London: Verso, 1992), 228–29. I describe a different musical representation of the *objet a* in the chapter on Diamanda Galás. There, I describe abjection as a representation of a downward spiral from the *objet a;* the sublime is an upward spiral from the *objet a.* My thanks to Eric Santner for this formulation. Thanks, as well, to Raphael Atlas for help in theorizing drive in "Der Doppelgänger."

18   See Kramer, "The Schubert Lied," 221.

19   Heinrich Heine, *Die Heimkehr* (Berlin: Fischer, n.d., 123.

20   Draper, trans., *The Complete Poems of Heinrich Heine,* 86.

21   The word *ach* suggests a fantasy of prelinguistic expression of pain. As such, it is an impossibility—a linguistic signifier that points to nothing but a primal cry. Since the word so often comes at the beginnings of lines (as *O* does in English poetry), it often suggests a fantasy of direct, unmediated sound out of which language emerges.

22   See Joseph Kerman, "A Romantic Detail in Schubert's *Schwanengesang,*" in Frisch, ed., *Schubert.*

23   See Heinrich Schenker, "Franz Schubert: 'Ihr Bild,'" in *Der Tonwille* (Vienna: Universal, 1921), vol. 1.

24   I agree with Schenker's perceptive notion that the music depicts staring and that the listener is placed in the subjective position of the narrator; I hear the signifier of staring in the music as the pitch class G♭ and the later key G♭ major. As will be suggested below, Schenker reinforces his notion of reiterated B♭s as staring at the beginning of the repeat of the A section mm. 22–24.

25   For a discussion of the relation between the look and the gaze, see chapter 1. I read this staring as a representation of castration as well. Freud points out that doubles and eyes are often displaced images of castration in dreams ("The Uncanny," 141). Freud also describes the evil eye as the transformed desires of the person who is gazed at: "One of the most uncanny and wide-spread forms of supersition is the dread of the evil eye. There never seems to have been any doubt about the source of this dread. Whoever possesses something at once valuable and fragile is afraid of the envy of others, in that he projects on to them the envy he would have felt in their place" (ibid., 147).

26   Schenker refers to this shift in the text as a *Wahnbild,* a representation of insanity,

unintentionally capturing precisely what this song is: a representation of a representation of insanity. See Schenker, "Franz Schubert: 'Ihr Bild,'" 47.

27 Recall how Schubert had undermined the conventional use of mode in *Winterreise*.

28 In tonal theory, stepwise motion in the upper voice is associated with organic, fully developed musical melody; leaps suggest spaces that must be filled (such as the diminished fifth discussed above from the C in m. 4 to the G♭ in m. 5). The theorist Leonard Meyer calls such leaps "structural gaps" that are "marked for memory"; the phrase suggests that, in tonal music, particularly significant notes are emphasized through a variety of harmonic, textural, metric, and gestural techniques. See his *Emotion and Meaning in Music* (Chicago: University of Chicago Press, 1956).

29 For Schenker, the goal of the melodic ascent to the E♭^{2} of m. 11 is the second scale degree C that supports a supertonic dominant-preparation chord. Schenker hears the G♭ in m. 5 prefiguring this "drive" to the supertonic; see Schenker, "Franz Schubert: 'Ihr Bild,'" 47.

30 Freud, "The Uncanny," 122, 123–24, 129.

31 Ibid., 131.

32 A voice exchange is a theoretical designation that points out a static structure among a number of chords. You can hear it in the example if you hear the E♭ in the upper voice in m. 11 being moved to the E♭ in the lowest voice and the C in the lowest voice being moved in the same measure to the C in the upper voice.

33 Schenker takes this idea one notch further by suggesting that the vocal suspension is mirrored in the accompaniment's 4-3 suspension at the beginning of m. 17. See Schenker, "Franz Schubert: 'Ihr Bild,'" 48.

34 I am using a Schenkerian sense of harmony in which cadential tonic chords in second inversion are heard as dominant chords waiting to happen.

35 Jonathan Crary argues that the crisis of modernism in the visual arts is linked to an epistemological shift in art theory in the early nineteenth century. Crary demonstrates that the camera obscura was at once the forerunner of the modern camera, a model for the representation of the stable position of the artist as mediator between the world and our perception of the world from the Renaissance to around 1800, and the site at which the crisis of modernism began. Crary shows that the camera obscura was a darkened room within which a detached observer could meditate on images from the external world projected through a tiny hole with epistemological security. Crary points out that Goethe was experimenting in such a room and paused to rub his eyes; the famous "Goethe shimmer" caused Goethe to realize that the physical organ of the eye both produced and received light and that the camera obscura must be abandoned as a metaphor for the artist's unmediated representation of "reality." His theories are contained in *Farbenlehre* of 1810, and Crary locates Goethe's shimmer as symptomatic of the beginnings of modernism in the early nineteenth century. See Jonathan Crary, *Techniques of the Observer* (Cambridge, Mass.: MIT Press, 1990). The turn on *Augen* in this song is a musical representation of the highly charged status of the eye in Romantic art in general and in this song in particular.

36 Schenker, "Franz Schubert: 'Ihr Bild,'" 48.

37 For a thorough discussion of third relations, see Robert Bailey, "Analytical Study," in *Prelude and Transfiguration from Tristan and Isolde* (New York: Norton, 1985).

38 One can understand the collapse of G♭ major back to B♭ minor in terms of notes arriving at their destination. See the chapter on *Winterreise* above. G♭ arrives at its first destination in mm. 18–22 as the conventionality of the illusion of representation seems in place; G♭ reaches its second destination in mm. 22–24 as the G♭ descends in an inner voice to F♮ and the narrator confronts his own image in the mirror, musically represented by the horrific return of B♭ minor.

39 I hear the two-chord progression at the outset of "Das Meer" echoing mm. 22–24 of "Ihr Bild." In both cases, Schubert moves from an augmented-sixth chord right to tonic.

40 Schubert often uses conventional textures ironically (think of the *Männerchor* texture at the beginning of "Das Wirtshaus" from *Winterreise*).

41 See Jacques Lacan, *Écrits,* trans. Alan Sheridan (New York: Norton, 1977), 1–2.

42 Ibid., 5.

43 "La reviviscence de *la* voix suppose toujours un écart, un parcours irréversible quant à l'objet perdu. Et dans cette distance l'agent même de la séparation, le père, a son répondant vocal. L'enfant distingue aussi la voix qui s'interpose entre la mère et lui et capte électivement l'intérêt, le désir de celle-ci. C'est là une différence de *registre,* d'ailleurs strictement liée à la différence des sexes, en étant la première marque à laquelle il se familiarise. Si l'on conçoit cette perte, cet abandon premier, repris, remémoré comme distance par *la* voix elle-même, un jeu subtil d'évocation sacrificielle s'engagera entre celle de l'homme et celle de la femme. Car à la séparation de la mère, assurée par le père, doit s'ajouter un redoublement, avec la mort du père, cette fois-ci au principe même du système symbolique: ce qui a pour effet le dépassement et tout à la fois le maintien—la relève—du manque" (Guy Rosdato, "La voix: Entre corps et langage," *Revue française de psychanalyse* 37 [1974]: 80).

5 Peter Gabriel's "Intruder"

1 See Scott Isler, "Peter Gabriel Finds Life after Genesis," *Rolling Stone,* no. 326 (18 September 1980): 16.

2 The texture of the music is quite full and highly mediated as a glance at the complete layout of the performers suggests: Jerry Marotta and Phil Collins play drums; Morris Pert, Jerry Marotta, and Peter Gabriel play percussion; John Giblin plays the bass; Larry Fast and Peter Gabriel play bass synthesizer; Tony Levin plays the "stick"; David Rhodes, Paul Weller, Robert Fripp, and Dave Gregory play guitar; Larry Fast and Peter Gabriel play synthesizers; Dick Morrisey plays the saxophone; Peter Gabriel plays the piano; and David Rhodes and Kate Bush sing background vocals (CD liner notes, Charisma Records, 1980).

3 One must be careful not to overinterpret this point; Debra Rae Cohen points out that there is no cymbal on the entire LP. Cohen, "Peter Gabriel Finds His Voice," 61. For a discussion of the backbeat and another (mis)usage of 1950s and 1960s rock conventions, see the Oi chapter.

4 Acoustic proximity and listening subjectivity are theorized by Michel Chion in *La voix au cinéma* (Paris: Cahiers du cinéma, 1982) and Slavoj Žižek in *Looking Awry* (Cambridge, Mass.: MIT Press, 1991). Voices that sound close tend to suggest identification between character and listener; voices that are far away tend to suggest subjective as well as literal distance. This simple binary will be shown in the discussion below on Primus to be far from simple because of crucial differences between how images and sound work in film and music.

5 See Anahid Kassabian, *Songs of Subjectivities: Theorizing Hollywood Film Music of the 1980s and 1990s* (Durham, N.C.: Duke University Press, in press), chap. 4.

6 For an example in the classical repertory of ambiguous perfect fifths, see Beethoven's Symphony no. 9 in D Minor (the very opening of the first movement) and Franz Schubert's song "Der Leiermann," which concludes *Winterreise.* For a discussion of the perfect-fifth drone in "Der Leiermann," see the chapter "Why Notes Always Reach Their Destinations (at Least Once) in Schubert's *Winterreise.*"

7 For a discussion of noise in rock and roll, see the chapter on the Beatles. In general, there are several approaches one can take to noise. It can refer acoustically to a representation of a sound in which frequencies are so numerous and confused that we cannot hear any one as primary and others as secondary (static, e.g.). Such an acoustic definition is compelling, but poor in terms of its positing an absolute subject. To hear noise as a culturally and textually specific "other" can illuminate how codes of meaning are produced in musical texts.

8 There are numerous discussions of mode and gender in the musical-critical literature. For an excellent recent article, see Gretchen A. Wheelock, "*Schwarze Gretel* and the Engendered Minor Mode in Mozart's Operas," in *Musicology and Difference,* ed. Ruth A. Solie (Berkeley and Los Angeles: University of California Press, 1993). See also Joke Dames's excellent study of voice and gender in the criticism of Roland Barthes, "Unveiled Voices: Sexual Difference and the Castrato," in *Queering the Pitch,* ed. Philip Brett, Elizabeth Wood, and Gary C. Thomas (New York: Routledge, 1994).

9 Think of the importance of Buffalo Bill's cross-dressing and the visual erasure of his penis in the mirror in *The Silence of the Lambs;* think of Frank Booth's oral obsession of stuffing a thin, long piece of (umbilical) velvet into his mouth after one of his rampages; think of the haunting, high voice of Mick Jagger at the outset of "Gimme Shelter."

10 See Chion, *La voix au cinéma,* 26–27. Chion discusses how some voices become stripped of their acousmatic status, marking a shift in the subjective position of a character—e.g., the end of *The Wizard of Oz,* when Dorothy is first terrified by the voice of Oz (loud, resonating, reinforced by smoke) and then relieved when she sees that its source is a small, weak man (p. 33). Chion discusses two different kinds of acousmatic voices in *Psycho.* As we see Norman in the jail cell having been "cannibalized" (Chion's term) by the voice of the mother, her voice is represented by Hitchcock as flat, insistent, "close" to the screen, forcing the viewer to identify with Norman's psychosis. As we see (much earlier in the film) Marion driving in her car having stolen money from a client of her company, we hear *her* hear

the voices of the men in her office earlier in the day. In this example, the voices reverberate in a space clearly beyond the listener; this is the space of Marion's conscience (pp. 47–50, 116–23). See also Žižek, *Looking Awry,* 125–28.

11 Debra Rae Cohen might hear such a passage as an example of "the distinctive let-me-strain-to-bear-witness leaps of his tenor" ("Peter Gabriel Finds His Voice," 61).

12 The song of the wicked witch's guards in *The Wizard of Oz* contains *only* a single fifth, rising, falling, rising, and then falling again.

13 An alternate interpretation is suggested by Debra Rae Cohen: "Gabriel has often used musical idiom in ironic juxtaposition to his lyrics" ("Peter Gabriel Finds His Voice," 61).

14 Debra Rae Cohen points out that the whistle connects songs on the album: the "whistling first heard on the brooding 'Intruder' brings shadow to the deceptively blithe 'Games without Borders' " (ibid., 61). There is an expression in German that embodies collective aggression against women who whistle: "Mädchen, die pfeifen, und Hühnern, die krähen / Soll man beizeiten den Hals umdrehen" (Girls who whistle and chickens that crow / Should have their necks broken as soon as possible). My thanks to Professor Mieder of the German Department at the University of Vermont for this expression.

15 For a similar use of a shift in percussion texture to represent a shift from a fantasy of impotence to one of empowerment in Störkraft's "Mann für Mann," see the chapter on Oi Musik.

16 See Kaja Silverman, *The Acoustic Mirror* (Bloomington: Indiana University Press, 1988), 149.

17 The scream of a woman is crucial in both operas of Alban Berg, *Wozzeck* and *Lulu,* as well as in Strauss's *Elecktra.* My thanks to Jenny Kallick for pointing this out to me.

18 Dissonance can be discussed in three ways: (1) impressionistically, as a sound that one dislikes; (2) acoustically, as an unstable sound; or (3) culturally, as a sound that is heard as unstable and demanding resolution within a specific cultural, aesthetic, and formal context. In classical, common-practice harmony, a fourth between two voices (particularly between soprano and bass) is a dissonance that demands resolution in some contexts. The tonality of rock and roll seems, on the one hand, obviously tonal and, on the other, ambiguously diatonic. That is, most rock and roll uses harmonic materials that are fundamental to common-practice harmony; but, in many cases, these harmonies are not dealt with "rigorously" or "structurally." Strumming chords on a guitar, e.g., eliminates the significance of inversions—a crucial criterion for stability and instability in common-practice harmony. Much blues-based rock also relies in a variety of ways on the importance of *subdominant* harmonies (such as the I-IV-I-V-IV-I scheme of the twelve-bar blues). And it is doubtful whether it is culturally responsible to describe relations between details of harmony and "structural" features in rock and roll as we are fond of doing, e.g., in Beethoven.

19 Like dissonance, *noise* is a term that can be defined aesthetically, acoustically, or

culturally. I am referring here to an acoustic definition of noise as a representation of a "sound" whose overtones cannot be distinguished from one another.

20 Modern art criticism shows how important it is not to confuse the surface of a painting with its picture plane; much modern art moves images up to and beyond the picture plane, beginning, perhaps, with Cézanne's objects in his still lifes that seem about to topple into the laps of his viewers.

21 Remember that Les Claypool plays the bass guitar and sings the vocals; he thus incorporates the close/distant binary.

22 See Claude Bailblé, "Programmation de l'écoute," *Cahiers du cinéma,* no. 293 (1978): 5–12.

23 For an introduction to the listening gaze, see the chapter on music as sonorous envelope and acoustic mirror. In "It's Gonna Rain" by Steve Reich, I argue that the word *gonna* gets fragmented and repeated, with the syllable *go* gazing out at the listener in its unanswered imperative. In the chapter on the sonorous envelope and acoustic mirror, I am less concerned with a threshold that such a gaze crosses than in the music seeming to come alive and address the listener.

24 For a discussion of how an acoustic mirror is also held up to the male viewing subject at the end of *Peeping Tom* by Michael Powell, see Silverman, *The Acoustic Mirror,* 39–40.

25 See Andreas Huyssen, "Mapping the Postmodern," *New German Critique,* no. 33 (Fall 1984): 5–52.

26 For a discussion of postmodernism that connects cultural and textual issues, see Fredric Jameson, "Postmodernism and Consumer Society," in *The Anti-Aesthetic,* ed. Hal Foster (Port Townsend, Wash.: Bay Press, 1983). Jameson discusses pastiche and schizophrenia as structures characteristic of representations of postmodernism.

6 Oi: Music, Politics, and Violence

1 My thanks to Vito Avantario, Rolf Suhl, and Matthias Weber for help in gathering articles, music, and personal contacts, without which this chapter would have been impossible.

2 For a thorough discussion of the history of Oi Musik, see Klaus Farin and Seidel-Pielen, *Skinheads* (Munich: Beck Publishers, 1993).

3 See *Frankfurter Rundschau,* 22 December 1992, 15. These numbers suggest the tip-of-the-iceberg metaphor that dominates much of the coverage of German skins in contemporary German journalism. The metaphor is apt since there seems to be an enormous number of economically and socially marginal young people, particularly in that part of Germany that used to be the German Democratic Republic. Michael Fuchs asserts that there are around forty thousand radical right-wingers in Germany, around four thousand of whom are active skins, around three thousand of whom come out of the former German Democratic Republic. See *Die Welt,* 28 December 1992, 8. Thus, like their British antecedents, German skins are produced or made possible at least in part by economic and social marginaliza-

tion. After the opening of the Berlin Wall, Oi sales to new customers in the east rose from 60 to 80 percent. See *Die Tageszeitung*, 10 June 1992, 5. At the bottom of this metaphoric iceberg, a study suggests that 87 percent of German youths feel betrayed by German public policy. See *Die Weltwoche*, 3 December 1992, 41. The pyramid metaphor also allows for the fact that members of Oi bands and their sympathizers are not all necessarily unemployed, marginal, white men. A report has determined, e.g., that the members of the band Tonstörung met each other at a *Gymnasium*. See *Stuttgarter Zeitung*, 4 December 1993, 7.

4 The most celebrated of these mail-order addresses is Rock-O-Rama in Brühl near Cologne. Rock-O-Rama is also a record label, the label with which Die böhse Onkelz recorded until 1988. See *Frankfurter Rundschau*, 22 December 1992, 15. As of April 1993, Rock-O-Rama represented and recorded a total of twenty-eight skin bands. *Frankfurter Rundschau*, 4 February 1993, 4. As of the present writing (spring 1996), Rock-O-Rama has been closed down.

5 See *Neue Züricher Zeitung*, 16 December 1992, 29. It is also a documented fact that, before the celebrated attack on foreigners in Hunxe, the attackers pumped themselves up by listening to Oi Musik; drinking and listening to Oi Musik also preceded attacks against foreigners in Eberswalde. See *Frankfurter Rundschau*, 27 November 1992, 3. See also *Kölner Stadtanzeiger*, 23 October 1992. For a general study of the connection between drinking, listening to Oi Musik, and violence, see *Der Spiegel*, 11 May 1992, 238. A German Press International release also connects drinking to skin violence: particularly "Skinhead-Mix," one bottle of rum and one bottle of beer (deutsche presse agentur, 2 June 1993). A German Press International story by Jutta Lehmer also documents the connection between Oi Musik and violence (deutsche presse agentur, 23 October 1992). *Stern* also reports that, shortly before the attack on a Turkish family in Solingen, Christian (one of the suspects) joined the other alleged attackers with cassettes of Oi Musik that he had borrowed from a friend. *Stern*, 9 June 1993, 28. A connection between music and violence is also suggested by the reported fact that a musician from the band Störkraft (Stefan Rasche) worked out in the same fitness studio as the alleged murderers of Solingen. See *Münchener Abendzeitung*, 8 November 1993, 3. The young men arrested in the Solingen attack were found guilty of murder. Felix K. (18), Christian R. (19), and Christian B. (22) were sentenced to ten years in a jail for juveniles. Markus Gartmann (25) was sentenced to fifteen years in prison. See deutsche presse agentur 0184, 14 October 1995.

6 See Farin and Seidel-Pielen, *Skinheads*, 25. The parallel between England and Germany is strong here. Germany, too, depended on large numbers of foreign workers after the war to support the economic recovery of the 1950s and 1960s. German *Gastarbeiter* (guest workers) came primarily from Turkey, (the former) Yugoslavia, Greece, Italy, and Africa. The German word contains the seeds for contemporary violence. These foreign workers were never deeply thought of as Germans; rather, they were guests who come, "visit," and then go home.

7 Ibid., 23–26.

8 See Jon Savage, *England's Dreaming* (New York: St. Martin's, 1992), chap. 1.

9 Farin and Seidel-Pielen, *Skinheads,* 27.

10 Ibid., 24.

11 My thanks to Rolf Suhl for pointing this idea out to me.

12 Translation mine. See *Emma,* 1 January 1993, 39.

13 Contemporary German journalists state quite flatly that Oi takes over rock and roll—a black musical form. Rock and roll was a style that came together in the mid-1950s from three different styles: (1) country western (white), (2) Tin Pan Alley (white, with some black influence from jazz), and (3) the blues traditions (black). Elvis Presley typifies the birth of rock and roll because (in addition to having a great voice and being a natural talent) he *covered* songs across all rock's three musical heritages. I will show below that Oi does emphasize black music, but with a qualification: the blackness of Oi is a carefully and well-constructed fantasy of a musical Other. It is also crucial to remember that Oi Musik has paradoxically evacuated most *white* aspects of rock and roll—Tin Pan Alley and country western.

14 See Farin and Seidel-Pielen, *Skinheads,* 29–35. I think that the word *ska* is an abbreviation of *skat song.* For a psychoanalytic reading of scatting in 1960s rock and roll, see the chapter on the Beatles. If *ska* is an abbreviation for scatting, then ska suggests a musical redoubling. Just as themes in jazz are mirrored, scatted, by a singer who improvises on the melody, imitating the sounds of the original instrument, so, too, ska is a large-scale improvisation based on jazz and 1950s rock and roll.

15 Ibid., 32, 37–43. Farin and Seidel-Pielen point out that the number of immigrants to England in the 1950s averaged 30,000 per year; by 1961, the number had risen to 141,000 (p. 40). They assert that post–World War II British public policy always sought to divide elements of the working class in order to prevent the emergence of a strong socialist movement that might threaten postwar capital expansion (p. 40). This has powerful implications for the argument that I will develop below, that Oi subjectivity is intimately linked in conscious and unconscious ways with "normal" social space and power. Although embarrassing, threatening, and dangerous, skin groups and their music are a product in a variety of ways of dominant culture and function crucially within and without it.

16 Ibid., chap. 1.

17 For a thorough account of the origins of the punk movement with particular attention to the nature of its production as an aesthetic and commercial phenomenon, see Savage, *England's Dreaming,* chaps. 1, 2.

18 The role of the rock-and-roll producer/promoter has been powerful ever since Colonel Tom Parker orchestrated Elvis Presley's career and Brian Epstein got the Beatles off the ground. Savage discusses how crucial Malcolm McClaren and his wife, Vivienne Westwood, were for the Sex Pistols and for the British punk movement in general. McClaren put the group together, loaned them money, arranged tours, and even supported *other* bands to give the movement a sense of fullness (ibid., chaps. 2, 3). The lines to the infamous song "Anarchy in the UK" were written by Vivienne Westwood: "I am an antichrist / I am an anarchist."

19   Stuart Hall, quoted in ibid., 229.

20   In this sense, contemporary German Oi Musik seems apolitical, as musicians emphasize over and over in interviews. I accept the assertion in a limited sense, but I think that the crucial fact about German Oi Musik is the complicity of "Left" and "Right" in text and music, as will be suggested below.

21   The typical rock-and-roll band became crystallized with Buddy Holly's band of the mid-1950s: lead guitar, rhythm guitar, bass guitar, and percussion, with one or more of the guitar players singing. Throughout the 1960s, many bands held on to this format; the quintessential group that used it was the Beatles. German Oi Musik bands often have only one guitar, which combines the function of rhythm and lead parts. One sound that German Oi Musik bands avoid like the plague is *strumming* (there are only a very few exceptions); thus, there is no need to have a separate rhythm guitar part.

22   Journalists continue to make the simplistic claim that punk has emptied itself of its black roots. For a clear exposition of this flawed argument, see Diedrich Diedrichson, "Als die Kinder noch in Ordnung waren," in *Neue Soundtracks für den Volksempfänger,* ed. Ralph Christoph and Max Annas (Berlin: ID-Archiv, 1993), 15. Punk is marked by two unmistakably *black* sounds: (1) the steady stream of eighth notes (from rhythm and blues of the 1950s) and (2) the perfect fourth, which suggests the plagal harmonies of the blues. Hebdige makes the point, as well, that punk hair and clothes style were taken directly from West Indian and Rasta styles. See Dick Hebdige, *Subculture: the Meaning of Style* (London: Methuen, 1979), 66–67.

23   The backbeat is the essence of rock and roll; it is usually played on the snare drum on beats 2 and 4. I think it originated in jazz of the 1920s, 1930s, and 1940s; in jazz, beats 2 and 4 are played on the cymbals. It also has roots in the black tradition of blues. The fourth beats of many of Robert Johnson's songs that have quarter notes for beats 1, 2, and 3 have a dotted eighth note/sixteenth note figure on beat 4 that is an acoustic forerunner of the backbeat of the 1950s. It developed as a mainstream white fantasy as rock and roll emerged in the mid-1950s and continues to dominate popular styles as diverse as German Oi Musik and commercial Muzak. In the 1960s, musicians varied the backbeat, often with spectacular effect; listen, for example, to Jimi Hendrix's "I Don't Live Today" for second beats that have an eighth *rest* followed by two very dry sixteenth notes on the snare and fourth beats that are very wet cymbal crashes. By *dry* I mean that there is a minimum of overtones; by *wet* I mean that there is a maximum of overtones. Wet cymbal crashes are played by hitting the cymbal hard *at the rim* so that the entire surface of the instrument sounds at once.

24   In pictures of punks of the era, I see wounds that suggest the violence of commodification (earrings that pierce noses, lips, etc.) and wounds that suggest the neglect and abuse of children (such as safety pins that have pierced cheeks, ears, etc.).

25   Savage, *England's Dreaming,* 373.

26   Farin and Seidel-Pielen, *Skinheads,* 45.

27   For a concise discussion of the history of British Oi, see Andrew Nevill, "The

Good, the Bad, and the Skins," in Christoph and Annas, eds., *Neue Soundtracks für den Volksempfänger*.

28 Savage, *England's Dreaming*, 330.

29 This was confirmed by a student of mine, Tim Abraham, a heavy metal musician who grew up in Birmingham, London, and Liverpool. My thanks to him for this information. My comments on Oi Musik and subjectivity will discuss music as interpellation—a kind of conscious/unconscious "calling" or "hailing." Oi as working class for "Hey you!" marks the connection between the sound *oi* and the production of subjectivity through music.

30 Farin and Seidel-Pielen, *Skinheads*, 46. The translation from the German is mine; the English may well sound different than this version; Farin and Seidel-Pielen give no title to the song.

31 Ibid., 47. Whether consciously or unconsciously, this call-and-response element of second-generation skin music recalls the A A B form of lyrics in the blues. This is the form of much West African poetry; a poet/performer reads a line, and the audience repeats it while he composes the B line in his head.

32 Farin and Seidel-Pielen, *Skinheads*, 116.

33 Since London's East End used to be a Jewish section of the city, it is possible that the sound *oi* condenses British working-class hailing and the Yiddish exclamation *Oy!* The sound is frequently indexed in song titles and names of Oi bands: *Doitschland* instead of *Deutschland, Noie Werte* instead of *Neue Werte,* etc.

34 Farin and Seidel-Pielen, *Skinheads*, 50.

35 The public identified the right-wing danger of Oi with the title of Gary Bushell's anthology of Oi Musik. His substitution of *oi* for *eu* or *oy* is typical of Oi manipulation of language. The phrase conveniently merges the Nazi phrase "Kraft durch Freude" with "Strength through Joy"; the *oi* for *eu* substitution condenses the two phrases. "Kraft durch Freude" was a phrase from the Third Reich that was used to encourage the internalization of fascist ideology through group outings in the countryside. These outings were intended to disrupt the connections between workers and union organizations.

36 I will refer to German Oi Musik throughout this study in order to keep the distinction between British and German Oi clear. It must also be pointed out that (German) skins, (German) skin music, and Oi overlap. German Oi Musik is one form of expression of one subordinate component of the German skin scene. There are progressive skins—the so-called Redskins—and there are the "Sharp Skins" (Skins against Racial Prejudice). There are also reports in Germany of "Gay Skins." See *Die Tageszeitung,* 7 May 1993, 12. Some scholars prefer to assign a limited meaning to the term *Oi Musik,* arguing, e.g., that the recent double album *Schwarz/Weiss* by Die böhse Onkelz is no longer Oi Musik. I use the term *Oi Musik* broadly since I argue throughout this chapter that Oi crosses musical, social, and psychoanalytic registers with fluidity. It is precisely the speed and ease of threshold crossing that makes Oi Musik work so powerfully on its listeners' unconscious. As of the present writing (Fall 1996), the Oi phenomenon has changed. Hard-core skins and

their music have gone underground; some groups, such as Die böhse Onkelz, have
partially joined mainstream popular culture.

37 Sometimes the last name is spelled with an *s;* sometimes it is spelled with a *z.* I
spell the name with a *z* since this spelling is most common.

38 Here is a list of their albums since 1984: *Der nette Mann* (1984), *Böse Menschen—
böse Lieder* (1985), *Mexico* (1986), *Onkelz wie wir* (1987), *Kneipenterroristen* (1988),
Lügenmarsch (1989), *Es ist soweit* (1990), *Wir ham noch lange nicht genug* (1991),
Live in Vienna (1992), *Heilige Lieder* (1992), and *Schwarz/Weiss* (1993). As of this
writing, the album *Hier sind die böhse Onkelz* is scheduled to be released in 1996
("Biographie" Bellaphon Records).

39 Oi lyrics actually fluctuate freely from urgency to protect the politically defined
nation-state Germany from impure elements from abroad (foreigners, leftists, Jews
[rarely]) and urgency to protect the Nordic *race* from pollution. This should not
be seen as a contradiction between two logical classes—the national and the racial.
The ease with which Oi lyrics shift the definition of the enemy shows how mobile
and therefore artificially constructed Oi's *Other* is.

40 *Emma,* 1 January 1993, 39.

41 The song is a fantasy of the torture, murder, mutilation, and cannibalization of
children. In the above-mentioned *Emma* interview, Stephan Weidner argues that
the song works out anxieties that he had as a child waiting alone for his mother to
come home from work and watching television news reports about the child mass
murderer Helmut Kroll, who was at that time still at large. See ibid. Although the
song is incredibly fast, demonic, and disturbing, this explanation cannot be cate-
gorically dismissed.

42 *Die Welt,* 28 December 1992.

43 *Süddeutsche Zeitung,* 23 October 1992, 12.

44 Unless otherwise noted, all German-English translations are mine.

45 See Klaus Theweleit, *Male Fantasies,* trans. Stephen Conway (Minneapolis: University of Minnesota Press, 1987–89), vol. 1. In "Der destruktive Charakter," Walter
Benjamin describes much the same kind of male subject. While Theweleit is historical in his treatment of the fascist subject, Benjamin describes a transhistorical
destructive personality: "Der destruktive Charakter kennt nur eine Parole: Platz
schaffen; nur eine Tätigkeit: räumen. Sein Bedürfnis nach frischer Luft und freiem
Raum ist stärker als jeder Hass" (The destructive character knows only one phrase:
to make space; only one activity: to clear away obstacles. His need for fresh air
and open space is stronger than hate). And, further on in the essay: "Der destruktive Charakter steht in der Front der Traditionalisten" (The destructive character
stands with the traditionalists). And: "Der destruktive Charakter lebt nicht aus
dem Gefühl, dass das Leben lebenswert sei, sondern dass der Selbstmord die Mühe
nicht lohnt" (The destructive character lives from the feeling not that life is worth
it but that suicide is not worth the trouble). Walter Benjamin, "Der destruktive
Charakter," in *Illuminations* (Frankfurt: Suhrkamp, 1977), 289–90; the translations
are mine.

46 The Other for the Oi subject is often the liberal establishment within German social space as well as ethnic and/or religious others from foreign countries.

47 As of October 1991, the Interior Department of the Lower Saxon government estimated that 97 percent of German skins were men and 3 percent women (*Skinheads: Fakten und Hintergründe* [Interior Department of Lower Saxony, 1991], 2). Considering that these numbers include the progressive skins, the number of women right-wing German Oi skins must be incredibly low. I have listened to no song that speaks well of women in German Oi Musik, with one exception: "Renees wir lieben euch" (Renees we love you) from Endstufe. *Renee* is the German expression for a female skin; it is pronounced with long, drawn-out *e*'s.

48 *Die Welt,* 28 December 1992. The "Hitler Gruss" (Heil Hitler!) is included under paragraph 86a; Die böhse Onkelz had to pay a fine of DM 5,000 for every "Hitler Gruss" at a concert in Rottweil. *Stuttgarter Zeitung,* 28 November 1992. Legal actions against Rock-O-Rama and a host of German Oi bands are ongoing and are difficult to synthesize briefly. Here are a few key events concerning the German government's actions against German Oi Musik as of 1 May 1993. The band Radikahl was fined between DM 10,800 and DM 7,200 for disseminating propagandistic material. They played the infamous "Hakenkreuz Song." *Tageszeitung,* 31 March 1993, 2. Activities of the Oi band Störkraft were curtailed after agents of the government executed a massive raid of band members' apartments and the headquarters of the firm Rock-O-Rama. *Die Welt,* 26 March 1993, 3. The band Kraftschlag was charged in early 1993 with violations of paragraph 131; as of the summer of 1993, the trial is ongoing.

49 I transcribed the musical examples for this chapter on a piano in Germany; on my return to the United States, I noticed that the music sounded different. It was excruciatingly difficult to transcribe the music, aside from the ideological problems involved, since some songs sounded in tune with a tonic pitch that was "between" notes on a keyboard. "Deutschland," e.g., sounded close to B♭ minor on my German piano; in America, it was quite close to A minor.

50 *Kölner Stadtanzeiger,* 23 October 1992, 4. The roman numerals that follow refer to notes that imply harmonies.

51 Farin and Seidel-Pielen made a few mistakes or transcribed slight variations in the text (see their *Skinheads*); my versions are given in brackets.

52 Listen to Jimi Hendrix's "I Don't Live Today" for a delicate use of feedback that is incorporated into the musical texture of a rock song. Artificially produced noise has since become a basic musical material in contemporary rock; consider the exquisite use of noise in "Downward Spiral" by Nine Inch Nails. The chapter on Diamanda Galás argues that "noise" within the voice can also signify the abject.

53 Max Annas discusses (and dismisses as frivolous) the similar ballad "Deutsches Mädchen" by the group Oi Dramz in his article "Diktatur und Alltag," in Christoph and Annas, eds., *Neue Soundtracks für den Volksempfänger.*

54 Klaus Walter, "Dicker Stephan, gutes Kind, in Christophe and Annas, eds., *Neue Soundtracks für den Volksempfänger,* 29 (my translation).

55 See *Emma*, 1 January 1993, 39; *Frankfurter Allgemeine*, 31 December 1992, 26; *Süddeutsche Zeitung*, 28 December 1992, 13; *Frankfurter Rundschau*, 24 December 1992, 20; 22 December 1992, 15; 17 December 1992, 28.

56 *Frankfurter Allgemeine*, 31 December 1992, 26. This is a powerful number in itself. Considering the fact that German Oi Musik is an underground phenomenon, the fact that 500,000 copies of a record were sold is incredible—a record that is never played on the radio and is never advertised. As of December 1992, 300,000 copies had been sold. As of 26 September 1992, only 190,000 copies had been sold—a testimonial to the slow, underground nature of the distribution of German Oi Musik. *Berliner Zeitung*, 26 October 1992, 3. A cautionary note: this record was produced by the mainstream label Bellaphon, and it is possible that its distribution was not, therefore, as under the table as the work of other Oi bands. See Walter, "Dicker Stephan, gutes Kind."

57 Keep in mind that Oi Musik rarely uses full harmonies; I am referring here and elsewhere to harmonies *implied* through monophonic lines of single pitches.

58 *Skinheads: Fakten und Hintergründe*, 15. Many German Oi bands have names that are associated with violence, some explicitly reminiscent of the Third Reich and the Final Solution, some implicitly laden with Teutonic references. Here are some examples: from England, Brutal Attack, Skullhead, and Celtic Dawn; from France, Legion 88 and Evil Skins; from Italy, Verde Bianco Rosso; from Sweden, Dirlewanger; from the United States, Bound for Glory and the Allegiance (*Skinheads: Fakten und Hintergründe*, 12); and from Germany, Radikahl, Endsieg, Noie Werte, Volkszorn, Kahlkopf, and Werwolf. The band Radikahl has an unusually resonant naming history. The group was first called Giftgas—a direct reference to the gas that killed Jews, Gypsies, and others at Auschwitz. The change of name to Radikahl is typical of Oi fascination with having violence emerge out of the sounds of language itself—as suggested by the obsessive substitution of *oi* for the German *eu* sound. The name also stands in general for the way Oi Musik has robbed "leftist" or alternative music of its power; *radikal* (radical) becomes turned inside out with the insertion of an *h* between the second *a* and the final *l*.

59 *Die Welt*, 26 March 1993. Since the initial research was completed for this chapter, the status of the group is in doubt, and some journalists and scholars assert that, as of spring 1995, the band does not retain its earlier status as an entity. My thanks to Rainer Erb of the Technische Universität Berlin for this idea.

60 Esther Bick, "The Experience of the Skin in Early Object Relations, *International Journal of Psycho-Analysis* 49 (1969): 484.

61 See Didier Anzieu, *The Skin Ego*, trans. Chris Turner (New Haven, Conn.: Yale University Press, 1989), pt. 3.

62 *Der Spiegel*, 28 December 1992, 40.

63 It would be interesting, for example, to compare the texts and music of the progressive British Oi groups the Cockney Rejects and the Angelic Upstarts and the music on Gary Bushell's *Oi! the Album* and *Strength through Oi*. This chapter focuses on right-wing Oi Musik; a study of so-called progressive Oi might refigure some of the categories this chapter has established.

64 Slavoj Žižek, *Enjoy Your Symptom!* (New York: Routledge, 1992), 117.

65 The quintessential Petritsch performance is on a song called "Terror" from a record produced under the label Street Rock and Roll. The record is a thirty-three, although it looks more like a forty-five. Here, Petritsch's voice is barely comprehensible; I can hear only the phrase "Deutschland Terror!" in the chorus. There is massive feedback and distortion in the guitar part, clear percussion, and a vocal part that sounds like a human voice turned inside out.

66 I am unsure of the pitch content of the notes of this song owing to distortion on the tape I was using.

67 For another musical representation of an erection with different implications for subjectivity, see the "Intruder" chapter, where I discuss what happens to the percussion at the line "I am the Intruder" in the Peter Gabriel version of the song.

68 Two other songs by Störkraft use sounds to represent the listener as victim. "Kampfhund" opens with a snarling dog; "Imperator der G." opens with thunder and the words "wir sind wieder da!" Compare this notion of return to "Back in Black" by Screwdriver. Contemporary high-tech cinemas exploit this phenomenon to inscribe the viewer into the purity of viewing and listening space not yet inscribed with content. Think of the Dolby demonstration so common now at the outset of movies. A wide spectrum, all-around sound narrows, moves forward, and closes on one low, focused pitch at the screen.

69 One might object that I narrowly equate German Oi Musik to right-wing music and politics, ignoring progressive Oi Musik. In this chapter, I am interested in interrogating connections among right-wing German Oi Musik, the history of rock and roll, and right-wing Oi Musik's listeners. Even if progressive Oi Musik sounds "just the same" as right-wing Oi, its rhetorical, psychoanalytic, and musical effects on listeners must be interrogated outside the parameters of this discussion.

70 For an excellent discussion of the role of television in the representation of German Oi music, see Jens Hohmann, "Wilder Westen inklusive," in Christoph and Annas, eds., *Neue Soundtracks für den Volksempfänger.* See, particularly, Hohmann's argument that German television coverage treats the viewer to a voyeuristic eroticism in which filthy fascists (the members of Störkraft) are turned into aesthetic objects of desire through the television (pp. 96–97).

71 See "Jetzt singen die Böhsen Onkelz gegen die 'braune Scheisse' an," *Frankfurter Rundschau,* 19 October 1993, 24; and "Blinde Wut," *Der Spiegel,* 15 November 1993, 278.

72 For an excellent article on Oi Musik, see "Wie Nazi-Rock zur Waffe wird," *Hamburger Abendblatt,* 18 November 1993, 5. For an opinion that differs from my own, see "Heute hier, morgen dort" by Klaus Farin. In this article, Farin argues that Die böhse Onkelz have made a shift away from right-wing politics in their recent music. Farin is heavily invested in the clarity of the Right/Left binary; I would like to suggest that Oi Musik functions precisely with and through intricately imbricated structures that have right-wing and left-wing histories. *Die Tageszeitung,* 24 June 1994, 15.

73 See Slavoj Žižek, *Metastases of Enjoyment* (London: Verso, 1994), 55.

74 Ibid., 54–55.

75 See Slavoj Žižek, ed., *Everything You Always Wanted to Know about Lacan but Were Afraid to Ask Hitchcock* (London: Verso, 1990), 220.

76 Ibid., 228–29.

77 For an analysis of the musical representation of drive, see the discussion of "Der Doppelgänger" in the chapter on Schubert and the gaze.

78 For an excellent discussion of the social and intellectual context of Western European life that provided fertile ground for the emergence of Oi subjectivity, see Oliver Günther, "Utopie und 'Überlebenskampf,'" *Frankfurter Rundschau,* 10 December 1992, 12.

79 In his "Diktatur und Alltag" (in Christoph and Annas, eds., *Neue Soundtracks für den Volksempfänger*), Max Annas argues that the affect of this music is a proletarian complaint about social conditions on the level of loud teeth gnashing. He refers to the ideology behind Oi Musik as less fascist than "musizierende Biederkeit." This characterization of Oi Musik is both classist and dismissive; it sounds very much like the caricatures of Hitler before 1933, the crazy prol whom no one need take seriously.

80 Émile Benveniste locates within the pronouns *I* and *you* the structure of subjectivity *in a nutshell.* The pronouns at once stand for ourselves, for our proper names, *and* for our function in social, linguistic space. *I* suggests a speaker, *you* a listener; and they both shift back and forth in discourse. See Émile Benveniste, *Problems in General Linguistics,* trans. Mary Elizabeth Meek (Coral Gables, Fla.: University of Miami Press, 1971). Louis Althusser discusses interpellation as a crucial component of subjectivity. For Althusser, interpellation connects individuals (subjects with a lowercase *s*) to the state (Subject with a capital *S*). The act of interpellation is "hailing," through language, naming customs, the law, and performative gestures made and encoded in public space. Althusser's famous example of interpellation is the policeman's call "Hey You!" through which, in returning the policeman's gaze, we become subjects. See Louis Althusser, "Ideology and Ideological State Apparatuses," in *Lenin and Philosophy,* trans. Ben Brewster (New York: Monthly Review Press, 1971), 170–77. Žižek takes Althusser's structure a notch further. Žižek argues that interpellation consists of two "moments" that occur simultaneously: (1) a moment of indeterminate guilt and (2) a moment of identification with the structure that supports the hail from public space. For Žižek, the law supports identification; its "obscene superego" supports indeterminate guilt. See *Metastases of Enjoyment,* 57–62.

81 Nazi rock and its ideology in racist skinhead culture have found their way onto the Internet from sites in Canada and the United States. A recent article suggests that acts of violence in the United States and Canada can be linked to Nazi rock. See "The Method of a Neo-Nazi Mogul," *New York Times Magazine,* 25 February 1996, 40–43.

7   The Music of Diamanda Galás

1   Apparently, Galás is actually soaked in blood, or stage blood, for performances of *Plague Mass*. My thanks to Richard Morrison of Duke University Press for this information and his perceptive comments on an early draft of this chapter.

2   The issue of gender and musical representation is crucial for any discussion of Diamanda Galás. Susan McClary suggests that Galás takes what might be considered the worst female stereotypes that link women with uncontrollable rage and madness and turns them into a radical critique of the very ideology that produces these stereotypes. See Susan McClary, *Feminine Endings: Music, Gender, and Sexuality* (Minnesota: University of Minnesota Press, 1991).

3   In a personal interview, Galás told me that her father performed Rebetika music, or hashish music, and did not want his daughter to sing. My thanks to Ms. Galás for this information.

4   See Gracie and Zarkow, "The Killing Floor," *Mondo 2000,* no. 8 (1990): 79.

5   Diamanda Galás, "Intravenal Song," *Perspectives of New Music* 20 (Fall–Winter 1981/Spring–Summer 1982): 59–62.

6   For an excellent interview with Diamanda Galás, see Richard Morrison, "We Are All HIV Positive: A Conversation with Diamanda Galás, Singer, Composer, Performance Artist, AIDS Activist," *Art and Understanding* (January/February 1993): 18–22.

7   In addition to her musical studies, as a college student she majored in biochemistry with special interests in immunology and hematology. There is an eerie coincidence in this early academic interest and the importance AIDS has in her mature work.

8   Gracie and Zarkow, "The Killing Floor," 76.

9   See Loring M. Danforth, *The Death Rituals of Ancient Greece* (Princeton, N.J.: Princeton University Press, 1982). Danforth describes the elaborate rituals of preparing the corpse, singing laments, tending the grave, attending to other mourners, and attending and facilitating the exhumation in his chapter "Death in Potamia."

10 See Gail Holst-Warhaft, *Dangerous Voices: Women's Laments and Greek Literature* (London: Routledge, 1992), 20.

11 See Danforth, *Death Rituals,* 35–38, 102–3, 126.

12 See Holst-Warhaft, *Dangerous Voices,* 3–6, 114–18.

13 Danforth, *Death Rituals,* 73; Holst-Warhaft, *Dangerous Voices,* 6, 67.

14 Danforth, *Death Rituals,* 66, 83, 94.

15 Holst-Warhaft, *Dangerous Voices,* 50.

16 See Paraski's lament (ibid., 76–80).

17 Ibid., 70; see also 69, 75. We are now in a position to reevaluate the binary distinction in Michel Chion's *La voix au cinéma* (Paris: Cahiers du cinéma, 1982). As mentioned above in the chapter on the Beatles, Chion points out that we are used to associating the female cry with the expression of limit, of total violation and fear, on the one hand, and the male cry with a phallic territoriality, on the other. Chion gives Tarzan's cry as an example of the latter. Such a binary is completely

arbitrary, however, as this discussion of women's cries in Greek lament suggests. Yes, Hollywood has coded cries as Chion suggests, but this coding is part of an ideology that is gender and culture specific, as Holst-Warhaft's two women's cries suggest. Another explanation for the power of the cry may lie in psychoanalytic theory; recall psychoanalytic research that concerns the cry as the first act of communication in developing subjectivity.

18 Holst-Warhaft, *Dangerous Voices,* 70.

19 Danforth, *Death Rituals,* 38.

20 Holst-Warhaft points out that architecture of houses in the Mani region of southern Greece today (houses shaped like towers) reflects an unbroken tradition of blood feuds fueled by lament from the fourteenth century until shortly after World War II. The Nazi occupation of Greece refigured the logic of familial blood feud into opposing political factions: the left-wing resistance (EAM) and right-wing collaborators. After the Greek civil war of the 1950s, the blood feuds died out, and massive emigration brought Maniot families to western Europe and the United States (*Dangerous Voices,* 91–96).

21 Ibid., 97.

22 Ibid., 38. What Holst-Warhaft means by the word *pitch* is unclear. I think that the word refers not to pitch-specific tones but to register within a singer's range.

23 Ibid., 156.

24 Danforth, *Death Rituals,* 74.

25 I borrow this term from Roland Barthes's "The Grain of the Voice." In this essay, Barthes discusses two approaches to music that he borrows from Julia Kristeva: the pheno-song and the geno-song. The former signifies the traditional parameters of music as a semiotic system that can be described as a series of transformations from basic material to immanent text. The latter (in which Barthes is much more interested) signifies the "volume of the speaking and singing voice, the space in which the significations germinate." The "grain of the voice" connects the signifying systems of music to the body, to the act of breathing, sweating, making sounds at and within an instrument, to the act of writing. See Roland Barthes, "The Grain of the Voice," in *The Responsibility of Forms,* trans. Richard Howard (New York: Hill & Wang, 1985), 270.

26 Danforth, *Death Rituals,* 112.

27 This phenomenon is manifestly clear when you learn to play a string instrument. My violin teacher always encouraged me to play with lots of "consonance"—bite—because such articulations make the musical phrases clear and do not project beyond a few feet of the instrument.

28 For a definition of *listening plane,* see the "Intruder" chapter. Recall, as well, Didier Anzieu's point that it is through sound that developing subjects first gain a sense of space—of our bodies as containers in which sounds resound and of the external world as a space into which sounds penetrate. See Didier Anzieu, *The Skin Ego,* trans. Chris Turner (New Haven, Conn.: Yale University Press, 1989), pt. 2, chap. 7.

29 Throughout this chapter, I will be discussing Galás's radical vocal technique. One

should point out, however, that, since at least the nineteenth century, musicians have been extending the technical resources of instruments. The great virtuosi took music out of the hands of the middle-class amateur and put it in the hands of the professional musician. Composers also extended the technical and musical resources of music throughout the nineteenth and twentieth centuries. To take just one example, the violin concerti of the following composers extend violin technique one notch further than their predecessor: Beethoven, Mendelssohn, Brahms, Schoenberg. Recent classical and jazz technique has extended the use of wind instruments and the voice, as well. What Galás does with her voice is similar to advanced jazz techniques of overblowing to produce multiphonics.

30   This heavy breathing might also imitate the sound of a respirator in an intensive care unit; my thanks to Richard Morrison for this idea.

31   One of the clearest representations of abjection and boundary crossing is the movie *The Cook, the Thief, His Wife, and Her Lover.* The camera often tracks shots through partitions between the kitchen and the dining room, the dining room and the bathroom, and the kitchen and the street outside. The movie is also pervaded by abject admixtures of oral, anal, and genital representations.

32   For a discussion of abjection in Freud and Lacan, see Jean Laplanche and Jean-Baptiste Pontalis, "Foreclosure," in *The Language of Psycho-Analysis,* trans. Donald Nicholson Smith (New York: Norton, 1973), 166–69. The authors point out that Freud used the term *Verwerfung* to signify a putting aside that is similar sometimes to repression, sometimes to a rejection of a piece of reality that leads to psychosis—a more radical exclusion of a part of reality that one cannot deal with, *Verleugnung.* Lacan uses the term foreclosure (*forclusion*) as an operation at the oedipal stage that initiates the establishment of both the Real and the Symbolic Order: "What has been foreclosed from the Symbolic appears in the Real" (p. 168).

33   Julia Kristeva, *Powers of Horror,* trans. Leon S. Roudiez (New York: Columbia University Press, 1982), 2.

34   See Peter Winkler, "The Politics of Transcription," in *Keeping Score: Music, Disciplinarity, Culture,* ed. David Schwarz, Anahid Kassabian, and Lawrence Siegel (Charlottesville: University Press of Virginia, in press).

35   This may sound confusing to readers who have never played a string instrument or who have never manipulated their voices in vocal instruction. Since I am a violinist, I think of these two registers of noise as follows. If you pull a violin bow across a string with too much pressure and too little speed, you "crush" the sound. But there is not a binary relation between pure and crushed sounds. You can produce a continuous note that begins pure and ends crushed or begins crushed and ends pure. Most "beautifully" played notes in the classical, standard repertoire are played in the middle of this continuum. If, on the other hand, you pull the bow along a string with too little pressure and too much speed, you will produce another kind of noise—a fluty, thin, wispy sound with no "center." Galás sings with the former type of noise much more often than the latter.

36   Kristeva, *Powers of Horror,* 2, 6.

37   Ibid., 2.

38   My thanks to Eric Santner for pointing out this idea to me.

39   Slavoj Žižek, *Enjoy Your Symptom!* (New York: Routledge, 1992), 77.

40   Kristeva, *Powers of Horror*, 49.

41   For another spectacular example of the emergence of the Real in a contemporary rock song, see the first song of *Downward Spiral* by Nine Inch Nails; noise as a filthy residue begins as a secondary sound and engulfs the music toward its conclusion.

42   Kristeva, *Powers of Horror*, 13. Anzieu suggests another reason for connecting the body, sound, and abjection. We have seen in earlier chapters how the sonorous envelope opens in a variety of stages for developing infants and prepares the way for the visual mirror stage and language acquisition. Anzieu suggests that the sounds of coughing, sneezing, farting, and shitting are also crucial elements of the sonorous envelope. At first, these sounds are simple elements of the sonorous envelope; as sounds become differentiated from one another at the outset of the acoustic-mirror stage, they also become *spatial* and *temporal*. Anzieu suggests that the noises that the body makes and hears give us our first sense that our bodies can be vessels in which sounds resound. See *The Skin Ego*, pt. 3.

43   Kristeva, *Powers of Horror*, 8–9. This is similar to Bataille's sense of the abject: "Ecstatic time can only find itself in the vision of things that puerile chance causes brusquely to appear: cadavers, nudity, explosions, spilled blood, abysses, sunbursts, and thunder." See Georges Bataille, *Visions of Excess*, ed. and trans. Allan Stoekl (Minneapolis: University of Minnesota Press, 1985), 200. Although there are other ways in which Kristeva and Bataille intersect as theorists of abjection, I focus in this chapter on Kristeva since I find her theory more appropriate for the music of Diamanda Galás. Bataille's abjection is quite male, with his insistence on erection and male orgasm as a central metaphor in his metaphysical cosmology of the abject; Kristeva's connection between abjection and representations of the female work much better for Galás's art.

44   Bataille, *Visions of Excess*, 12.

45   For a discussion of the similarities and differences between Bataille and Kristeva, see "The Politics of the Signifier II: A Conversation on the Informe and the Abject," *October*, no. 67 (Winter 1994): 3–21. Rosalind Krauss suggests there that "the notion of the *informe*, as Bataille enunciates it, is about attacking the very imposition of categories, since they imply that certain forms of action are tied to certain types of objects. But Kristeva's project is all about recuperating certain objects as abject—waste products, filth, body fluids, etc." (p. 3).

46   For a discussion of musical sneaking, see the "Intruder" chapter.

47   Richard Morrison pointed out to me that the voices are actually singing the word *Selah*—a Hebrew word similar in function to the Christian *Amen*.

48   Kristeva, *Powers of Horror*, 4, 118.

49   For a similar sense of the abject as a cycle in which beauty rots to the abject, out of which beauty arises in a perpetual cycle, see Bataille's "The Language of Flowers," in *Visions of Excess*.

50 This theme predates the nineteenth century, although I think that most listeners would identify it as a quote from the final movement of Berlioz's *Symphonie fantastique* in which the artist who has killed his beloved is judged and damned.

51 The reader will remember that such a distance between performer and audience also informed live punk concerts as discussed above in the Oi chapter. Punk gobbing can now be understood as an ambivalent form of interpellation in which a bond is created between audience and performer through expelled and spit body fluids.

52 Compare this introduction of "Let My People Go" to Schubert's "Ihr Bild," discussed above. In Schubert, the octaves are explicitly linked to the gaze that both reveals and empties; in Galás, the octaves suggest a musical frame that is going to be filled with the rich sonorities of the blues B-minor scale.

53 Kristeva, *Powers of Horror*, 1.

54 My thanks to Eric Santner for suggesting a clear way of mapping abjection and the sublime onto the circle that marks Lacanian drive.

55 Žižek, *Enjoy Your Symptom!* 48–49.

56 See Žižek's discussion of a story by Patricia Highsmith for a compelling illustration of how images, or representations of objects, can signify psychoanalytic objects such as the *objet a*. Slavoj Žižek, *Looking Awry* (Cambridge, Mass.: MIT Press, 1991). See also Slavoj Žižek, *The Sublime Object of Ideology* (London: Verso, 1989), 182–85. In the chapter on Schubert, I argue as well that the hint of E minor in "Der Doppelgänger" is a rare example in music of a representation of the *objet a*.

57 Kristeva, *Powers of Horror*, 68.

58 Immanuel Kant, *The Critique of Judgement*, trans. James Creed Meredith (Oxford: Clarendon, 1952), 90.

59 For an extended definition of the mathematical sublime, see ibid., 98–105.

60 Ibid., 104.

61 Žižek, *The Sublime Object of Ideology*, 203.

62 Slavoj Žižek, *Tarrying with the Negative* (Durham, N.C.: Duke University Press, 1993), 36.

BIBLIOGRAPHY

Abbate, Carolyn. *Unsung Voices*. Princeton, N.J.: Princeton University Press, 1991.

Agawu, V. Kofi. *Playing with Signs*. Princeton, N.J.: Princeton University Press, 1991.

Althusser, Louis. "Ideology and Ideological State Apparatuses." In *Lenin and Philosophy*, trans. Ben Brewster. New York: Monthly Review Press, 1971.

Annas, Max. "Diktatur und Alltag." In *Neue Soundtracks für den Volksempfänger*, ed. Ralph Christoph and Max Annas. Berlin: ID-Archiv, 1993.

Anzieu, Didier. "L'envelope sonore du soi." *Revue française de psychanalyse* 37, no. 1 (1974): 161–79.

Anzieu, Didier. *Le peau-moi*. Paris: Bordas, 1985. Translated by Chris Turner as *The Skin Ego*. New Haven, Conn.: Yale University Press, 1989.

Bailblé, Claude. "Programation de l'écoute." *Cahiers du cinéma* 293 (1978): 5–12.

Bailey, Robert. "Analytical Study." In *Prelude and Transfiguration from Tristan and Isolde*. New York: Norton, 1985.

Barthes, Roland. "The Grain of the Voice." In *The Responsibility of Forms*, trans. Richard Howard. New York: Hill & Wang, 1985.

Bataille, Georges. *Visions of Excess*. Edited and translated by Allan Stoekl. Minneapolis: University of Minnesota Press, 1985.

Beatles. Milwaukee: Hal Leonard, 1989.

Beatles in Their Own Words. Edited by Barry Miles. New York: Omnibus, 1978.

Benjamin, Walter. "Der destruktive Charakter." In *Illuminations*. Frankfurt: Suhrkamp, 1977.

Benveniste, Émile. *Problems in General Linguistics*. Translated by Mary Elizabeth Meek. Coral Gables, Fla.: University of Miami Press, 1971.

Bick, Esther. "The Experience of the Skin in Early Object Relations." *International Journal of Psycho-Analysis* 49 (1968): 484–86.

Brown, Matthew. "The Diatonic and Chromatic in Schenker's Theory of Harmonic Relations." *Journal of Music Theory* 30, no. 1 (Spring 1986): 1–34.

Charlton, Katherine. *Rock Music Styles*. Madison, Wis.: Wm. C. Brown, 1990.

Chion, Michel. *La voix au cinéma*. Paris: Cahiers du cinéma, 1982.

"Cinema/Sound." *Yale French Studies,* no. 60 (1980).

The Complete Poems of Heinrich Heine. Translated by Hal Draper. Boston: Suhrkamp/ Insel, 1982.

Crary, Jonathan. *Techniques of the Observer*. Cambridge, Mass.: MIT Press, 1990.

Dame, Joke. "Unveiled Voices." In *Queering the Pitch,* ed. Philip Brett, Elizabeth Wood, and Gary Thomas. New York: Routledge, 1994.

Danforth, Lorin. *The Death Rituals of Ancient Greece*. Princeton, N.J.: Princeton University Press, 1982.

Everett, Walter. *Music of the Beatles: An Analytical History*. Oxford: Oxford University Press, in press.

Everett, Walter. "A Schenkerian View of Text-Painting in Schubert's Song Cycle *Winterreise*." Ph.D. diss., University of Michigan, 1988.

Farin, Klaus, and Eberhart Seidel-Pielen. *Skinheads*. Munich: Beck Publishers, 1993.

Forte, Allen. "Schenker's Conception of Musical Structure." *Journal of Music Theory* 3, no. 1 (April 1959): 1–30.

Forte, Allen, and Steven E. Gilbert. *An Introduction to Schenkerian Analysis*. New York: Norton, 1982.

Freud, Sigmund. *Beyond the Pleasure Principle*. Translated and edited by James Strachey. New York: Norton, 1961.

Freud, Sigmund. *Civilization and Its Discontents*. Translated and edited by James Strachey. New York: Norton, 1961.

Freud, Sigmund. "The Uncanny." In *On Creativity and the Unconscious,* trans. Joan Riviere. New York: Harper & Row, 1958.

Galás, Diamanda. "Intravenal Song." *Perspectives of New Music* 20 (Fall–Winter 1981/ Spring–Summer 1982): 59–62.

Hohmann, Jens. "Wilder Westen inklusive." In *Neue Soundtracks für den Volksempfänger,* ed. Raph Christoph and Max Annas. Berlin: ID-Archiv, 1993.

Holst-Warhaft, Gail. *Dangerous Voices: Women's Lament and Greek Literature*. London: Routledge, 1992.

Huyssen, Andreas. "Mapping the Postmodern." *New German Critique,* no. 33 (Fall 1984): 5–52.

Jameson, Fredric. "The Imaginary and Symbolic in Lacan." In *Ideologies of Theory*, vol. 1. Minneapolis: University of Minnesota Press, 1988.

Jameson, Fredric. "Postmodernism and Consumer Society." In *The Anti-Aesthetic,* ed. Hal Foster. Port Townsend, Wash.: Bay Press, 1983.

Jarman, Douglass. *The Music of Alban Berg*. Berkeley: University of California Press, 1979.

Juno, Andrea. "Interview with Diamanda Galás." In *Angry Women*. San Francisco: Re/ Search Publications, 1991.

Kant, Immanuel. *The Critique of Judgement*. Translated by James Creed Meredith. Oxford: Clarendon, 1952.

Kassabian, Anahid. *Songs of Subjectivities: Theorizing Hollywood Film Music of the 1980s and 1990s*. Durham, N.C.: Duke University Press, in press.

Kerman, Joseph. "A Romantic Detail in Schubert's *Schwanengesang.*" In *Schubert: Critical and Analytical Studies,* ed. Walter Frisch. Lincoln: University of Nebraska Press, 1986.

Kramer, Lawrence. *Music as Cultural Practice.* Berkeley: University of California Press, 1990.

Kramer, Lawrence. "The Schubert Lied: Romantic Form and Romantic Consciousness." In *Schubert: Critical and Analytical Studies,* ed. Walter Frisch. Lincoln: University of Nebraska Press, 1986.

Kramer, Richard. *Distant Cycles.* Chicago: University of Chicago Press, 1994.

Kramer, Richard. "Schubert's Heine." *19th-Century Music* 8, no. 3 (1985): 213–25.

Kristeva, Julia. *Powers of Horror.* Translated by Leon S. Roudiez. New York: Columbia University Press, 1982.

Lacan, Jacques. *Four Fundamental Principles of Psychoanalysis.* Edited by Jacques-Alain Miller. Translated by Alan Sheridan. New York: Norton, 1978.

Lacan, Jacques. "The Mirror Stage." In *Écrits,* trans. Alan Sheridan. New York: Norton, 1977.

Laplanche, Jean, and Jean-Baptiste Pontalis. *The Language of Psycho-Analysis.* Translated by Donald Nicholson Smith. New York: Norton, 1973.

Lewin, David. "Auf dem Flusse: Image and Background in a Schubert Song." In *Schubert: Critical and Analytical Studies,* ed. Walter Frisch. Lincoln: University of Nebraska Press, 1986.

Lewisohn, Mark. *The Beatles Recording Sessions.* New York: Harmony, 1988.

Mapping Ideologies. Edited by Slavoj Žižek. New York: Verso, 1994.

McClary, Susan. *Feminine Endings.* Minneapolis: University of Minnesota Press, 1991.

McCreless, Patrick. "Schenker and Chromatic Tonicization: A Reappraisal." In *Schenkerian Studies,* ed. Hedi Siegel. Cambridge: Cambridge University Press, 1990.

Meyer, Leonard. *Emotion and Meaning in Music.* Chicago: University of Chicago Press, 1956.

Morrison, Richard. "We Are All HIV Positive: A Conversation with Diamanda Galás." *Art and Understanding* (January–February 1993): 18–22.

Nevill, Andrew. "The Good, the Bad, and the Skins." In *Neue Soundtracks für den Volksempfänger,* ed. Ralph Christoph and Max Annas. Berlin: ID-Archiv, 1993.

New Grove Dictionary of Musical Instruments. Edited by Stanley Sadie. New York: Macmillan, 1984.

Ovid. *The Metamorphoses.* Translated by Rolf Humphries. Bloomington: Indiana University Press, 1955.

"The Politics of the Signifier II: A Conversation on the Informe and the Abject." *October,* no. 67 (Winter 1994): 3–21.

Proctor, Gregory. "Technical Bases of Nineteenth-Century Chromatic Tonality." Ph.D. diss., Princeton University, 1978.

Rosen, Charles. *The Romantic Generation.* Cambridge, Mass.: Harvard University Press, 1995.

Rosolato, Guy. "La voix." In *Essais sur le symbolique.* Paris: Gallimard, 1969.

Rosolato, Guy. "La voix: Entre corps et langage." *Revue française de psychanalyse* 37 (1974): 75–94.

Savage, Jon. *England's Dreaming*. New York: St. Martin's, 1992.

Schenker, Heinrich. "Ihr Bild." In *Der Tonwille*, vol. 1. Vienna: Universal, 1921.

Schubert: The Complete Song Texts. Translated by Richard Wigmore. New York: Schirmer Books, 1988.

Schwarz, David. "The Ascent and Arpeggiation in 'Die Stadt,' 'Der Atlas,' and 'Der Doppelgänger' of Franz Schubert." *Indiana Theory Review* 7, no. 1 (Spring 1986): 38–50.

Schwarz, David. "Listening Subjects: Music, Psychoanalysis, and the Music of John Adams and Steve Reich." In *Keeping Score: Music, Disciplinarity, Culture*, ed. David Schwarz, Anahid Kassabian, and Lawrence Siegel. Charlottesville: University Press of Virginia, in press.

Silverman, Kaja. *The Acoustic Mirror*. Bloomington: Indiana University Press, 1988.

Silverman, Kaja. *Male Subjectivities at the Margins*. London: Routledge, 1992.

Silverman, Kaja. *The Subject of Semiotics*. London: Oxford University Press, 1982.

Skinheads: Fakten und Hintergründe. Interior Department of Lower Saxony, 1991.

Theweleit, Klaus. *Male Fantasies*. Translated by Stephen Conway. Minneapolis: University of Minnesota Press, 1987–89.

Vasse, Denis. *L'ombilique et la voix*. Paris: du Seuil, 1974.

Walter, Klaus. "Dicker Stephan, gutes Kind." In *Neue Soundtracks für den Volksempfänger*, ed. Ralph Christoph and Max Annas. Berlin: ID-Archiv, 1993.

Wheelock, Gretchen. "*Schwarze Gretel* and the Engendered Minor Mode in Mozart's Operas." In *Musicology and Difference*, ed. Ruth A. Solie. Berkeley: University of California Press, 1993.

Winkler, Peter. "The Politics of Transcription." In *Keeping Score: Music, Disciplinarity, Culture*, ed. David Schwarz, Anahid Kassabian, and Lawrence Siegel. Charlottesville: University Press of Virginia, in press.

Youens, Susan. *Retracing a Winter's Journey: Schubert's Winterreise*. Ithaca, N.Y.: Cornell University Press, 1991.

Žižek, Slavoj. *Enjoy Your Symptom!* New York: Routledge, 1992.

Žižek, Slavoj. *For They Know Not What They Do*. London: Verso, 1991.

Žižek, Slavoj. "In His Bold Gaze My Ruin Is Writ Large." In *Everything You Always Wanted to Know about Lacan but Were Afraid to Ask Hitchcock*, ed. Slavoj Žižek. London: Verso, 1992.

Žižek, Slavoj. *Looking Awry*. Cambridge, Mass.: MIT Press, 1991.

Žižek, Slavoj. *The Metastases of Enjoyment*. London: Verso, 1994.

Žižek, Slavoj. *The Sublime Object of Ideology*. London: Verso, 1989.

Žižek, Slavoj. *Tarrying with the Negative*. Durham, N.C.: Duke University Press, 1993.

INDEX

Abjection: and developing subjectivity, 200 n.42; as drawing/erasing boundaries, 150; and lamentation, 160; and the maternal, 150; as opposed to repression, 148; registers of, 143; as a representation of separation, 149; and the sublime, 163; and the Symbolic Order, 161; and temporality, 150

Acoustic mirror, 16–17, 21–22; and developing subjectivity, 20–21; and imitation, 169 n.27; and Ovid, 170 n.29; and performance art, 156; and the Real, 150; representations of in "Ihr Bild," 75; representations of in "I Want You (She's So Heavy)," 27–28; representations of in 1950s rock, 171 n.14; and the visual mirror stage, 169 n.25

Adams, John, 9–15

Alterity, 2, 39

"Amazing Grace," 143; and abjection, 145

Ambivalence: in "I Want You (She's So Heavy)," 29; in Oi Musik, 130

Analysis: applications of in classical and popular music, 24

Angelic Upstarts, 106

Anxiety: in relation to fear and fright, 169 n.24

Anzieu, Didier, 21, 29, 121, 169 n.25, 200 n.42; and Oi subjectivity, 121

Backbeat: and the history of popular musics, 190 n.23

Bailey, Robert: and thirds, 80

Bataille, Georges, 151; and abjection, 200 n.43, 200 n.49

Barthes, Roland: "The Grain of the Voice," 198 n.25

The Beatles: and the cry, 29–30; "I Want You (She's So Heavy)," 25–37; and the Real, 31–35; *Sgt. Pepper's Lonely Hearts Club Band* and *Abbey Road,* 23

Beginnings: of rock songs, 173 n.26

Benjamin, Walter, 192 n.45

Benveniste, Émile, 196 n.80

Berg, Alban: Piano Sonata, Opus 1, 10–13

Bick, Esther: and Oi subjectivity, 121; and the signification of skin, 169 n.25

Bill Haley and the Comets, 112

Binaries: in the Imaginary and Symbolic Order, 167 n.11

Castration anxiety: and music, 94, 97

Chion, Michel, 30, 91, 185 n.10

Cooder, Ry: and Oi Musik, 117

Cockney Rejects, 106

The Cook, the Thief, His Wife, and Her Lover: and abjection, 149

Crary, Jonathan, 183 n.35

Cries: and abjection, 146–147; and the blues, 172 n.19; in classic Hollywood

84, 184 n.43; and the Furies, 137; and gender, 89; and instrumental music, 92; of the mother, 16, 20–22; and prohibitions, 135; and proximity to the listener, 91–92, 185–186 n.10; and silence, 123

Wagner, Richard, 13–15
Whistling: and gender, 92–93; and violence, 186 n.14

Youens, Susan, 39, 176 n.8, 176 n.12, 179 n.27

Žižek, Slavoj, 2, 35, 40–41, 69, 129–130, 149, 161, 162, 171–172 n.15, 174 n.35, 174 n.38, 176 n.10, 182 n.17, 196 n.80, 201 n.56; and *Flaschenpost,* 53; and forgetting to forget, 40; and remembering to forget, 40. *See also* Imaginary Order; *Objet a;* Real; Symbolic Order

David Schwarz is Valentine Professor of Music at Amherst College.

Library of Congress Cataloging-in-Publication Data

Schwarz, David, 1952–

Listening subjects : music, psychoanalysis, culture /
David Schwarz.

Includes bibliographical references (p. ***) and index.

ISBN 0-8223-1929-2 (alk. paper). — ISBN 0-8223-1922-5 (pbk. : alk.
paper)

1. Music—Psychology.   2. Psychoanalysis.   3. Music—Philosophy
and aesthetics.   I. Title.

ML3830.S28   1997

781'.11—dc21   96-39870 CIP   M